real world economic outlook

the legacy of globalization:
debt and deflation

real world economic outlook

the legacy of globalization: debt and deflation

edited by
ann pettifor

editorial consultant
janet bush

Jubilee Research at the
New Economics Foundation

First published 2003 by
PALGRAVE MACMILLAN
Houndmills, Basingstoke, Hampshire RG21 6XS and
175 Fifth Avenue, New York, N. Y. 10010
Companies and representatives throughout the world

PALGRAVE MACMILLAN is the global academic imprint of the Palgrave Macmillan division of St. Martin's Press, LLC and of Palgrave Macmillan Ltd. Macmillan® is a registered trademark in the United States, United Kingdom and other countries. Palgrave is a registered trademark in the European Union and other countries.

ISBN 1–4039–1794–9 hardback
ISBN 1–4039–1795–7 paperback

This book is printed on paper suitable for recycling and made from fully managed and sustained forest sources.

A catalogue record for this book is available from the British Library.

A catalogue record for this book is available from the Library of Congress.

10   9   8   7   6   5   4   3
12   11   10   09   08   07   06   05   04   03

Text design by cyandesign.co.uk

Printed and bound in Great Britain by
Antony Rowe Ltd, Chippenham and Eastbourne

This book is dedicated to four people who have backed this project when other funders would not: Galahad and Tom Clark (of the J.A. Clark Charitable Trust) and Angela and Ian Marks (of the AIM Foundation). We are immensely grateful for their confidence, their vision, and their generosity.

We would also like to dedicate this book to a small group of economists working in official institutions who have given us invaluable encouragement, and pointed us towards helpful analyses and data. Sadly, given the current censorious climate, they cannot be named. We wish them to know their support is deeply appreciated.

contents

PART 05 **new era?**

list of figures

PART 03

PART 04

list of tables

foreword

For all the prominence and sophistication of capital markets and financial services in the new global economy, it is rare that we ask questions of our financial system itself. The way that credit is extended and debt incurred seems so ingrained that it is hard to question. It is, in the words of George Orwell, 'the air we breathe'. Like air, it is everywhere, we are dependent on it, and perhaps most important, until it is really dirty, it cannot be seen. We see the financial system that underpins global economic activity as something natural. But it's not.

The 24 million citizens across the world that took an active part in the Jubilee 2000 campaign on the debts of the poorest countries were the first to call into public question a system in which spiraling debts gave creditors all the rights and debtors all the responsibilities. The campaign spoke for a worldwide hunger among citizens for global justice, and demonstrated that the constituency of concern was far greater than the narrow membership of traditional NGOs. Those involved were describing afresh their relations as individuals with the world around them. As Hazel Henderson, the US futurist, remarked, 'It represented the arrival of the global citizen, well in advance of the structures of global governance.'

Global citizens, particularly those engaged in campaigning, are however not necessarily popular with those in power. No organization did more to block, delay, and filibuster progress on the debts of the poorest countries than the IMF. The rebuttal that such critics made was that NGOs of this kind were unaccountable, unfactual, and unrealistic. The paradox is that there is an element of truth in each charge; these characteristics also talk to their strengths. After all, campaigning NGOs:

- Don't seek to mimic the accountability of representative politics, but give voice to those typically marginalized by it.

- Are unashamedly emotional and not just factual (a better balance perhaps, as empirical data tends to be skewed to the interests of the powerful).

- Are not in the business of being realistic, in terms of accommodating the interests of those in power, but instead aim to speak the truth, however uncomfortable.

But the publication of the first *Real World Economic Outlook* is a sign of the fast-growing maturity of the global justice movement. The creativity and innovation of the new transnational networks of civil society, from churches and trade unions through to consumer and environmental NGOs, are shaping an economic agenda that offers credible policy alternatives. They argue that more equitable human development or ecological balance can be achieved by a redirection of economic activity. And they expose the reality that debt is as systemic a by-product as pollution or global warming of a global political economy locked into inequality and unsustainability.

The emergence of a new era of geopolitical insecurity means that any such ideas, emerging from the alternative legitimacy of civil society rather than the captured institutions of the rich, may come to define our future. With no more subtle a goal than material advancement, Western secular capitalism appears, in the words of James Hillman, the American psychoanalyst, to generate 'insensitive feeling with no looking around at life values'. The search set out in this landmark book for a more meaningful understanding of prosperity may be the only way humanity has, to move from insecurity, competition, and conflict towards peace and inter-dependence.

Ed Mayo is Director of the National Consumer Council in the UK. He was Director of the New Economics Foundation from 1992–2003 and Chair of the UK Jubilee 2000 Coalition from 1996–2000.

preface

This is the first edition of the *Real World Economic Outlook* (*RWEO*). Aimed at both economists and the general public, its purpose is to review the world economy from the perspective of economic and environmental justice, and to broaden understanding of economics amongst those profoundly affected by economic policies.

RWEO seeks to make economics accessible and comprehensible to those who wish to get a grip on their own domestic, household economics; but also to understand and influence national, regional, and global economic policy. In other words, *Real World Economic Outlook* is aimed at those who not only want to change their own world, but also our shared world.

Each year, we will tackle a different topic. The theme for 2003/4 is 'debt and deflation'.

> Deflation is usually defined as a generalized fall in prices, the consequence of which is often a fall in wages. Deflation is the converse of inflation, a rise in prices. In a deflationary environment, when prices are falling, the **real** value of debts will rise. Interest rates can never fall below zero (or else no-one would ever lend) even if prices are falling by say, 10 per cent. The **real** rate of interest in these circumstances would therefore be 10 per cent. In other words in a defla-tionary environment **real** interest rates, or the cost of debt rises. Once nominal interest rates reach zero, central bankers have no control over real interest rates. In a recession, this means that central bankers have no levers with which to 'reflate' the economy. Moreover, in a context of high levels of debt, even mild deflation risks triggering a 'debt-deflationary' spiral when people are forced to reduce expenditure or sell off assets in order to pay off debts, thereby forcing prices down, and causing debt to rise even further in **real** terms.

Debt and deflation we argue are the legacy of the economic experiment that was globalization. We are concerned that economists, central bankers, and politicians fail to tell the truth, the whole truth, about the impact of these often-reckless policies on ordinary wage-earning consumers. We are particu-larly dismayed because consumers, in all parts of the world, have obliged cen-tral bankers and economists by joining the money merry-go-round, borrowing heavily and then propping up economies with their spending. When the music stops, these consumers will be heavily indebted and badly hurt. They will suffer some of the disastrous consequences faced by developing countries, which also joined the international money-go-round, lured by the siren voices of central bankers and IMF staff.

RWEO is for those managers in corporations and companies who now find their companies massively over-indebted and with substantial pension liabilities. In addition, *Real World Economic Outlook* will, we hope, be helpful to readers who may be unaware of the implications of deflation and the threat it poses to livelihoods and jobs, and to the ability to repay debts.

Another reason for producing an alternative economic outlook is because economists, on the whole, fail to take into account key economic costs; for example the costs and impacts of climate change and the subsidies provided by women. By limiting their remit and excluding these 'scarce resources', we argue, economists create a 'false economy'. We note that the words *economy* and *ecology* both have their root in 'eco', the home or hearth—and that the discipline of economics needs to embrace all the scarce resources associated with our home, the earth. We will point the way to a new form of economics, making positive proposals for change.

While *RWEO* has been produced in the North, we have sought the advice and collaboration of distinguished economists from the South. The censorship exercised by neoliberal economists and their supporters motivated us to provide a platform for those who do not share in the consensus of 'the single economic theory' that lies behind globalization. So this volume gives a voice to those economists who live the reality of globalization's spectacular failures and whose opinions have been drowned out by highly-paid economists and commentators located far away from poverty and turmoil, in the ivory towers of Washington, London, and Geneva.

With their help, we believe that the analyses contained within this volume will give a clearer picture to all of us of our inter-connected world. We aim to shed some light on an economic doctrine, known popularly as 'market fundamentalism', which has undermined the state and democratic institutions in developing countries; and in the words of the international Jubilee movement, led to the 'extraction and transfer of assets from the poor to the rich'. These transfers have been achieved in the context of a global economy addicted to fossil fuels, a dependency which is a source of conflict in the Middle East and elsewhere and which worsens climate change and in turn exacerbates floods and droughts in the poorest parts of the world.

The genesis of the idea for this annual review of the global economy lies within the international Jubilee 2000 campaign. Jubilee 2000 was backed by 24 million people, campaigners in both creditor and debtor nations.[1] The leaders of the campaign were convinced that rhetoric and appeals for charity were a weak basis for mobilizing and energizing millions of decent people concerned about the injustice of the international financial system. Instead, campaigners needed to be empowered with facts, information, and analyses. So we prepared accurate, credible, and accessible briefing materials on sovereign debt and the international financial system—and educated millions of people in the arcane processes of international lending, sovereign borrowing, and debt negotiations. In just a few years, these millions of supporters used their newfound understanding to challenge the economic arguments of powerful governments and international financial institutions, in particular the IMF. We learned from the Jubilee 2000 campaign that economic rigour and statistical accuracy are powerful weapons in transforming broader public opinion, but also the opinions of those who stand as the gatekeepers to knowledge and power.

The campaign's resulting achievement was considerable: to persuade the G8 to cancel $110 billion of the debts of 42 countries. But the Jubilee 2000 campaign failed to deflect the G8, through the IMF, imposing and extending economic policies (so-called 'structural adjustment policies' or 'austerity programmes') onto these countries. The purpose of these policies and conditions, in our considered view, is not to increase economic efficiency or stimulate economic growth—the very opposite has often occurred—rather it is to extract and transfer assets from indebted nations to their foreign creditors. The IMF used these conditions systematically to block and slow down the process of debt relief campaigned for by Jubilee 2000. As a result, as we go to press, after five years, only eight of the 42 countries have obtained the relief promised in 1999.

A group involved in the Jubilee 2000 campaign resolved that, if poverty was to be tackled worldwide, the IMF's deflationary economic policies and the institution's stubborn defence of creditors and resistance to debt cancellation, had to be challenged. This could best be done, we believed, by producing an annual alternative to the IMF's influential biennial *World Economic Outlook*—a *Real* *World Economic Outlook*.

At the end of the millennium campaign, I moved to the New Economics Foundation (NEF) to lead the Jubilee Research programme[2] and continue research and analysis of sovereign debt, to expand and deepen that work, and to begin the project that has resulted in this volume. NEF was at that time led by Ed Mayo, chair of Jubilee 2000 UK for the duration of the campaign. With the backing of thousands of Jubilee 2000 supporters and the Network for Social Change, we used our precious, but very scarce, resources to embark on this ambitious venture.

We have worked with NEF's Andrew Simms to incorporate ecological debts into the Jubilee 2000 remit; and are undertaking research (with OXFAM) into alternatives to debt for financing development. We worked too, with NEF's 'localization' experts, Sarah Forster, Bernie Ward, David Boyle, and Pat Conaty—who are developing alternatives to globalization.[3]

While those of us who have helped put together this volume are angered by the injustices of the international financial system, we are not convinced or comfortable with our own correctness. We have many questions and not enough answers. But we are convinced of this: that the world has been turned upside down without the understanding, consent, or authority of the majority.

We intend to be open about our own principles, prejudices, and perspectives, while at the same time exercising intellectual rigour in developing our analyses. We will not pretend to be independent of the constituencies we care about: those who have been impoverished needlessly by unwise economic and environmental policies.

We rely on you, our readers, to assess whether we have achieved our goals in this issue. We welcome your feedback, your comments, and your corrections.[4] Indeed, we hope you will help us build *communities of RWEO* readers (which could meet, just as book clubs do) to discuss, debate, and critique the chapters and essays in **Real World Economic Outlook**. We hope that some of these analyses could be used as a prism to explore the real economics of your local communities, countries, and regions. That way we can collectively share, learn, argue, and expand our economic knowledge, understanding, advocacy, and influence.

Your backing, support, and participation in forthcoming Real World Economic Outlooks will be of great value to the authors.

So we welcome you, our readers, to this ambitious project: the economics of our real world.

Ann Pettifor
Editor

references

[1] 24 million people worldwide, signed the Jubilee 2000 petition—which has entered the Guinness Book of Records, as the first-ever, and largest global petition.

[2] See www.jubileeresearch.org.

[3] See www.neweconomics.org.

[4] Email comments to rweo@neweconomics.org.

acknowledgements

Many people have helped this book evolve from a 'big idea' to reality. It is an ambitious project, and would not have been possible without the confidence and support of our key funders. Their commitment is both our motivation and our inspiration. We hope this volume justifies their faith and investment in us.

The incisive mind and intellectual skills of Jubilee Research's senior economist, Romilly Greenhill, my partner in this project, have been fundamental to the achievement of our objectives, and I thank her for her dedication, enthusiasm and hard work. **Real** *World Economic Outlook* has also been enormously enhanced by the contributions of our guest authors. They are, without exception, distinguished and renowned in their fields, and face enormous pressures on their time. We thank them for their excellent contributions. Geoff Tiley from the Office for National Statistics provided advice with sources of data, but cannot be held responsible for the use they were put to.

One of our distinguished authors, Janet Bush, assisted in the editing of the book as a whole, much improving its overall style and content.

We owe special thanks to our associates in the Jubilee Research team, Susanna Mitchell, Claus Gruber, and Elena Sisti who gave precious time and their special skills to this project. We owe a debt to NEF staff, including Stuart Freeman who kept laptops and PCs humming; Elna Kotze and her team for administrative support; and to Andrea Westall for encouragement and editorial comments.

We owe a great deal to Amanda Watkins at Palgrave Macmillan for believing in and supporting this book; and to Scott Graham, our designer, for his immense patience as we stumbled up a steep learning curve.

While this project would never have started without the support of two funders, it would never have been finished without the dedicated professionalism of our project manager—Mary Murphy. She corralled and marshalled authors, designers, typesetters, words, grammar, and syntax into final shape. The book is very much the better for her ferocious attention to detail and her charming but firm management of us all.

Finally, Jeremy Smith, my best friend and partner, has always believed in me and gave unstinting support to this project, as did my sons Thomas and Christopher Pettifor. They listened patiently as I rehearsed analyses and arguments, challenged my thinking, helped me refine and hone points more effectively, and were only mildly grumpy as holidays and weekends were lost to *Real* World Economic Outlook! For which support, my grateful thanks.

Ann Pettifor

notes on contributors

Dean Baker is Co-Director of the Center for Economic and Policy Research (CEPR) in Washington, DC. He is also author of the Economic Reporting Review, a weekly examination of the economic reporting in the New York Times and the Washington Post, and periodic analyses of the Federal Government's economic data on prices, employment, corporate profits, and the GDP. He received his PhD in economics from the University of Michigan.

David Boyle is an associate of the New Economics Foundation, and the author of *Funny Money, The Tyranny of Numbers* (both HarperCollins), *The Money Changers* (Earthscan) and *Authenticity: Brands, Fakes, Spin and the Lust for Real Life* (HarperCollins/Flamingo 2003).

Janet Bush is an economics journalist. Having started her career at Reuters, she joined the Financial Times as Deputy Economics Correspondent and then New York Correspondent. In 1990, she became a presenter of economics documentaries for BBC Two's *The Money Programme*, before joining the *Times* as Economics Correspondent in 1992. She became Economics Editor in 1997, and subsequently Leader Writer. In 1999, she was appointed Director of New Europe, the cross-party campaign against UK membership of the euro, and then Co-Director of the no campaign in 2000

Pat Conaty currently works as a consultant with the New Economics Foundation. An Honorary Research Fellow at the University of Birmingham he has published many reports in the fields of money advice, fuel poverty, ecological enterprise, the social economy and community reinvestment.

Jane D'Arista is Director of Programs for the Financial Markets Center. She has written on the history of US monetary policy and financial regulation, international and domestic monetary systems, and capital flows to emerging economies. From 1988 to 1999, she taught and administered a program in international finance at Boston University School of Law. Before that, she served for 20 years as a staff economist for the US Congress.

Herman E. Daly is Professor at the University of Maryland, School of Public Affairs. From 1988 to 1994 he was Senior Economist in the Environment Department of the World Bank. Prior to 1988 he was Alumni Professor of Economics at Louisiana State University, where he taught economics for 20 years. He holds a BA from Rice University and a PhD from Vanderbilt University. In 1996 he received Sweden's Honorary Right Livelihood Award, and the Heineken Prize for Environmental Science awarded by the Royal Netherlands Academy of Arts and Sciences. In 1999 he was awarded the Sophie Prize (Norway) for contributions in the area of Environment and Development.

Alan Freeman is a visiting Fellow of the University of Greenwich, and an economist with the Greater London Authority. He is co-editor of a forthcoming collaborative critical book on globalization.

Jayati Ghosh is Professor at the Centre of Economic Studies and Planning in the School of Social Sciences at Jawanharlal Nehru University, New Delhi, India. She writes a regular current affairs column for Frontline Magazine, Businessline Financial daily and other journals and is currently the Executive Secretary of the International Development Associates (IDEAs), a South-based network of development economists seeking to promote heterodox approaches to economics.

Wynne Godley has for a number of years been working with The Levy Economics Institute of Bard College. He is Professor Emeritus of Applied Economics at Cambridge University, a fellow of King's College, Cambridge, and Senior Visiting Scholar at the Cambridge Endowment for Research in Finance (CERF) at the Judge Institute of Management Studies in Cambridge. A member of HM Treasury's Panel of Independent Forecasters, the so-called 'Wise Men' he worked for 13 years (1956–70) in the Treasury where he became deputy director of the Economic Section.

Romilly Greenhill is the Senior Economist at Jubilee Research at the New Economics Foundation. Prior to joining Jubilee Research, she worked as an economist in the Ugandan Ministry of Finance, Planning and Economic Development and has also worked in a research capacity for the UN Conference on Trade and Development (UNCTAD) and the Institute of Development Studies (IDS.)

Claus Gruber is currently an associate of the New Economics Foundation. A 20-year veteran of Deutsche Bank, he is focusing on the impact of stock options on wealth inequality, corporate behavior and profitability, as well as analyzing the pension industry.

Michael Hudson is an independent Wall Street Financial Analyst with much of his work being for US money managers: Chase Manhattan, Scudder Stevens & Clark, and Arthur Anderson, as well as Kemper Financial and Zurich International. A Distinguished Professor of Economics at the

University of Missouri (Kansas City), he has also taught at the New School (Graduate Faculty) in New York.

Jomo K. S. (Kwame Sundaram) is Professor in the Applied Economics Department, University of Malaya, Kuala Lumpur, Malaysia. He has taught at the Science University of Malaysia (USM), Harvard, Yale College, National University of Malaysia (UKM) and Cornell University, and has spent two sabbaticals at Cambridge University. Studying at Yale (BA, 1973) and Harvard (MPA, 1974; PhD, 1978), he is founding chairman of IDEAs, International Development Economics Associates (www.networkideas.org).

Nic Marks leads the New Economics Foundations Well-being programme, exploring the links between personal, social, economic, and environmental well-being - particularly in regard to public policy formation. An Associate of NEF since 2000 he is also a qualified psychotherapist

Ann Pettifor is a Director at the New Economics Foundation, leading NEF's work on international finance; and is editor of *Real World Economic Outlook*. In 1996 she co-founded and was for five years director of the Jubilee 2000 campaign for the cancellation of poor country debts. She is on the board of the UN's Human Development Report; has a degree in English from Wits. University, Johannesburg, and an honorary doctorate from the University of Newcastle.

Zo Randriamaro is a human rights and gender activist from Madagascar. A sociologist by training she currently works with Third World Network-Africa as the Manager of the Gender and Economic Reforms in Africa (GERA) Programme.

Dani Rodrik is Professor of international political economy at the John F. Kennedy School of Government, Harvard University. He has published widely in the areas of international economics, economic development, and political economy. He is affiliated with the National Bureau of Economic Research, Centre for Economic Policy Research (London), Center for Global Development, Institute for International Economics, and Council on Foreign Relations. Among other honours, he was presented the Leontief Award for Advancing the Frontiers of Economic Thought in 2002.

Gita Sen is Sir Ratan Tata Chair Professor at the Indian Institute of Management in Bangalore, India, and Adjunct Professor at the Faculty of Public Health, Harvard University. She is a founding member of DAWN (Development Alternatives with Women for a New Era), a network of Third World researchers, activists, and policy-makers committed to alternative development and gender justice.

Franklin Serrano is an Associate Professor at the Instituto de Economia of the Universidade Federal do Rio de Janeiro, Argentina where he does research and teaches macroeconomics, economic development and (Sraffian) political economy. He got his PhD from Cambridge University (UK) in 1996.

Andrew Simms is Policy Director at NEF. A regular contributor to the *World Disasters Report*, published by the International Federation of Red Cross and Red Crescent Societies, Andrew spent four years leading campaigns for Christian Aid where he did original work on the ecological debt concept.

Joseph E. Stiglitz is Professor of Economics and Finance at Columbia University in New York. In 2001, he was awarded the Nobel Prize in economics. He has taught at Princeton, Stanford, and MIT. He was the Drummond Professor and a fellow of All Souls College, Oxford. A member of the Council of Economic Advisors from 1993–95 during the Clinton Administration, he served as CEA chairman from 1995–97. He then became Chief Economist and Senior Vice-President of the World Bank from 1997–2000. His book *Globalization and Its Discontents* (Norton June 2001) has been translated into 20 languages and is an international bestseller.

Robert Hunter Wade is Professor of Politics and Development at the London School of Economics. He has taught at Victoria University (Wellington), UCSD, Sussex, Princeton, MIT, Brown; been a fellow of the Institute for Advanced Study, Princeton, at the Institute for Advanced Study, Berlin, and at the Russell Sage Foundation, New York City; and worked as an economist in the World Bank and in the Office of Technology Assessment (US Congress).

Peter Warburton is an independent economic consultant and a director of Rhombus Research. For 15 years he was a City economist with Shearson Lehman (now Lehman Brothers) and Robert Fleming (now J P Morgan Chase). Before this, he worked as an economic researcher, forecaster, and lecturer at the London Business School and the City University. A member of the Institute of Economic Affairs' Shadow Monetary Policy Committee he published *Debt and Delusion* in 1999 and the *IEA Yearbook of Government Performance* in 2002.

Erinc Yeldan is Professor of Economics at Bilkent University in Ankara, Turkey. Receiving his PhD from the University of Minnesota, Minneapolis, his recent work focuses on empirical, dynamic general equilibrium models of the Turkish economy and applications of endogenous growth systems. His areas of interest are International Economics and General Equilibrium Modelling.

executive summary

This book reviews, analyzes, and provides an outlook for the global economy. We examine in depth the consequences of the transformation that has taken place over these last 30 years: the global deregulation and empowerment of financial markets within the economic framework of 'globalization' and the widespread debt-deflation that has resulted.

We show that:

- Globalization has not been 'corporate-driven' nor is 'technology' responsible. Instead, we contend, the origins lie with the United States' need to finance the post Vietnam War-deficit, and to do so without making 'structural adjustments' to the US economy. This led US politicians, backed by the UK Government, to lift controls over capital markets—so as to tap their resources to fund the US deficit.

- Globalization, therefore, was created by politicians and can be reversed by politicians.

- The three pillars that make up the architecture of globalization are: a) the removal of restraints on money, national and international; b) the 'downsizing' of the government or state; and c) the attempt to create a single global market in goods and services.

- Removing controls over the finance sector paved the way for its rise to dominance, which in turn has led to a transformation of the global economy and increased instability. Financial institutions, we contend, no longer act as servants to the real economy but as its masters.

- In the process, elected governments have stripped themselves of key economic powers, hollowing out democratic institutions, transferring powers to markets, and undermining their ability to meet the democratic mandates of their electorates. The democratic vacuum has been filled by NGOs and other organizations.

- Independent central bankers, supported by finance ministers and governments, have acted recklessly and abdicated their role as guardians of the credit and financial system.

The consequences for the global economy are grave:

- An enormous increase (or 'bubble') in the stock of financial assets in relation to the 'real' economy, as measured by GDP or the stock of physical, human, and technological capital.

- As a counterpart to this huge increase in assets, an explosion in the level of indebtedness amongst households, corporations, and governments.
- Central bankers and institutions like the IMF have presided over a combination of asset price inflation and consumer price deflation, including the deflation of wages.
- This careless approach to *asset price* inflation has greatly benefited the rich.
- Economic research over the last decade has shown convincingly that the inflationary paranoia of earlier years was just that—largely paranoia. Low to moderate levels of inflation have had no significant adverse *real* consequences; further reductions in inflation do not lead to faster economic growth, lower unemployment, and higher real wages but threaten deflation.
- At the same time the obsession with *consumer price* inflation, and a preference for deflation, have led to falls in wages and in the prices of commodities—and have hurt the poor.
- Under this transformation of the global economy, there has been a marked increase in global inequalities of income and wealth; and a net transfer of resources from poor people and poor countries to rich people and rich countries, in particular the United States.
- That inequalities in *wealth* (assets minus debt) have increased much more than inequalities in *incomes* over the past two decades; and that this fact is unrecognized by economists, who focus only on income inequalities.
- That far from bringing about increased efficiency, productivity, and economic growth, finance-led globalization has actually led to lower investment rates, higher unemployment, and economic stagnation.
- That the global economy is dangerously addicted to fossil fuels, driving conflict, climate change, volatile energy costs, and unresolved confrontation over how to share the global commons of the atmosphere.

As a result, the *Real* world economic outlook is that

- There will be a further collapse in the credit system in the rich world, led by the United States, leading to soaring personal and corporate bankruptcies.
- Once default rates approach 1 per cent of the value of debt across the whole lending spectrum, the profitability of banks is called into question. If default rates reach 2 per cent, then the probability of a financial crisis rises appreciably.
- The risks of a debt-deflationary spiral in the rich world are significant.

- Europe will continue to experience low levels of growth as a result of the region's neoliberal policies, most notably the Stability and Growth Pact.
- East and South Asia will continue to experience deflation; that East Asia will be hard hit by its dependence on the United States; and that South Asia will continue to see high levels of poverty.
- South and Central America will continue to experience economic stagnation and state decline.
- The economic outlook for Middle East and North Africa is grim, particularly in light of high debt burdens and social and political instability.
- Africa faces an uncertain future as a result of deflationary economic policies, falling commodity prices; high levels of external debt, and AIDS.

Finally, we urge the replacement of the three pillars of the architecture of globalization. We make proposals for the

- Taming of financial markets,
- 'Upsizing' the state, and
- 'Downsizing' the single global market.

introduction

ann pettifor

In this first edition of **Real** *World Economic Outlook*, we conclude that the crises now endemic in our economies, and afflicting millions of ordinary, innocent citizens, were not induced by 'technology', by the 'eternal behaviour of the market'[1], or indeed by the foolish behaviour of investors. Nor do we blame 'corporate-driven globalization' and 'the system'. Instead, we lay responsibility for these crises at the door of elected politicians and 'responsible' central bankers, who have pursued with extraordinary single-mindedness a single economic policy, market fundamentalism (often celebrated as 'globalization'), despite this policy's well-established record in accelerating and deepening financial crises. We note that the consequences of following such a disastrous single policy have included record rises in personal, household, and corporate debt and defaults; a collapse in productive investment and in stock and commodity markets; high, and rising levels of unemployment; and a growing polarity in wealth and poverty, which is, in turn, fuelling crime, random violence, terrorism, and war.

In Chapter 25 we propose a different set of economic policies, which we believe will go some way to remedying the imbalances and insecurities inflicted unnecessarily on our world by this single economic policy.

As we go to press in 2003, the world is mesmerized by the threatened economic and political instability of the Middle East, caused by a pre-emptive invasion of a sovereign state, Iraq. To the west, economists and financial journalists are spooked by the huge US imbalances—its massive foreign trade deficit, historically high household debts, and runaway federal and state budget deficits. Looking south, Bolivia is erupting with the anger of impoverished coca farmers deprived of their livelihoods by a government more concerned about foreign debts than domestic stability. In Africa, there are precious few resources to help the millions of people dying of disease and a lethal plague, unprecedented in history. This is laying the ground for future social and economic instability. And in South East Asia economies are being damaged by the sudden appearance of a new, virulent, killer disease, severe acute respiratory syndrome (SARS).

At the same time, the world is lapsing into recession for the second time in three years. Deflation is now hurting and undermining the economies of Japan and Hong Kong and threatening the economies of China and Germany. Given the inter-connectedness of the global economy, the spread of deflation to yet more countries is very real.

RWEO analyzes and examines the economic background to these developments, and challenges traditional, mainstream economic approaches. Neoliberal analyses are deeply flawed, we argue, and as a result mainstream economists are either blind to, or else complacent about, the deeply disturbing developments outlined above.

The IMF's *World Economic Outlook* (published in April 2003) provides a clear example of such complacency. It is relatively upbeat, assuring us that 'provided equity prices [as if Western equity prices were one of the fundamentals of the global economy] do not fall further, the drag on GDP growth— while still significant—should start to diminish. . . . United States expected to continue to lead the recovery…in emerging markets growth prospects have fallen moderately' . . . and so on.

On the worrying threat of deflation, about which many economists are now expressing grave concerns, IMF staff, obsessed by inflation over these last 30 years, shrug off the risks: 'The risk of a generalized global deflation, or even of a deflationary spiral in the major economies, appears small: financial markets and institutions have remained broadly resilient *so far: corporate and household debt burdens appear manageable;* and there remains scope for policy adjustment in most countries.'[2] [our italics]

The effect is to numb readers into false comfort and to obscure reality.[3] This would not matter, but the *World Economic Outlook*, like the World Bank's *Global Economic Prospects*, is read in university libraries, investment bank research departments, government economic policy and international development departments, and by the staff of presidents and prime ministers. These reviews and reports are transmitted as gospel in the mainstream media throughout the world. Both institutions are dismissive, defiant even, in the face of deflation, growing inequality, high and increasing unemployment, and chronic impoverishment. Complacency and indifference are dangerous in our increasingly unstable world. This *Real World Economic Outlook* sets out to counter the irresponsible smugness of mainstream economists, and to alert readers both to the reality of the global economy and the grave risks.

challenging economic dogma

We note that it is scarcely possible to be recruited to the staff of the IMF or the World Bank, to influential institutions like the Bank for International

Settlements (BIS), or indeed to any major Western university economics department, without holding fervently to a set of economic principles that have been elevated to a doctrine; even, some would argue, an ideology. These economic principles are often loosely defined as 'neoliberal', 'orthodox', 'market fundamentalist', or 'monetarist'.

The following tenets, simplified but not distorted, will, we hope, illuminate for our readers the intellectual armoury of this body of economic thought:[4]

- Economic growth, more than distribution, environmental sustainability, or well-being is the supreme aim of economic policy-making

- Economic efficiency, not economic justice, is, and should be, one of the ultimate goals of all economic policy; markets are the most reliable deliverers of economic efficiency; they should therefore be elevated to become the *supreme organizing principle* of society.

- Markets, (not governments, and least of all parliaments), should be tasked with allocating and distributing resources, like income from taxation. They should mobilize and allocate the resources needed for pensions, hospitals, and health provision; schools and universities; public transport; and cultural activities—from opera to public broadcasting to international cricket and football clubs. Indeed markets, it is argued, should allocate resources for almost every aspect of the economy, except perhaps *warfare*.

- Governments are 'rent-seeking' and should be marginalized.

- Economic policy (monetary and fiscal) should be privatized in the hands of financial markets that, surprisingly, are regarded as having no such 'rent-seeking' instincts.

- Distribution of income is, and must remain, beyond the control of economists and the 'vested interests' of governments; markets are better at redistributing income than, say, elected democratic institutions.[5]

- The environment, like human happiness, is an 'externality'.

- Individuals are what matter, not collectively organized communities, groups, or even nation states.

- The interests of the owners and lenders of capital (creditors, financiers, investors, bankers, bond holders) should take precedence over the interests of the users of capital, the productive sector, or governments.

- Inflation hurts the interests of creditors, as it transfers assets from creditors to debtors; therefore inflation is elevated to Public Enemy No. 1 in the global economy. All economic policy-making must be geared towards its defeat.

- Deflation, or the suppression of prices, on the other hand, is at the heart of most IMF 'structural adjustment programmes'; deflation, of course, transfers assets from debtors to creditors.

Human security, love, friendship, mutual trust, community, harmony, and stability, as well as environmental sustainability are, on the whole, considered external to the central organizing principle of the economy—the market. Vital to the well-being of us all, and central to human development, these issues are of supreme indifference to the IMF, the World Bank, and other orthodox economists. *Their* major goal is the achievement of economic efficiency under the government of markets—regardless of the human, social, or political costs or of damage to the environment. We believe it is time that economists, particularly those who make their living at the expense of global taxpayers, are reined in to meet society's goals.

The now-dominant economic dogma is not new. These ideas and concepts are amongst the most antiquated models or explanations of how economies work or should work. The 'globalization' model was, after all, applied way back in the period between 1870 and 1914, and again after the First World War. The Great Depression and its contingent disasters led to widespread demand for the overthrow of this economic ideology; demand that could no longer be ignored.[6]

Then, as now, these economic policies and models have led humanity and the environment into unbearable degradation, poverty, and misery. Dangerous international tensions have arisen. The response has been entirely predictable. Society—locally, nationally, and internationally—is making 'concerted efforts to protect itself from the market'. History is repeating itself. Current resistance to market liberalism echoes past resistance. As Karl Polanyi argued in his great, and increasingly relevant, work, *The Great Transformation*, the second 'great transformation' of the 20th century, the rise of fascism, was a result of the first 'great transformation'—the rise of market liberalism.[7]

Today, the rise of terrorism, militarism, nationalism, protectionism, and fundamentalism is an irrational and inadequate response to a global economic transformation brought about by 'government of and by the markets'. In short, societies and communities are resisting, sometimes with violence, the rise in poverty, the polarization of inequality, and the frequency of financial crises. Society, however clumsily and self-destructively, is seeking to protect itself from the wildly utopian, some would say delusional, project of orthodox economists and their supporters in governments around the world—the subordination of human, social, political, and environmental relations to the actions of 'the invisible hand'.

The ideology driving the marketization or 'globalization' of society is pervasive, and enjoys a consensus amongst the political classes of almost all most nations. Modern governments are as proactive as the Soviet Union was, in *planning* changes to societies so that markets can function and take over from government. Nowhere is this more evident than in Britain. The country has been transformed, by successive Conservative and Labour governments, from its post-war co-operative and collective condition to a society, which if present trends continue, will be directed 'from the cradle to the grave' by the 'invisible hand' of the market.

In elevating markets to a central role, governments abandon their responsibility to provide for the weak and defenceless; for vital public infrastructure and services; and for the environment; and divest themselves of power. This helps explain why our political institutions, our parliaments, congresses, and political parties are increasingly hollowed out and impotent; why citizens are abstaining in elections to powerless parliaments, or else choosing to elect controlling, authoritarian leaders, who promise stability and continuity. It helps explain why so many are taking to the streets, or resorting to random violence, criminality, and terrorism, desperately seeking effective outlets for the expression of anger, humiliation, frustration, and powerlessness.

We, the authors of **Real** *World Economic Outlook*, do not doubt the efficacy or importance of markets. Markets have been with us, argue some anthropologists, for more than 5000 years. They are a natural and inevitable part of the interchange and exchange that takes place in and between human communities. However, throughout history, and with brief exceptions during the early 20th century, markets have been *subordinated* to the interests and control of human communities and the environment—through regulation. Orthodox economists have tried to turn that world upside down.

This obsession with the efficiency of markets includes labour markets of course. Labour markets are most efficient when the lowest number of people is employed, at minimal wages. Unemployment is not of great concern to orthodox economists. While rarely asserting this explicitly, these economists regard unemployment as a necessary, if unpleasant, by-product of that higher goal: economic efficiency. While the IMF does 'track' unemployment in that it provides figures for it in its *World Economic Outlook*, it does not really take unemployment seriously as a focus of economic policy; and rarely assesses policies in terms of the effects on unemployment. Nor do central bankers, even though they may have mandates to do so.

RWEO takes a different approach. A population engaged in gainful employment is fundamental, we argue, to the mental, social, political, and economic health of any nation, and of the international community as a whole. High levels of unemployment, as Keynes argued, lead to 'privation and—what is sometimes worse—the extreme anxiety which exists today in millions of homes all over the world'.[8] It is this anxiety that lies behind today's growing resistance to the marketization of society.

Next to markets, argue these economists, individuals—not states, groups, communities, or classes—are the most important units in society. Again, we at *Real World Economic Outlook* do not contest the power and genius of individual human action. *However, we believe the shackling of human invention only to the making of money is ultimately to diminish that invention.* Moreover, we will not isolate the individual from her neighbourhood, community, class, ethnic identity, state, or environment.

Orthodox economists do not regard the growth of inequality as significant; nor do they believe that their policy decisions exacerbate inequality. In his review of neoliberal economics, Prof. Gilpin tells us, 'Concern over the distribution of income lies outside the primary focus of the discipline.'[9] Inequality, assert these economists, is hellishly difficult to measure—and so will not be measured. We beg to differ. Inequality is not too difficult for us to measure—as Robert Wade suggests in Chapter 15—and measure it we will. We will track unemployment and will make the inequality of both income and assets a primary focus of each annual review.

Sadly economics, as taught today, is not just a dismal science; it is a dreary discipline. Little more than a subdivision of applied mathematics, it is based on assumptions that do not hold in reality and which have scant relevance to our complex, diverse, *real* world. The obsession with a) the promotion of economic efficiency achieved through government by markets; b) the self-interested optimizing behaviour of individuals; and c) the wisdom of usurious financial markets, means that today, the economics taught in universities ignores reality and is narrow and exclusive. In its assumed world of rational agents, neoliberal economics simply concludes that unsustainable debt is impossible!

Little wonder then that a group of students at one of France's leading universities, the *Ecole Normale Superieure*, revolted, and formed the 'Post-Autistic Economics (PAE) Network.[10] We share their concerns. In our annual *Outlooks*, we will attempt to treat economics in a holistic and balanced way, placing economic developments in political, social, environmental, historical, and cultural contexts.

Neoliberal economics is not just a hopelessly utopian view of society. It has also eroded the key principles of economic, social, and political justice:

the principles of *taxation, regulation, and democracy*. *RWEO* will argue for these principles to once again take their place at the heart of economic debate.

Finally, official economic forecasting, locked in the grip of ideologues and vested interests, now produces *deeply flawed economic analyses and forecasting*. Does this matter? Yes, of course it does, because bad forecasting rooted in false analyses, can—and does—lead to disastrous consequences for ordinary investors and for government policy makers. Examples come readily to hand. Very few economists, with the notable exception of Brian Reading,[11] predicted Japan's descent into a deflationary economic morass. Japan's decline has inflicted widespread pain and suffering on individuals and communities within that country, and continues to impact both on Asian economies and the wider global economy. Yet mainstream economists appear impotent, if not indifferent, to Japan's economic malaise.

Back in 1994, World Bank economists were apparently nonplussed by the high interest rates that attracted foreign investors like bees to the honey pot of Mexican bonds or *tesobonos*. Their forecast for the forthcoming year reinforced their own prejudices. These were that Latin America was prospering and enjoyed 'improved economic prospects', thanks to 'trade liberalisation, improved public finances (such as taxation reforms and lower fiscal deficits), and structural reforms to encourage the private sector....making [Latin American countries] much more creditworthy (sic) and much more attractive to foreign investors'.[12] While Mexico did not actually default in 1994, her threatened default triggered a major international financial crisis. The US Government (with the reluctant support of the European Central Bank) moved in with a $55 billion credit line, which staved off the immediate liquidity problem, and forced US banks to reschedule their Mexican debt. In return for this, the IMF imposed an 'adjustment' package, intended to generate the money needed to repay the debts. This adjustment has shifted the burden of repayment onto the shoulders of Mexican workers and peasants. The Mexican economy has still not recovered.

No-one, least of all the two Nobel Prize-winning economists running the Long Term Capital Management (LTCM) Fund, predicted Russia's default in 1998, and the impact that default was to have on highly leveraged US hedge funds and banks. 'The losses came from every corner. They were so swift, so encyclopaedic in their breadth, so utterly unexpected that the LTCM partners felt abandoned. They had suddenly lost control, as though the gods of science had been dislodged and some unseen diabolical power had taken hold of their fates.'[13]

No one, least of all the chief economic adviser to the Bush Administration,

Larry Lindsey (once a well-paid adviser to ENRON), predicted the then biggest ever-corporate collapse and bankruptcy in US history in 2001.[14]

Even well after the US economy began to contract in 2001, Wall Street analysts and neoliberal enthusiasts were still talking up stocks. Alfred Broaddus, the President of the Richmond Federal Reserve Bank, told the *Washington Post* that 'it's quite possible that the near- and intermediate-term outlook for the next year, year and a half, could be *very bright indeed*' [our italics]. And his judgement was offered even as deflation loomed and stock markets crashed, inflicting long-term pain on corporations, pension funds, and individual investors. Partly as a result of such advice, millions removed their precious savings from safe havens, invested them in dangerously unstable stock markets, and, egged on by analysts, kept them there until too late. Worse still, over-optimistic predictions of the stock market's progress duped pension-fund holders into keeping their funds in stocks and shares that were very obviously heading for a fall.

greenspan's policy of malign neglect

From the 1970s until the present, influential policy-makers—mainstream economists, central bankers, finance ministers, and IMF economists—have appeared obsessed by *inflation*. Representing the finance sector, they have consistently argued that policies for attacking and subduing inflation must take priority over almost every other public policy objective, including the redistribution of wealth; and the defence of the weak and vulnerable through publicly-funded services. So central bankers and like-minded colleagues in the IMF have repressed inflation of inputs like wages, commodity prices, and goods. With brutal efficiency, they achieved their aim by applying deflationary economic policies, the so-called 'structural adjustment' or 'growth and stability' policies so pervasive in developing countries and Europe.

But the evidence shows that central bankers had only a *partial* concern with inflation. While deflating prices in one part of the economy, they recklessly ignored asset *price inflation*—which massively enriched the already rich. Central bankers like Alan Greenspan refused to apply the brakes on this inflationary spiral (by raising interest rates) despite warnings from none other than Milton Friedman, University of Chicago Nobel laureate. 'I think there is a good deal of comparison between the market in 1929 and the market today,' he told the *New Yorker* magazine. 'If anything, I suspect there is more of a bubble in today's market than there was in 1929.'[15]

John Cassidy, author of *dot.con* and writer for the *New Yorker*, is in no doubt of the culpability of the Chairman of the US Federal Reserve, 'Alan Greenspan will go down in the history books as the Fed chairman who oversaw the greatest speculative boom and bust that the US has ever seen. He wasn't the only person responsible for the Internet bubble, but his actions encouraged and prolonged the speculative mania.'[16] This has not, however, prevented the likes of Greenspan from receiving honorary knighthoods, or indeed extended periods in office.

What is the *real* story behind the combination of an obsession with consumer price inflation and malign neglect of asset price inflation? Why do most Western central banks have targets for inflation of anywhere between zero and 3 per cent and yet allow asset price inflation to run riot?

The reason is simple. Inflation transfers assets *from* creditors to debtors. Inflation will erode the real value of any debt, meaning that the debtor pays back less in real terms. Conversely deflation—where prices are falling—increases the real value of debts.

The combination of consumer price deflation and asset price inflation is every wealth-holder's dream. Under deflation, the costs of wages, commodities, and other inputs fall, while asset price inflation means that capital gains steadily rise and are not eroded in real terms. Lowering costs can make higher profits. Capital gains can be recycled into further capital purchases leading to yet more capital gains. So the rich make money from money while those reliant for their income on current wages, and not from capital gains, receive a smaller and smaller share of national income.

Alan Greenspan and his colleagues in the neoliberal establishment have truly been guilty of robbing the poor to pay the rich on a global scale.

The cost of these wrong analyses and predictions is almost immeasurable. Over the past three years, pension funds have built up $2500 billion of liabilities. The impact of those losses on the weak and elderly will be devastating, adversely affecting millions of individuals, their families, and their communities for years to come. But these events were entirely predictable—and were indeed accurately predicted by those who take a more objective view of markets, like the Center for Economic Policy Research in Washington.[17]

Real World Economic Outlook will avoid ideological rigidity and fixed belief systems. We will adopt a broader, deeper approach to economic forces. We will be open and honest about our world-view and provide space for those who do not share that world-view. At the same time, we believe it is now urgent for the health both of our democratic institutions, but also the stability of the global economy, to provide a platform for dissidents: those who have been ruthlessly silenced and marginalized by mainstream neoliberal ideologues. Above all we hope to provide platforms for the promotion of new economics—economic policies that will, we believe, lead humanity and the earth into an era of economic justice and sustainability.

references

[1] See Martin Wolf's reservations about the Anglo-Saxon model of shareholder capitalism in 'Managers should not listen too carefully to the market', *Financial Times*, 7 May 2003.

[2] *World Economic Outlook: Growth and Institutions*, (Washington DC: IMF, 2000) p. 13.

[3] It is tempting to be cynical about the IMF's complacency on the issue of deflation. The IMF is a creditor-dominated institution. In a deflationary environment, assets are transferred from debtors to creditors. The reverse occurs in an inflationary environment, which is why creditors are so hostile to inflation.

[4] Prof. Robert Gilpin, in his book *Global Political Economy: understanding the international economic order* (New Jersey: Princeton University Press, 2001) provides an excellent analysis of the 'neoclassical synthesis', the theoretical consensus of mainstream, orthodox, or conventional economists.

[5] See 'Thinking the Unthinkable—think tanks and the economic counter-revolution, 1931–1983: p. 101. Hayek to Merrian: 'you are inclined to burden democracy with tasks which it cannot achieve'.

[6] See P. Hirst and G. Thompson, *Globalisation in Question* (Cambridge: Polity Press, 1996) and H. James, *The End of Globalization: the lessons from the Great Depression* (Harvard: Harvard University Press, 2001).

[7] See K. Polanyi, *The Great Transformation: the political and economic origins of our time* (Boston: Beacon Press 2001) with an introduction by Fred Block and a foreword by Joseph Stiglitz.

[8] J. M. Keynes, *Essays in persuasion* (London: Macmillan Cambridge University Press, 1972) Ch 6 'Economy', p. 135.

[9] Gilpin, op. cit. p. 67.

10 See www.paecon.net.

11 B. Reading, *Japan, the Coming Collapse* (Orien Books Ltd., 1992).

12 World Bank Debt Tables, 1994 p. 17.

13 R. Lowenstein, *When Genius Failed. The rise and fall of Long Term Capital Management* (London: Fourth Estate, 2001).

14 Mr. Lindsey was, according to Robert Bryce 'on Enron's payroll before going to the White House, earning $100,000 in consulting fees from the Houston company'. *Guardian* 6 November 2002 'Enron: the inside story'—an extract from Bryce's book on Enron: *Pipe Dreams*.

15 J. Cassidy, *dot.con: the greatest story ever told* (London: HarperCollins, 2002) p. 183.

16 *Financial Times*, 2 March 2002.

17 See www.cepr.net.

PART 01

---

global transformation and global outlook

introduction

Part 01 is written by staff of the New Economics Foundation (NEF), in particular by the Jubilee Research team (which majors on international finance and debt), with contributions from Joseph Stiglitz. While we share many common values and principles, we have distinct voices, and these are reflected in the various contributions. We review the transformation of the global economy over the last 30 years, laying out the groundwork for an analysis of how this seismic shift impacts on today's economy, and of the future outlook.

In Chapter 1, we analyze the key forces that have shaped globalization, and challenge the frequently expressed but superficial explanation of 'new technology' as the key driver. We draw on the work of Eric Helleiner, who has a comprehensive grasp of the background to the deregulation of capital markets.

In Chapter 2, we present original research and data on the *consequences* of globalization: the growth of a massive credit bubble and its counterpart—the huge growth of debt; the 'hoover' effect of transfers from poor to rich; the predominance of speculation over enterprise; the threat of deflation; and the way in which governments—rich and poor—have lost, or given up, control over their economies.

Chapters 3 and 4 outline both the economic and the environmental outlooks respectively, which we conclude are bleak. We note that it is ordinary wage-earning consumers that are propping up the 'engine' economies of the world, by spending and borrowing excessively. When the bubble bursts, they will be left with unpayable debts. We examine the global economy's dangerous addiction to fossil fuels, a dependency that drives conflict, climate change, volatile energy costs, and unresolved confrontation over how to share the global commons of the atmosphere.

making sense of our world: 1970–2003

ann pettifor

turning the world upside down

We used to build our cities and towns around churches. Now banks are at their centres . . .

John Densmore, drummer for the Doors, explaining why he could not accept $1.5 million from Apple Mac for the use in their commercials of: "When the Music's Over . . ."   (Guardian 12 August 2002).

In just over 30 years, our world has been turned upside down. When Jim Morrison and the Doors were making music and rocking audiences in San Francisco, a form of economic regulation—the Judaeo Christian principle of the Sabbath—prevailed; namely that one day of each week would be set aside for rest, for a short respite to the exploitation of land (in its broadest sense) and people. On each seventh day, moneylenders were expected to retreat from the temple.

In the Western world, and in many parts of the Third World, Sunday had, for more than 2000 years, been a strict form of regulation: a periodic correction to imbalances and injustice. With the onset of the deregulated, globalized economy, this form of regulation had to be banished, along with other forms of regulation. Sunday was 'liberalized'—to use the loaded language of economists—implying that people and the land were emancipated from a forced day of rest. Instead they were 'freed' to work, consume, and make money, for long hours, seven days a week.

Since 1970, as a result of this and many other forms of deregulation, the world of people like John Densmore has changed beyond recognition. Today, banks and other financial institutions are indeed at the centre of cities and towns, promoting credit cards to all and sundry. Moneylenders use electronic equipment ('holes in the wall') to do business around the clock and every day of the week. Their presence in communities across the world is indicative and symbolic of much broader changes wrought by the remarkable economic experiment known as 'globalization' or market liberalism over the period

1970–2003. These changes have transformed our world, and rendered it much more unstable than the period 1945–70.

The post-war era was a period of relative economic and social stability and rising material welfare in all parts of the world. These advances were distributed unequally between the North and the South, the East and the West; yet there is widespread intellectual agreement that over this period world living standards were rising. As Robert Wade and Alan Freeman demonstrate in Part 03, this progress has now stopped. Instead, our world has for some years now become more polarized and divergent, with the rich countries 'pulling away' not just from the poorer countries, but also from middle-income countries. Gita Sen notes in Chapter 13 that global markets have acted to extract and transfer assets from poor countries to rich countries—engaging in what Sen reminds us is a form of 'primitive accumulation'.

This polarization and divergence, is we argue, not accidental or 'natural'. It is not because human ingenuity, geography, new technology, and advancement are present in one part of the world, and lacking in others. Instead, it is a direct consequence of the remarkable economic experiment of market liberalism, which has, we contend, brought our world to a point of grave peril.

The danger is expressed in the growing divergence between rich and poor; in the high rate of corporate defaults; in the collapse of world commodity markets; in the crashing of Western stock markets; and the bursting of the dot.com and telecoms 'bubbles'. It is reflected in the increasing number of conflicts brought about by our addiction to fossil fuels. It finds expression in a world made insecure by rises in crime, random violence, opportunistic diseases, and the threat of nuclear weapons. A world ruptured by terrorism on the one hand, and the military aggression of the United States, backed by the United Kingdom, on the other; a world divided by the shattering of UN authority, the splintering of European alliances, and destabilized by the ungovernability of much of Africa and Latin America.

These destructive and frightening consequences are not very different from the consequences of a similar experiment in market liberalism, tried out in the 1920s and 1930s but abandoned between 1945 and 1970. The cheerleaders of the earlier experiment deployed many of the same arguments and defences used by orthodox economists today. Then, as now, they expressed supreme confidence in the success of the experiment. Then, as now, politicians were advised that economic cycles had come to an end; that the 'end of history' was nigh. A New Economy had been designed and engineered, which would bring continuous and uninterrupted benefits. Winston Churchill reflected on this optimism in his history of the period:

The year 1929 reached almost the end of its third quarter under the promise and appearance of increasing prosperity, particularly in the United States. Extraordinary optimism sustained an orgy of speculation. Books were written to prove that economic crisis was a phase, which expanding business organisation and science had at last mastered, We are apparently finished and done with economic cycles as we have known them, said the President of the New York Stock Exchange in September. But in October a sudden and violent tempest swept over Wall Street . . .

The whole wealth so swiftly gathered in the paper values of previous years vanished. The prosperity of millions of American homes had grown up a gigantic structure of inflated credit, now suddenly proved phantom. Apart from the nation-wide speculation in shares which even the most famous banks had encouraged by easy loans, a vast system of purchase by instalment of houses, furniture, cars and numberless kinds of household conveniences and indulgences had grown up. All now fell together. But yesterday, there had been the urgent question of parking the motor-cars in which thousands of artisans and craftsmen were beginning to travel to their daily work. Today the grievous pangs of falling wages and rising unemployment afflicted the whole community, engaged till this moment in the most active creation of all kinds of desirable articles . . .[1]

Substitute the phrase 'the urgent question of parking motor-cars' with 'the urgent question of parking SUVs (Sports Utility Vehicles)' and Churchill's picture reflects pretty much the state of Western economies today.

Like the globalization experiment of the period 1970–2000, the 1920s were a period of 'extraordinary optimism sustained by an orgy of speculation' before it came to a catastrophic end after 1929—fuelled by greed and by the kind of fraud and deception that has today become commonplace in Wall Street and other financial centres. It was a period when, just as today, economic policies made the finance sector dominant: Moneychangers occupied the high seats of the temple. Then, as in the 1990s, economies were afflicted by a credit bubble conjured up by moneylenders who duped 'practical men'—those who believed themselves to be quite exempt from any intellectual influences, but who were nevertheless, in the words of Keynes, 'the slaves of some defunct economist'.

In a remarkable inaugural speech, which has a contemporary resonance for those millions who have lost pension savings, dot.com, or stock market investments, President Roosevelt attacked the role the financial community played in bringing his country to its knees in the 1930s:

. . . the withered leaves of industrial enterprise lie on every side; farmers find no markets for their produce; the savings of many years in thousands of families are gone. More important, a host of unemployed citizens face the grim problem of existence, and an equally great number toil with little return.

Yet our distress comes from no failure of substance. We are stricken by no plague of locusts. Plenty is at our doorstep, but a generous use of it languishes in the very sight of the supply. Primarily this is because the rulers of the exchange of mankind's goods have failed, through their own stubbornness and their own incompetence, have admitted their failure, and abdicated.

Practices of the unscrupulous money changers stand indicted in the court of public opinion, rejected by the hearts and minds of men.

True they have tried, but their efforts have been cast in the pattern of an out-worn tradition. Faced by failure of credit they have proposed only the lending of more money. Stripped of the lure of profit by which to induce our people to follow their false leadership, they have resorted to exhortations, pleading tearfully for restored confidence. They know only the rules of a generation of self-seekers. They have no vision, and when there is no vision the people perish.

The money changers have fled from their high seats in the temple of our civi-lization. We may now restore that temple to the ancient truths. The measure of the restoration lies in the extent to which we apply social values more noble than mere monetary profit. Recognition of the falsity of material wealth as the stan-dard of success goes hand in hand with the abandonment of the false belief that public office and high political position are to be valued only by the standards of pride of place and personal profit; and there must be an end to a conduct in banking and in business which too often has given to a sacred trust the likeness of callous and selfish wrongdoing.

Small wonder that confidence languishes, for it thrives only on honesty, on honor, on the sacredness of obligations, on faithful protection, on unselfish performance; without them it cannot live.[2]

the post-war revival of market liberalism

During the Second World War, and in the immediate post-war years, politi-cians and economists tried hard to restore stability and equity to the inter-national financial system: to 'restore the temple to the ancient truths'. In Part 04, we outline their designs, which culminated in the decisions of the Bretton Woods conference in 1944, for a more stable and equitable international finan-cial architecture. They had learnt from the disasters of the 1920s and 1930s that unrestrained capital flows led to financial instability and more and more 'Ponzi finance' schemes—financing old liabilities with new liabilities—and further-more, that these unregulated capital flows were incompatible with, and hin-dered, free trade. Central to their plans for the new international financial architecture were controls over capital and the restoration of policy autonomy to governments and states.

Yet at almost the same time, neoliberal economists were preparing to revive the economic ideas that had so devastated capitalist economies in the 1930s.[3] As the horrors of financial catastrophe and world war began to recede from public memory, economists like F.A. Hayek approached the politicians of a country whose foreign traders and colonial empire had for long oriented the economy towards openness and market liberalism: Britain. From 1970-2000, thanks to the extraordinary perseverance of Hayek and his colleagues in right-wing think tanks, academics, journalists, and most importantly politicians and governments (of both the left and right) were slowly re-educated in the virtues and powers of market liberalism.

But it was not the power of ideas only that persuaded politicians of the virtues of market liberalism; economic and political circumstances conspired to make the liberalization of capital flows attractive to US politicians in particular.

why our world was turned upside down

Many argue that the phenomenon known as 'globalization' came about largely because of advances in new technology and communications. For example, Walter Wriston, once Chief Executive Officer of Citibank, one of the world's largest banks, has argued that

> . . . today we are witnessing a galloping new system of international finance (which) differs radically from its precursors in that it was not built by politicians, economists, central bankers or finance ministers, nor did high-level international conferences produce a master plan. It was built by technology . . . by men and women who interconnected the planet with telecommunications and computers.[4]

Others, particularly anti-globalization activists, hold strongly to the view that globalization, (often broadened into 'corporate globalization') was, or is, promoted by big, aggressive corporations, keen to expand their markets and brutal in promoting self-interest.[5]

We contest this view of the driving force behind financial globalization— central to the whole globalization project. On the contrary, we argue, democratic governments and their elected leaders have been the real driving force behind financial liberalization. These leaders were motivated to embark on the 'globalization' project, as Eric Helleiner has cogently argued,[6] because of the costs of the Vietnam War, and the steady expansion of the US trade deficit in the 1960s and 1970s. This led to deliberate decisions by the US and UK governments to remove statutory controls over movements of capital.

The US trade deficit had to be financed, and the United States was determined to get the money without having to make any unpleasant 'structural adjustments' to the US economy and without giving up policy autonomy to foreign creditors. The City of London, backed by the UK Government, was only too happy to broker financing for the US deficit through the 'stateless'

Eurodollar market based in London—a market carefully created by elected representatives of two of the world's most powerful states.

As Helleiner has argued:

> *Ever since the first dollar crisis in late 1960, the (US) government had attempted to postpone adjustment measures by persuading foreign central banks to finance its external deficit through dollar holdings . . . Taking an approach that would prevail throughout the 1970s and 1980s, Washington policymakers fostered a more liberal international financial system as a way of preserving their policy autonomy in the face of growing external constraints.*

The emergence of the Eurodollar market began the process of dismantling capital controls in the 1960s. But as Helleiner notes, the other:

> *advanced industrial states remained wary of international capital movements for the reason discussed at Bretton Woods: Disequilibriating speculative capital movements could restrict their policy autonomy and disrupt both the Bretton Woods system of stable exchange rates and liberal trading relations.*

The removal of these capital controls, which gained terrific momentum as the US deficit ballooned, was pushed by the United States and the United Kingdom and has been central to the process of 'globalization'. Today, the US deficit can only be sustained by mobilizing a staggering $4 billion of foreign savings each working day of the year.

it was not always thus

Back in 1944, as part of the Bretton Woods Agreement, the United States had helped construct the post-war economic order with other Western governments. The new order, which the IMF and the UN were tasked to defend, set out to:

- prevent and limit the imbalances and disorder brought about by the capital liberalization of the 1920s and 1930s;
- restore policy autonomy to nation states (primarily by imposing controls on the movement of capital); while
- liberalizing trade, which included challenging the UK's protectionist policies for imperial preferences.

Two decades after the Bretton Woods Agreement, the Eurodollar market represented the first attempt at bypassing the exchange controls of nation states, and enabled the United States to mobilize additional finance from a foreign capital market. The existence of the Eurodollar market gradually led to the erosion of capital controls by all major Western governments and, finally, most developing country governments. This in turn laid the ground for a massive expansion in the role of finance capital in the global economy, and, as a consequence, for greater trade liberalization.

how our world was turned upside down

In promoting market liberalism, advocates of these policies often called for what spin-doctors describe as 'reforms'—of the financial system, of labour markets, and of trade. The word 'reforms' suggests incremental changes but, on the contrary, they are often fundamental both to social and political relationships, and their impact has been revolutionary.

These radical 'reforms' were sold to the broader public on terms that suggested that, while they might benefit the rich, wealth would 'trickle down' to the poor. Instead, they have achieved the reverse, and, in the process, transformed the world economy for the worse. This is an outcome we analyze in greater detail in Chapter 2, and which we call the 'hoover effect' of globalization. As a result, rich societies enjoy levels of consumption 200 times greater than other societies.

The three 'reforms' or pillars that make up the architecture of globalization are:

- The removal of regulations and controls over capital, both national and international.
- The 'downsizing' of government or the state.
- Attempts by the G8 (through the WTO and other institutions) to create a single global market in goods and services.

Of these three 'reforms', we regard the first as the most important because it led to the second and third—marginalizing the state; removing policy autonomy from elected governments; and facilitating the creation of a single global market. Finally, capital deregulation has helped create the crisis of debt now threatening the stability both of the developing and developed world.

Neoliberal economists and commentators tend to have a blind spot for the role played by deregulated capital in today's globalized world. Instead, as we have noted above, responsibility for globalization is often laid at the door of impersonal and disembodied 'technology'.[7]

One of the reasons why it is easier to identify technology as responsible for globalization is that the rapid development of technology is highly visible to all and sundry whereas the massive expansion in financial flows is not. Nor do neoclassical economists acknowledge expanded financial flows (as we demonstrate in the next chapter). In the words of Michael Hudson a 'protective cloak of invisibility has become a distinguishing feature of the economic analysis promoted by the financial sector'.[8]

> *The neo-classical synthesis became the economics of capitalism without capitalists, capital assets and financial markets.*   Hyman P. Minsky[9]

globalization's key 'reforms'
deregulating money or capital

The first of the policy changes advocated by neoliberal economists and required of governments is that regulations are removed over capital, over lending and borrowing, and over the creation of different financial instruments (see Peter Warburton's essay in Chapter 17). However a priority for these economists was the removal by governments of institutional controls and regulations over capital moving across national boundaries. Most governments, with the exception of those with the highest officially recorded rates of economic growth in the recent past (India and China) have obliged. Once removed, there is a general assumption that capital controls can never be re-imposed. Given the earlier experience of capital liberalization, and the subsequent imposition of capital controls under the Bretton Woods Agreement of 1944, we are not so sure.

The deregulation of capital meant effectively that elected politicians and governments abandoned their responsibility for managing finance, for preventing crises, for managing their country's exchange rate, and for protecting the weak, the elderly, the unemployed, and the infirm.

Central to the deregulation of capital was the release of the savings of millions of workers and employees. In the early days of deregulation, as governments were lifting capital controls and deregulating money lending, ordinary people were persuaded (by their elected politicians) to detach themselves from state pension provision; and to give up their hard-earned savings to speculators, disguised as merchant bankers, insurance companies, and other financial institutions. As Toporowski has noted, 'financial laissez-faire . . . provided a seemingly endless inflow into capital markets of money by compulsory prescription to pension funds levied on the workforce and their employers'.[10] These funds were recklessly deployed by merchant banks and insurance companies and used to enrich a few, while ultimately bankrupting or diminishing the value of pension funds. Having unleashed this torrent of money, elected politicians turned a blind eye as the people's savings were gambled on stock markets. Governments and regulators were either indifferent or negligent, as stock markets collapsed after the turn of the century and billions of dollars of pension fund value was destroyed.

The kind of speculation indulged in by pension fund managers, investment and merchant banks is well known—especially to those who have already been duped. It is 'Ponzi finance'. As Toporowski noted with prescience in 2000, because of their success, 'pension funds have become the newest and possibly the most catastrophic example of "Ponzi finance"'.[11] Three years later, after the collapse of the stock market and the closure and devaluation of many pension funds, he has been proved right.

ponzi finance

The term Ponzi finance was invented by the American economist Hyman P. Minsky as part of his analysis of financial market inflation. It describes a form of finance in which new liabilities are used to finance existing liabilities. Ponzi schemes are named after Charles Ponzi, an Italian immigrant who duped thousands of Boston investors in the 1920s with a postage stamp speculation scheme. Ponzi thought he could take advantage of differences between US and foreign currencies used to buy and sell international mail coupons. Ponzi told investors that he could provide a 40 per cent return in just 90 days compared with 5 per cent for bank savings accounts. Ponzi was deluged with funds from investors, taking in $1 million during one three-hour period—and this was in 1921. Though a few early investors were paid off to make the scheme look legitimate, an investigation found that Ponzi had only purchased about $30-worth of the international mail coupons.

Decades later, the Ponzi scheme continues to work on the 'rob-Peter-pay-Paul' principle, as money from new investors is used to pay off earlier investors until the whole scheme collapses.[12]

Minsky noted that Ponzi's scheme 'swept through the working classes and even affected respectable folk'. Because they prey on the poor and the ignorant, Ponzi schemes in banking are usually banned. However, this does not prevent them from occurring in countries where it is difficult to regulate them. Ponzi schemes have surfaced in Portugal and Eastern Europe.[13]

In the United Kingdom, private pensions were first proposed as an alternative to state earnings-related pensions in 1976. The banks and stock broking firms that promoted them (and the politicians that eagerly agreed because they saw an opportunity to divest themselves of responsibility for the care of the elderly and offered tax breaks to these firms) did not realize that, by the 1990s, pension schemes would effectively own stock markets—or at least most of the stocks and shares quoted on the world's stock markets. As a result, gains could be made as long as the market as a whole was rising but as the market fell, pension funds were caught, unable to withdraw without causing a bigger catastrophe, but needing to withdraw to protect the value of their own assets.

Virtually the only 'check' on the giant pensions Ponzi scheme is the fact that, inevitably, as the labour market becomes more 'flexible' and more people become unemployed or suffer falling wages, fewer savings can be compulsorily diverted to the capital markets in this way. In other words, government and regulatory institutions have failed to provide checks on the irresponsibility of the capital markets; instead, it is the declining economic activity caused by speculation that finally placed a limit on the speculators.

deregulation as freedom

The removal of regulation over capital is couched in terminology suggesting freedom: 'liberalization'. The use of this language enabled economists to depict changes, which ultimately empowered and enriched those with money while impoverishing those without, as a liberating experience.[14] It enabled them to argue that the state's regulatory framework was oppressive, and freedom from the state was an emancipation.

> To contain the evils that market systems can inflict, capitalist economies developed sets of institutions and authorities, which can be characterized as the equivalent of circuit breakers.   Hyman P. Minsky[15]

The removal of controls and regulation—of 'circuit breakers'—from capital is the most revolutionary of the economic doctrines promoted by neoliberal economists. Viewed from any perspective, this transformed and disrupted the economic landscape between 1970–2003.

The reason is straightforward: Removing controls over capital freed up the owners of money to move their funds to any part of the world. Naturally, they moved it to where returns, profits, or capital gains were highest. This made them richer, but also more powerful. As these 'reforms' have taken root, so the finance sector has come to dominate the global economy as a whole. In 1970, 90 per cent of international transactions were accounted for by trade and only

10 per cent by capital flows. Today, despite a vast increase in global trade, that ratio has been reversed, with 90 per cent of transactions accounted for by financial flows not directly related to trade in goods and services.[16]

As part of its expansion and growing dominance, the finance sector has fuelled and expanded credit, as we demonstrate in the next chapter. This has helped to create a vast 'credit bubble' which has, in turn, financed a 'bubble' in assets: stocks, shares, property, and dot-com companies. The easy availability of credit encouraged consumers, corporations, and governments to run up huge debts. In a deflationary environment, these debts will be transformed into heavy millstones.

banks and the corporate sector

The freedom for the owners of money to seek capital gains wherever they were highest between 1970 and 2003 revolutionized, in turn, relationships between the owners of capital and the owners and managers of productive capacity; those who engage in the real economy—growing, engineering, and manufacturing. They now have to deal with the unpredictability of land (in the broadest sense), resistance of labour, and the volatility of profits. By contrast, the capital gains from lending, speculating, and betting—until financial crisis strikes—are much higher. While the dynamics of profits might be unstable, the dynamics of capital gains (in particular, interest or compound interest) follow a straight line—upwards.

Because the free flow of capital enabled the owners of capital (creditors and investors) to capture the highest returns in any part of the world, this placed enormous pressure on the corporate sector (less mobile than the finance sector) to provide higher rates of return, or capital gains, that were comparable to those made from lending, speculating, and betting in parts of the world where costs were lower. Shareholders and creditors bullied managers, demanding that companies prioritize their interests, and compete with financial gains made elsewhere. The interests of consumers, employees, suppliers, local communities or, indeed, the environment, were downgraded. As shareholders were free to move their funds out and transfer them elsewhere to other parts of the globe, they were empowered effectively to hold a gun to the heads of the companies they invested in.

There can be no excuse or justification for corporate weakness, fraud, and malfeasance, in the face of this pressure. Nevertheless the intense pressure of the finance sector led CEOs and then managers to manipulate their balance sheets; to inflate the real value of their companies; to relentlessly merge and acquire new companies; ruthlessly to force down costs; and to carelessly harm the environment. If this did not prove sufficient, CEOs and their advisers did not hesitate to devise 'tricks, contrivances, and bogus transactions' to please and satisfy the finance sector.[17]

bankers and governments

Governments, in particular poor country governments, suffered similar pressures from the finance sector. Their creditors are often grouped together as 'global capital markets' and include bondholders, investors, official institutions like the IMF and the World Bank, but also rich country Treasuries. To satisfy these predatory lenders, and repay their ballooning debts, governments have had to re-orient their economies towards foreign creditors, and expand revenue-generating exports to raise money for debt repayments. While the United States is able to repay its debts in a currency that it prints itself, this option is not open to poor countries who have to repay in 'hard currency' (dollars, yen, euro, and sterling)—the only currencies that international creditors understand, or will accept. So the pressure has been on to expand exports, which generate hard currency; domestic priorities such as feeding its people and trying to keep them healthy have had to go by the board in many developing countries. It has also meant far too often, the continuous stripping of forests, the handing over of natural assets (minerals, oil), and the ruthless exploitation of the land.

When these efforts at raising revenues have proved insufficient, governments are forced to hand over state assets (the 'family silver') to repay creditors and investors. This transfer of assets from poor countries to their creditors was disguised as another favourite 'reform' of this period: privatization.

Above all, the power of international financial markets strips governments of policy autonomy—the power to decide, independently, on policies that serve the interests of their people and environment. Instead, governments are obliged to implement policies effectively dictated by foreign creditors/investors. By doing so, elected governments lose legitimacy with their populations, and democratic deficits are made worse.

minimizing the state

The second of the major upheavals proposed by neoliberal economists to governments was audacious—that governments should divest themselves of power, transferring control to unaccountable markets, including financial markets. Neoliberals are contemptuous of the state, dismissing it as 'rent-seeking', and have systematically tried to diminish the role of the state in the economy. Before 1970, governments on the whole allocated resources for the weak and defenceless in society; for public transport and infrastructure; for cultural activities and communication. Now, these roles are increasingly 'privatized' or 'marketized'. Public spending has been cut to please the markets. In sum, politicians have transferred to 'the market' those powers previously exercised democratically by parliaments and governments. The allocation of resources for health, clean water, sanitation, education, pensions, scientific research, transport, broadcasting, sport, culture, mineral extraction, and marketing are but a few of the government functions that, in many countries, are now carried out by 'the invisible hand of the market'.

And when the invisible market fails to allocate resources effectively— whether it is in employment, health care, public transport, or pensions—there is nobody to blame or hold to account. The weak, the unemployed, the isolated, the old, and the infirm are left in a democratic vacuum. NGOs and other extra-parliamentary organizations in the West have tried very hard to fill this vac-uum; but there is unfortunately room for anti-democratic forces, authoritarian and extremist organizations of both a religious and political nature which thrive most when economic times are hard for ordinary people.

We used to aspire to 'government of the people, by the people, for the people'; but the period 1970–2003 saw the perversion of this ideal with 'gov-ernment of the markets, by the markets, for the markets'. As Messner and Nuscheler note, 'the degeneration of political culture and the brutalization of social conflicts' are two of the characteristics of the last 20 years.[18]

We would go further and argue that the degeneration of political culture is a direct result of financial liberalization, which, in collaboration with elected politicians who chose to strip democratic institutions of political and economic power, has hollowed out the state.

a single global market

The third major change proposed to politicians and governments by econo-mists (and facilitated by technological change) was bold, and we repeat, strik-ingly utopian: that governments should remove restraints on trade, and try and build a single global market for goods and services ranging from toothpicks to equities to music CDs to health services to pornography. We believe this to be utopian, because the social, political, and environmental pressures brought on by the increased competitiveness of a single global market 'racing to the bottom' would—and will—prove literally unbearable for humanity and will therefore be resisted.

WTO agreements now commit its governmental members not just to liber-alize trade in goods, but also services, investment, and intellectual property.

Such a global market in goods and services, it is argued, is best freed from the constraints of public interest regulation and from tariffs imposed by elected governments. There is a need, the argument goes, to eliminate 'inefficiencies' in national and local markets, particularly in the 'inflexible' labour markets of highly-regulated welfare-state societies like those of Europe.

But free trade is imposing enormous and uncounted costs on the global economy, not least on the environment. As recently as 1995, trade accounted for 20–25 per cent of all carbon emission from energy use. By 2004, it is estimated that transport caused by international trade will have grown by 70 per cent. Such trends make a mockery of the reduction targets for carbon emissions set for industrialized countries.

conclusion

Global markets, above all, intensify 'international competitiveness', pitting groups, communities, and environments against each other in a futile 'race to the bottom'. Trade and investment liberalization, or 'beggar-your-neighbour' economics, as Colin Hines puts it, is harming the planet, and fostering international tensions.[19] And global markets transmit shocks more effectively. For example, the global market in travel has been hurt by the shock of a virulent, killer disease—SARS; and the shock of recession rolls from one country to another and then from one continent to another.[20] In this, perhaps, is the catalyst that will take us back to a world economic structure that has equity and social justice at its core. Once the developed world finds it cannot insulate itself from the damage it has done to its less privileged neighbours, thousands of miles away and bundled conveniently out of sight and mind, the time may have come when we can turn our world the right way up again.

references

[1] W. Churchill, *The Gathering Storm* (London: Mariner Books; Reissue edition 1986) p. 27.

[2] First Inaugural Address of Franklin D. Roosevelt, Saturday, 4 March 1933.

[3] R. Crockett, *Thinking the Unthinkable: Think-Tanks and the Economic Counter Revolution 1931–1983* (London: HarperCollins, 1994)

[4] W. Wriston, *Technology and Sovereignty* Foreign Affairs (1988) 67:63–75. Quoted in E. Helleiner, *States and the Reemergence of Global Finance* (Ithaca, NY: Cornell University Press, 1994).

[5] See, as examples of this thinking, D. Korten, *When Corporations Rule the World* (Connecticut: Kumarian Press: Berrett-Koehler, 1995) and N. Klein, No Logo (London: Flamingo, HarperCollins, 2000) in which she argues that; 'At the heart of this conver-

gence of anticorporate activism and research is the recognition that corporations are much more than the purveyors of the products we all want; they are also the most powerful political forces of our time. . . We have read how a handful of powerful CEOs are writing the new rules for the global economy, engineering what Canadian writer, John Ralston Saul has called "a *coup d'etat* in slow motion ". . . because corporations have become the ruling political bodies [our emphasis] of our era, setting the agenda of globalization. We must confront them, in other words, because that is where the power is.' p. 339–40.

6 E. Helleiner, *The Reemergence of Global Finance*, (Ithaca, NY: Cornell University Press, 1994) p. 90–1.

7 MF staff have written that 'at its most basic there is nothing mysterious about globalization. The term has come into common usage since the 1980s, reflecting technological advances that have made it easier and quicker to complete international transactions—both trade and financial flows.' From a paper on 'Globalisation: Threat or Opportunity?' published 12 April 2000.

8 See M. Hudson, 'Savings, Compound Interest and Asset-Price Inflation' presented at Eastern Economics Association Annual Meeting, 22 February 2003.

9 *Stabilizing an Unstable Economy* (New Haven: Yale University Press, 1986) p. 120.

10 J. Toporowski, 'Pension funds and Ponzi finance' in Ends of Finance (London: Routledge, 2000).

11 Ibid., p. 58.

12 Taken from US Securities and Exchange Commission www.sec.gov/answers/ponzi.htm

13 J. Toporowski, 'Pension funds and Ponzi finance' in *Ends of Finance* (London: Routledge, 2000).

14 We have had appeals from a number of true liberals, not to use the language of neoliberalism, because of its distortion of liberal ideals. However we feel we have no choice but to use the language that is now widely used to describe the neoliberal agenda.

15 H. P. Minsky, D. Delli Gatti, and M. Gallegati, 'Financial Institutions, Economic Policy and the Dynamic Behaviour of the Economy' Working Paper no. 126, Levy Institute, 1994. quoted in *Minsky's analysis of financial capitalism* by D. Papdimitriou and L. Randall Wray, Levy Institute, July 1999.

16 R. P. Cronin, 'Asian Financial Crisis: An Analysis of US Foreign Policy Interests and Options', Foreign Affairs and National Defense Division 28 January 1998.

17 'As we go to press, AOL Time Warner Inc., executives are being sued by two institutional shareholders who accuse Chairman Steve Case and other top executives of using dishonest methods to inflate the company's share price.' MSNBC News 14 April 2003; available at www.msnbc.com.

18 D. Messner and F. Nuscheler, 'World Politics—Structures and Trends' in P. Kennedy (ed) *Global Trends and Global Governance*, (London: Pluto Press, 2002).

19 C. Hines, *Localization: A Global Manifesto* (London: Earthscan, 2000).

20 'A survey of the global economy' *The Economist* 28 September 2002, p. 31.

CHAPTER 2

globalization and its consequences

romilly greenhill

In all the debate about the remarkable experiment of finance-led globalization, taking up acres of print and hours of discussion, one blindingly clear point has not been made—that the past two decades of finance-led globalization have been bad for the poor and bad for the global economy. Let me summarize the main negative consequences:

1. The growth of a massive credit bubble and its counterpart—a huge growth of debt at household, corporate, and government levels, threatening a new 'debt crisis of the rich'.

2. A 'hoover' effect transfers *wealth* (assets minus debt) from poor people and poor countries to rich people and rich countries.

3. A dramatic divergence in the distribution of wealth both nationally and globally, which has been much greater than the divergence in *incomes*.

4. The predominance of speculation over enterprise, and of finance over the 'real' economy, leading to a dramatic decline in economic growth and rising unemployment.

5. A growing threat of global deflation, including collapsing commodity prices and falling real-wage growth, so that ordinary wage earners are being forced into debt just to keep the economy going.

6. An increase in economic instability, particularly in poor countries.

7. A loss of policy autonomy in both Northern and Southern economies, leading in particular to conflicts between free trade and the free movement of capital.

This is what the global economy *really* is and we present the data and analysis to prove it.

the credit bubble

The decades since 1970 have been characterized by a near-total abrogation by governments of any control over the growth of credit. Banks and other financial institutions have been able to 'create' credit at will, leading to a massive escalation in the total stock of financial assets. The total stock of these assets—which include bonds, shares, bank loans, and mortgages, as well as complex financial instruments such as derivatives and options—has mushroomed in relation to GDP and the 'real' economy of goods, services, and people.

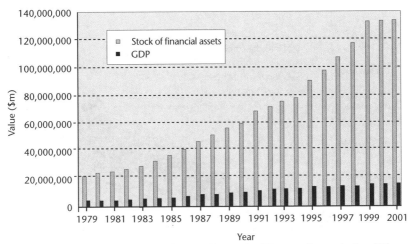

Figure 2.1 GDP and the stock of financial assets in G7 countries excluding UK and Japan

Source: US Federal Reserve: *Flow of Funds Accounts;* Statistics Canada: *National Balance Sheet Accounts by Sector;* Banque de France: *National Financial Accounts;* OECD: *National Financial Accounts;* Banca d'Italia: *Supplements to the Statistical Bulletin, Financial Accounts;* Deutsche Bundesbank: *Financial Accounts for Germany 1991 to 2001;* IMF: *International Financial Statistics*

In 1980, the total stock of financial assets in five of the major world economies was around $20 trillion—that is five times their combined GDP (see Figure 2.1). By 2000, this figure stood at almost $140 trillion, or *ten* times GDP. In some countries, the figures are even more dramatic—the financial stock in Japan rose from less than six times GDP to roughly *nine* times in just one decade, 1980 to 1990, a meteoric rise which may explain the country's equally rapid economic collapse.[1] In the United Kingdom, the total stock of financial assets stood at almost 15 times GDP[2] in 2000. Even taking into account the probability of some 'double counting'—an asset lent by a household to a bank or financial intermediary, and then on-lent to a company is counted twice—this growth has been spectacular.

So who is holding these assets? There has been a huge growth in assets held by households, albeit only the rich ones. But mostly the explosive growth has been in the finance sector—banks, investment funds, pension funds, mutual funds, and other forms of 'financial intermediary' (see Figure 2.2). Over the past 20 years, this sector has changed from being just that—an intermediary between savers and borrowers—to being one of the dominant sectors within the global economy, in both economic and political terms.

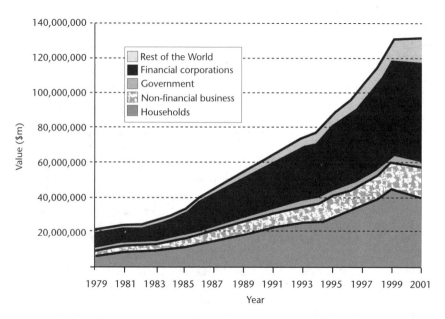

Figure 2.2 Trends in asset holdings by sector in G7 countries excluding UK and Japan, 1979–2001

Source: US Federal Reserve: *Flow of Funds Accounts;* Statistics Canada: *National Balance Sheet Accounts by Sector;* Banque de France: *National Financial Accounts;* OECD: *National Financial Accounts;* Banca d'Italia: *Supplements to the Statistical Bulletin, Financial Accounts;* Deutsche Bundesbank: *Financial Accounts for Germany 1991 to 2001;* IMF: *International Financial Statistics*

Does this matter? Does the dramatic growth in financial assets simply mean that we are all getting richer? And if the finance sector is getting more dominant, isn't that merely leading to greater risk-sharing and economic efficiency? The answer, quite simply, is no. The dramatic growth in the finance sector in relation to GDP has had a number of negative consequences. The huge growth in financial assets has become de-linked from any 'real' growth in the capital stock and it has forced millions of people and companies into debt. For these two reasons, it is unsustainable and threatens global economic stability.

Figure 2.3 compares the total stock of financial assets in five major economies with the stock of 'real wealth', defined as physical capital, human capital, and research and development expenditures. In the late 1970s and early 1980s, the two were roughly the same. By 2000, financial assets were worth about three times the value of the real assets underlying them.[3] There was a total divorce from economic reality.

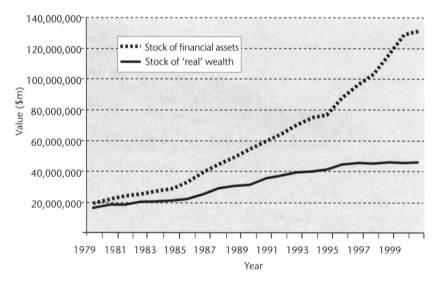

Figure 2.3 Stocks of 'real' wealth and financial assets in G7 countries excluding UK and Japan, 1979–2000

Source: The stock of financial assets is taken from Figure 2.1. The stock of 'real wealth' is calculated from data provided by the Centre for the Study of Living Standards, *'Latest Estimates for the Index of Economic Well-Being for OECD Countries' August 2002*

But how can financial assets not represent anything 'real'? The explanation is simple. Money has gone into speculation against currency movements and on the price of existing assets; into hedge funds which gamble against movements of future asset prices; into vastly complicated derivatives, options, and so on— a big betting game, in other words. The stock of credit and of financial assets has grown exponentially but there has been no discernible impact on the real, tangible, earthy economic realities.

All this might be a harmless gain if it were not for the fact that for every lender, there has to be a borrower. In the 1970s, the loan pushers of the Western banking system lent money to Third World governments, perceived at the time to be a source of ever-higher returns. Now, the financial sector is preying upon ordinary people on the high streets of London, New York, and Seoul.

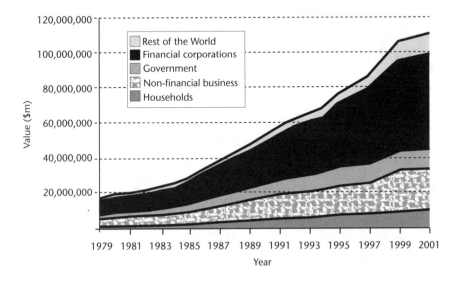

Figure 2.4 Trends in liabilities by sector in G7 countries excluding UK and Japan, 1979–2001

Source: US Federal Reserve: *Flow of Funds Accounts;* Statistics Canada: *National Balance Sheet Accounts by Sector;* Banque de France: *National Financial Accounts;* OECD: *National Financial Accounts;* Banca d'Italia: *Supplements to the Statistical Bulletin, Financial Accounts;* Deutsche Bundesbank: *Financial Accounts for Germany 1991 to 2001;* IMF: *International Financial Statistics*

The counterpart to growing financial assets is the increased liabilities of households, governments, and the corporate sector (see Figure 2.4). So we are now facing another kind of debt crisis. Unlike the Third World debt crisis, this one is taking place in the West, amongst the middle classes but also amongst the socially excluded underclass, preyed upon by predatory lenders. Lured by relentless pressure of the finance sector offering 'great deals', people are re-mortgaging their homes, running up credit card debts, overdrafts, student loans, hire purchase credit, and so on. In the United Kingdom, net credit card lending increased by 55 per cent between 2001 and 2002, net mortgage lending increased by 46 per cent, and personal loans and overdrafts by 13 per cent.[4] Debt is now financing about 10 per cent of all household spending. There is a similar story in the United States with personal sector liabilities now at 133 per cent of national income, four times the value in 1946, while mortgage credit expanded by $222 billion each year between 1988 and 1997.[5] Unlike corporate borrowing, much of this debt is not being taken on to make investments that will generate future incomes, but to meet consumer needs.

predatory lending in britain

pat conaty

The credit underground in Britain is thriving in the 21st century. Recession, social exclusion, and the widening gap between rich and poor have pushed increasing numbers into a financial twilight zone where borrowing, even for necessities, carries an extravagant price tag. Estimates suggest that one in five adults are denied the loans and cheap interest rates most middle class Britons take for granted. For over eight million people, the only credit available is that offered by predatory lenders—a market worth over £16 billion per year and with interest and credit charges ranging from 35 per cent to 2000 per cent annually. In a NEF pocketbook *Profiting from Poverty* (which calls for radical reform of the lending system and shows how it could be done), we show how sophisticated marketing techniques involving some of the best-known names in business are being employed to sell expensive credit to those low and moderate-income households that can least afford it. For those on the receiving end, the results involve a downward spiral of debt, court judgments, loss of homes, and evictions. Unlike most other EU countries and many American states, Britain has no ceiling on interest rates or effective legal controls against usury.

Figure 2.5 gives us some indication of the extent of the credit bubble in the United States. From about 1985 onwards, the value of all financial assets often grew much faster than could be justified by new purchases. From 1995, asset values lost touch with reality altogether, and only came crashing down when the bubble started to burst in 1999.

The credit bubble is particularly worrying given that people have borrowed in order to invest in assets on the expectation that their value will rise by more than the rate of interest paid. In 1999, purchase of financial assets by the UK

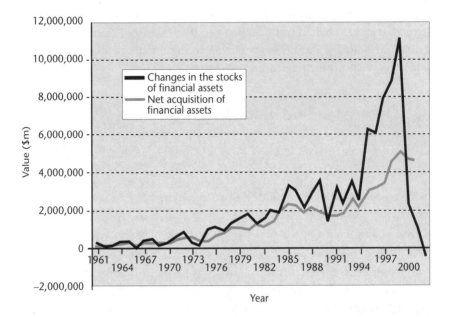

Figure 2.5 Changes in the stock of US financial assets against net acquisitions of financial assets, 1961–2001

Source: US Federal Reserve: *Flow of Funds Accounts*

Government, corporations, and households stood at £450 billion—around three times the value of gross national savings (see Figure 2.6).

The consumer debt phenomenon is not just an Anglo-Saxon or even a Northern Atlantic affair. There is now increasing pressure to get consumers into debt in other areas, particularly in Asia. As *The Economist* noted in its survey of consumer finance in February 2003, 'consumer finance is Asian banks' new thing'. Between 1999 and 2002, issuance of new credit cards in South Korea grew at an annual compound rate of 75 per cent. Aggregate household debt in South Korea has been growing at 25 per cent per year and now accounts for half of all bank lending. In Thailand, the credit card business has been growing by 15 per cent per year.[6] In January 2003, Citigroup, the world's biggest bank, won approval to take its first minority stake in a Chinese bank. The ability to promote credit cards and other consumer finance products in China was the chief attraction.

Moreover, as Peter Warburton explains in Chapter 17, corporations have also seen their debts spiraling out of control. Under pressure to massage their share price upwards, corporations have been borrowing by the billions, often to buy

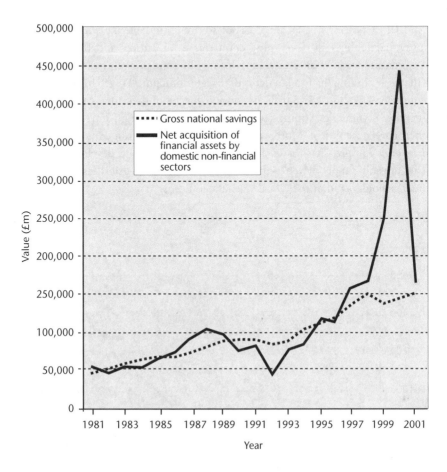

Figure 2.6 Gross national savings and net acquisition of financial assets by domestic non-financial sectors in the UK, 1981–2001

Source: UK Office of National Statistics: *UK Economic Accounts*

back their own stock. Much corporate debt has been hidden by accounting sleights of hand, a technique that has only come to light since the Enron scandal broke in 2001. So-called 'off balance-sheet' items include unfunded pension liabilities, stock options, property leases, derivative contracts, and joint ventures—liabilities which are now estimated to represent almost 40 per cent of long-term debt.[7] And, as with consumer indebtedness, the problem is not limited to the North American and European economies. In Asia, it has been estimated that the total stock of *non-performing loans*[8] is already at $2 trillion— quite apart from those loans which will, at least in theory, be paid back.[9]

And let us not forget that the crisis of sovereign indebtedness has not gone away, particularly in developing countries from Turkey and Indonesia to Uganda and Iraq. By 2001, total long-term public and publicly guaranteed debt (that is, excluding the foreign debts of private companies) owed by developing countries was almost $1.5 trillion—or one quarter of their total gross national income.[10] Many developing countries are paying sky-high interest rates on their government debt. Moreover, as the World Bank's latest edition of *Global Economic Prospects* has made clear, foreign capital flows to developing countries are still 'supply driven'—they flow according to the priorities of Western finance holders rather than locally generated needs.[11]

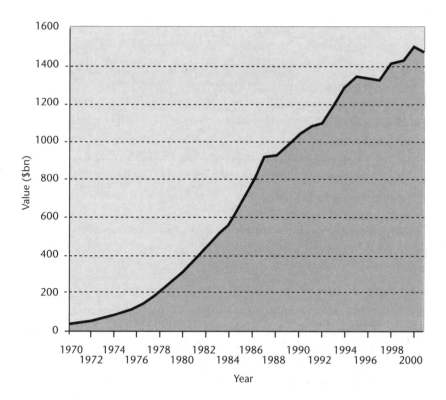

Figure 2.7 Total public and publicly guaranteed debt owed by developing countries

Source: World Bank: *Global Development Finance 2002*

This credit bubble, ultimately based on nothing more than expectations, cannot be maintained forever. There will be a crash. People will no longer be able to pay their debts, particularly if the values of the assets they hold against those debts start to fall as has already happened with equities, and will shortly spread to corporate debt and personal debt. The effect on people in both rich and poor countries will be profound.

pensions in crisis

The pension industry is in crisis. Globally, pension fund assets fall short of their liabilities by some $2500 billion.[12] This deficit is due to a combination of a collapsing stock market, plus company greed. When the going was good, many companies took pension holidays, failing to pay in what was needed to meet their overall liabilities while inflated share prices appeared to take up the slack. Now, employees are suffering the fall-out. In some cases, pension schemes have collapsed, wiping out a lifetime's worth of savings for the hapless employees who thought they were well protected. In other cases, companies are radically downgrading what they will be offering pension holders. At Maersk International Shipping Group, for example, employees may lose up to 60 per cent of their pension rights. Still, other companies are asking their employees to pay more. Sainsbury's, for example, is asking employees to increase contributions into its final salary scheme from 4.35 per cent to 7 per cent.[13]

The outlook for pensions is likely to get even worse, as the credit bubble collapses. Ordinary people, whose life savings have been handed over to risky and irresponsible pension funds, will see increasing levels of hardship in their old age.

national accounts and the finance sector

Economists and statisticians have developed ways of measuring the total output in any given economy. An economy's Gross Domestic Product (GDP) adds up everything produced. By definition, this is equal to total expenditure and total income. GDP figures, both in the aggregate and per person, are commonly used to assess economic performance across nations. Higher GDP growth is seen as a measure of success. Countries are also classified as 'developed' or 'developing' based on the level of GDP per person.

However, GDP measures are frequently criticized by 'alternative' economists for providing a distorted view of trends in economic welfare across time and across countries. Such economists rightly point out that GDP fails to account for the impacts of economic activity on the environment; that it counts clean up costs for environmental catastrophes, natural disasters, war, and conflict as 'goods' rather than 'bads'; that it neglects the work undertaken by women, and fails to take into account non-material aspects of well-being.

But GDP also excludes another important measure—trends in gross national wealth and indebtedness. GDP only measures annual flows. This means an economy such as the United States can become ever more indebted while still appearing to be the richest country in the world in GDP terms.

Our national accounts fail to fully understand capital, debt, and savings. 'Savings' are defined as any income that is not consumed. Debt repayments are therefore defined as savings! Similarly, people spending capital gains, for example mortgage equity withdrawal on their houses, is counted as running down savings. This is one of the reasons why economists fail to fully understand credit bubbles and the effect that these have on our economies and why they are unable to stop them occurring or deal with them when they do.

To be fair, national statistical offices are starting to produce 'national financial accounts' which track national wealth and indebtedness. But the data produced is often patchy, too short-term, and subject to large revisions. While data on GDP, exports, and consumption can be down-loaded from many a CD-ROM or website, financial accounts remain hidden in the depths of national statistics websites—if they are produced at all.

Maybe if we really want to compare the 'wealth of nations', in the seminal words of Adam Smith, we need to start taking 'wealth' a bit more seriously.

financial globalization and the 'hoover effect'

The huge growth in the finance sector and the abrogation of control by governments over the supply of credit have not happened by accident. Rather, they are the result of deliberate policy decisions of governments, particularly in the West. But if the resulting credit bubble is so dangerous, why have governments let it happen? Quite simply, financial globalization has taken place because it is in the interests of a small elite of politically and economically dominant people who have done extremely well out of it while ordinary people have found themselves increasingly indebted. It is indicative that the flow of resources from the poor South to the rich North has increased steadily.

stock options and their effect on wealth inequality

claus gruber

A stock option is a right to buy or sell a share for a defined price during a specified period of time. The movement of the underlying stock influences the value of this right. When the right is exercised, the owner gets the underlying stocks delivered into his account. The granting company is thus distributing wealth rather than income to the recipient.

Many companies are now granting stock options to employees as part of their compensation package. When they are exercised, these options are transferred into stocks and the company receives additional capital. But, given that the company has not changed in value at this very moment, the value due to other shareholders is diminished. In other words, the company is creating wealth to new potential shareholders at the expense of existing shareholders. Great, isn't it!

In 1935, the legendary investor Benjamin Graham wrote a brief satire about the accounting shenanigans at US Steel, explaining this wonderful value-creating circle. In those times, stock options were already granted to executives, but only on a small scale.

Nowadays, almost everybody—especially in publicly-traded companies— is playing the stock-options game. The United States is the leading country and the one in which most statistics are available as well. Standard & Poor's has compiled a database out of the company reports over the last years. It states that, in 1999, all employees of S&P 1500 companies were granted an equivalent of $2508 in stock options. On the surface, this looks moderate; but split between CEOs and middle management, the size of the iceberg is apparent. While a middle manager in general received $2159, his CEO received $2,468,000. Between 1999 and 2001, the 25 CEOs with the highest total compensation together accumulated $5,634,187,000—that's more than $75 million annually each. But what might have been available to 'normal' employees? The statistics do not tell us (in most countries, because wealth is not, or only partly, subject to tax, virtually no statistics are available and academic research turns a blind eye on wealth-distorting effects) but it is indicative that the average annual earning of US full-time working employees in 2001 was $44,848, according to the US Census Bureau.

Stock options have other worrying implications. The exercising of stock options has allowed CEOs to see growing levels of compensation in 2001, away from the prying eyes of their Boards of Directors even at a time when corporate profits were falling by 35 per cent, stock prices had fallen by 13 per cent and unemployment had risen by 35 per cent.

Stock options also allow companies to manipulate their accounts. Although they account for part of employee compensation, they are not formally treated as costs. Efforts by the Independent Accounting Standards Board in the US to force companies to list stock options as expenses were dropped under pressure from CEOs, who often defended themselves from scrutiny by making large political contributions.

inequality

In a market economy, people should be rewarded for showing entrepreneurship and taking risks and that inevitably creates limited inequalities. However, inequalities increase exponentially in a system where money is made from money. The more money a person or a country has, the more money is made. Conversely, people and countries without a bed-rock of capital to start off with are getting priced out of the market, and are forced further into debt just in order to survive.

Inequalities between people and between nations have been exhaustively studied. However, most of the work done to date has focused on inequalities in annual *incomes*, while the distribution of personal wealth and indebtedness has been hidden from view. This is despite the fact that wealth influences both a person's subjective well-being—how secure they feel—and increasingly also their ability to make money over their lifetime. Conversely, as Gita Sen points out in Chapter 13, people and nations that are in debt lose 'their resources, their control over their means of livelihood, the security of their old age, their children's futures and their ability to make decisions on their own assessments of their needs and realities'.

Unfortunately, there is a real paucity of reliable global data on inequalities in wealth. Institutions such as the World Bank, the IMF, and the UN have let us down badly; they do not collect the required figures, arguing that it would be too difficult to provide an accurate assessment. But in our view, there may also be another motive; if the numbers were made available, the polarization in wealth would be too unpalatable for words.

Perhaps unsurprisingly, the private sector tends to track the rich. In a ghoulish alternative to publications such as the UN's *Human Development Report* or the World Bank's *World Development Indicators*, investment banks Merrill Lynch and Cap Gemini Ernst and Young have developed a *World Wealth Report*. The report notes that there are now 7.1 million 'High Net Worth Individuals' (HNWI) around the globe, with a total financial-asset wealth of $26.2 trillion. Although 2001—the latest year for which data is available—was not a good year for HNWIs, at least they 'managed to protect their wealth better than less-affluent groups'.[14] In Latin America, for example, HNWIs managed to see their wealth grow by 8 per cent in 2001, despite the appalling economic decline in the region in that year. This is highly suggestive of growing wealth inequality.

At a national level, we can track some of the trends in the distribution of wealth and indebtedness. In the United States, almost all of the increase in the stock of financial assets since 1983 has accrued to the top 10 per cent of the population, while virtually all the increase in debt has accrued to the bottom 90 per cent (see Figures 2.8 and 2.9). The poorest 90 per cent now have debts equal to 75 per cent of their financial assets, while for the richest 10 per cent, debts amount to only 7 per cent of their assets. Of course, this leaves the poorest US households much more vulnerable to falls in asset values.

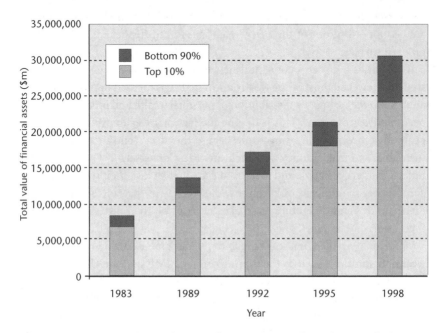

Figure 2.8 Growth of financial assets of top 10% versus bottom 90% of US households

Source: 'Recent Trends in Wealth Ownership 1983–1998' Working Paper No.300 by Edward N Wolff, Jerome Levy Economics Institute, April 2000

Growing inequality is evident in the United Kingdom too. Excluding household wealth, the bottom 50 per cent of the population now owns only 1 per cent of the wealth; in 1976, they had 12 per cent.[15] The richest 20 per cent of the UK population in income terms now has 41 per cent of the wealth but owes only 35 per cent of the total stock of debt. The poorest 20 per cent of the population has 7 per cent of the wealth but 11 per cent of the debt.[16]

The transfer of wealth from the poor to the rich is a global phenomenon; the 'hoover' effect is dramatic. Textbooks tell us that capital should flow from countries in which it is plentiful—the rich world—to those in which it is scarce—the poor world. But the opposite is happening. Even the World Bank,

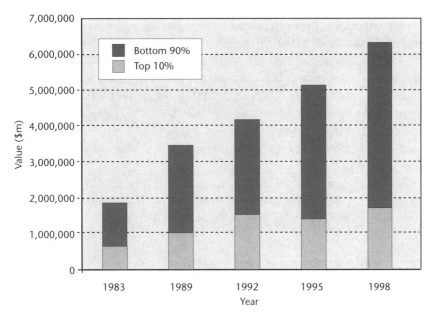

Figure 2.9 Distribution of debt amongst US households by household wealth class

Source: 'Recent Trends in Wealth Ownership 1983–1998' Working Paper No.300 by Edward N Wolff, Jerome Levy Economics Institute, April 2000

not known for its radical critique of globalization, has finally admitted that 'on a net basis, capital is no longer flowing from high-income countries to economies that need it to sustain their progress towards the Millennium Development Goals'.[17] What the Bank is saying, in essence, is that the poor are financing the rich.

A high proportion of these transfers from poor to rich are accounted for by interest payments and profit remittances. In 2001, developing countries paid a total of $122 billion in interest payments on their debt, and $55 billion in the form of profits sent back home by multinational corporations. In total, such countries were paying about 3 per cent of their GDP in such 'unproductive' payments. And this, of course, is in addition to the $260 billion loan principal they paid back to their creditors in rich countries.[18]

Such transfers also occur through the forced holdings of foreign currency reserves, usually US dollars. Countries have been radically increasing their foreign currency reserves as a result of the financial instability associated with globalization over the past decade. As Jane D'Arista points out in Chapter 24, such transfers 'constitute an immense and expanding transfer of wealth out of these economies' to the United States. In 2002, the World Bank estimated these flows amounted to $110 billion[19] or more than double the total volume of aid.

Moreover, the officially recorded transfers from poor to rich do not include illegal and thus unrecorded capital flight from poor countries. The volume of such flows is notoriously difficult to quantify, but in 1994 was estimated at some $122.4 billion for all developing countries.[20] This capital flight is not accidental but has, at least in part, been promoted deliberately by Western banks and finance ministries because they need this capital to prop up their own economies.[21]

'Trickle down' is a discredited idea; let us think instead of globalization as a 'hoover' effect, sucking resources away from poor people in both poor and rich countries, and concentrating them in the pockets of the rich.

the 'real' economy is not performing

Advocates of finance-led globalization have often claimed that, while globalization may worsen income distribution, the poor are still better off because growth is higher than it would otherwise be—in other words, the poor get a smaller share of a larger global cake. The reality is quite different; the global economy has performed *much worse* during the last two decades of finance-led globalization than during the earlier era of capital controls and government intervention.

While we must beware of treating growth as the Holy Grail of economic policy-making because of its environmental costs, let us nevertheless look at growth on its own terms. Globalization has failed on growth. As Alan Freeman shows in Chapter 16, growth per person during the 1970s was almost 4 per cent per year; while during the 1980s it was only 0.7 per cent per year. Over the 1990s, output per person actually *fell* by 0.2 per cent on an annual basis. Developing countries have performed particularly badly, especially in Latin America and Sub-Saharan Africa. As IMF Managing Director, Horst Köhler admitted recently, in Latin America 'real per capita income levels today are basically back to their levels of 25 years ago'.[22]

Even in rich countries, the majority has not seen much benefit. The median wage in the United States is the same as it was 27 years ago, while unemployment rates across the OECD have been steadily increasing since the 1960s (see Figure 2.10). Even the so-called 'productivity miracle' has been largely illusory, with the 1.2 per cent annual growth rate experienced in the 1990s only slightly higher than the 1 per cent seen in the 1980s, and well below the 2.5 per cent growth rate seen between 1945 and 1973.[23]

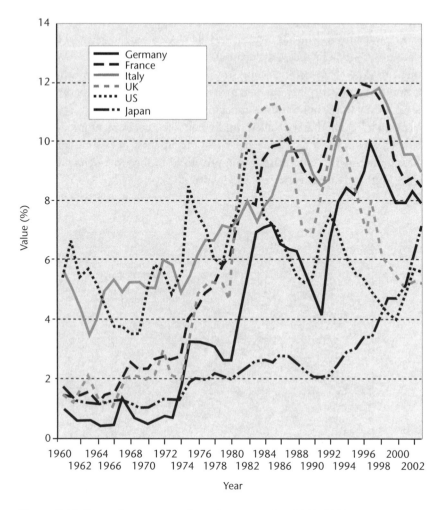

Figure 2.10 Unemployment rates in major economies, 1960–2003

Source: European Commission: *'European Economy' No.4, 2002*

One of the causes of low growth has been falling investment. As a share of GDP, investment was lower in the 1990s than the 1980s in all G7 countries, except Germany. Moreover, despite the stock market boom of the late 1990s, investment rates fell between the first and second half of the decade in all G7 countries except the United States,[24] where, as Dean Baker argues, the figures were inflated by some 10 per cent because of an exaggerated way of calculating the quality of computers. [25]

Given the growth in global finance, which is supposed to channel resources more productively, why has investment fallen? According to Michael Hudson, one answer is that finance-led globalization has encouraged speculative investment in *existing* assets, including stocks, bonds, and property, rather than creating new assets. 'When markets are rising, the way to get rich most quickly is to borrow to the hilt to buy as much property [or stocks, bonds and so on] as possible.' [26] This has a parallel with foreign direct investment in developing countries, which so often has been used for the purchase of existing companies –often state-owned enterprises being privatized to meet the demands of the IMF—rather than increasing the productive stock.

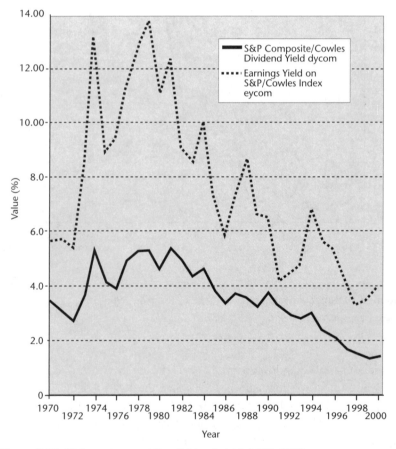

Figure 2.11 S&P earnings and the dividend yield, 1970–2000

Source: Wright (2001) Nonfinancial Stock Market Data

Moreover, companies have been reducing their levels of investment in order to increase dividend payouts to aggressive shareholders; dividends are now taking out a much larger share of profits than they were in the 1970s (see Figure 2.11).

the threat of global deflation

Since the 1970s, influential policy-makers and economists in both the North and South have been obsessed by inflation over all other economic priorities such as employment or tackling poverty. This monomania has even spread to Uganda where the government has rejected offers of new, grant-financed spending on areas such as agriculture and AIDS on the grounds that increasing government spending would be 'inflationary'. This inflationary obsession has, in fact, pushed us very close to deflation. Some countries are already suffering

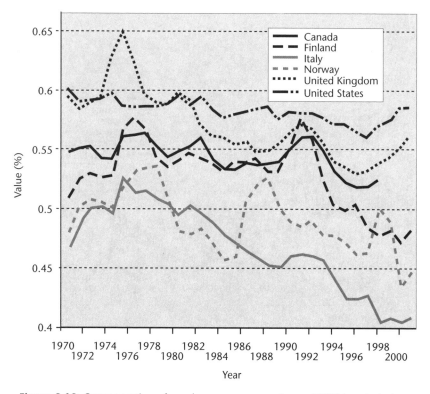

Figure 2.12 Compensation of employees as a percentage of GDP in selected OECD countries

Source: OECD

from it. Japan has been struggling with deflation for more than four years now, and a number of East Asian countries are seeing similar trends. Germany is on the brink of deflation, while inflation rates are at record lows in a number of OECD countries and have also fallen in other parts of the world under the influence of IMF-sponsored deflationary policies.

As we have noted in the Introduction to *RWEO*, a combination of consumer price deflation and asset price inflation is every wealth holder's dream. Under deflation, the costs of wages, commodities, and other inputs fall, while asset price inflation means that capital gains steadily rise and are not eroded in real terms. Lowering costs can make higher profits. Capital gains can be recycled into further capital purchases leading to yet more capital gains. In other words, money can be made from money—while those reliant for their income on current wages, and not from capital gains, receive a smaller and smaller share of national income.

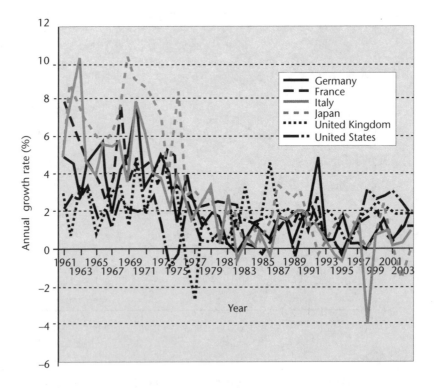

Figure 2.13 Growth in real wages in major western economies, 1961–2003

Source: European Commission: *European Economy, No 4. 2002*

The share of GDP going to employees in the form of wages and other compensation has fallen over the past three decades; despite high profile 'fat cat' pay
deals (see Figures 2.12–2.14). In almost every country, the growth rate of real
wages has been falling lower and lower. Similarly, commodity prices have been
in steep decline—and by 2001 were at only 60 per cent of their 1980 levels.[27]

Central bankers and finance capitalists may soon get their come-uppance.
Their obsession with inflation but laxity over asset prices has left us with
chronic instability, the risk of financial crisis, and perilously close to outright
deflation. What a stupid self-inflicted wound, particularly, as Joseph Stiglitz

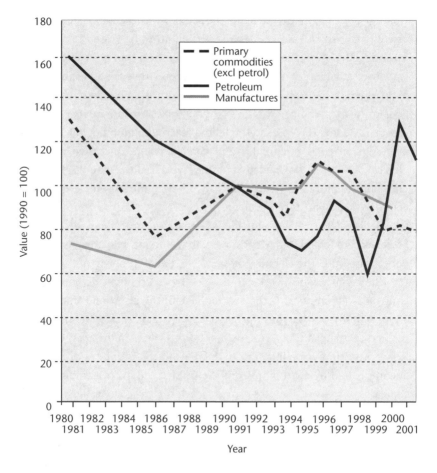

Figure 2.14 Trends in prices of manufactures and primary commodities, 1990 = 100

Source: UNCTAD *Handbook of Statistics 2002*, (Geneva: UNCTAD, 2002)

shows, given that low to moderate inflation does not have any significant adverse real consequences; being obsessive about driving down inflation ever further does.

inflation paranoia

joseph stiglitz

The oil price shocks of the 1970s set off a wave of inflation, and central bankers around the world took up the task of fighting inflation, no matter what the cost. They won the battle—today, in America, Europe, and Japan, as well as most developing countries, inflation has been tamed. We recognize that even the modest inflation numbers that we see may be a large overstatement of the true level of inflation. There are a host of biases, highlighted in the United States by the Commission headed by Michael Boskin, former Chairman of the Council of Economic Advisers under President George H. W. Bush. At the time, it was thought that inflation was overestimated by as much as 1 to 2 percentage points. Since then, methodological revisions in the United States have lowered the magnitude of the bias, but the problems remain in many other countries. Moreover, some countries, like Japan, face a problem of *deflation*.

Deflation—especially unanticipated deflation—is problematic because borrowers are forced to pay back more. In real terms, creditors benefit but debtors are hurt. The United States had a deflation problem at the end of the 19th century, which was accompanied by an economic downturn. The issue of deflation became the central issue of the electoral campaign of 1896, with the Democratic Presidential Candidate, William Jennings Bryant, running on the platform 'We should not be crucified on the cross of gold'. He wanted to reverse inflation by increasing the money supply, to be accomplished by switching from the gold standard to the bimetallic standard.

Economic research over the last decade has shown convincingly that the inflationary paranoia of earlier years was just that—largely paranoia. Low to moderate levels of inflation have no significant adverse real consequences; further reductions in inflation do not lead to faster economic growth, lower unemployment, and higher real wages. Indeed, pushing inflation too low may have serious adverse effects, as George Akerlof (who shared the 2001 Nobel Prize) and his co-authors have shown. There is a trade-off between inflation and unemployment, and if lower inflation does not bring faster economic growth, then there can be a high cost to pushing the battle against inflation too far. For there is a real cost to those who otherwise would have been gainfully employed. Moreover, economic research has shown that this cost is long lived. Lower economic growth in one year—as a result of excessively contractionary policies—leads to lower economic growth in future years; some of the extra output would have been spent on productivity-increasing investments.

One of the reasons that deflation (or even low inflation) can be such a problem is that real interest rates, interest rates taking account of changing price levels, cannot be reduced by central banks to the levels required. In the Great Depression, when prices were falling 10 per cent per year, even zero nominal interest rates were translated into 10 per cent real interest rates—an extremely high number. Today, even in Japan, deflation is far more moderate. But even in the United States, there is growing recognition that the 'room to manoeuvre' has been reduced enormously. With nominal interest rates at 1.25 per cent, there is not much room to lower them further, and to stimulate the economy through monetary policy.

This puts more of the burden on fiscal policies, but here again, in the case of Europe, hands are tied because of the strict limits on the size of fiscal deficits imposed by the Stability Pact—again, largely because policy-makers have both eyes on inflation. The Clinton Administration managed to stop the Republican attempt to force a balanced budget through a con-stitutional amendment in the United States, but now the Republicans are taking full advantage, turning the huge fiscal surplus into mounting deficits reminiscent of the Reagan era. The deficits are being used not to stimulate the economy, but to finance large tax reductions for the very wealthy, with little effect on the real economy, either through output expansion in the short run or productivity enhancement in the long run. The centrepiece of the most recent proposal is a dividend tax cut, largely of benefit to the 'old economy' industries, like the railroad and aluminium from which Bush has drawn his Secretaries of Treasury, and not to the 'new economy' sectors, which pay out little in dividends.

The institutional frameworks—especially central banks—are fixated on the problem of inflation. Most central banks, including the European Central Bank, now have a mandate, which focuses exclusively on inflation; many have adopted inflation targeting. The problems are evident in Europe, which is facing mounting unemployment but has a central bank that does nothing about it because it does not view unemployment as its problem.

The threat of deflation is now so serious that even conservative economic institutions including the IMF, the Federal Reserve, and the Bank of England are starting to propose highly unorthodox policy measures for dealing with the crisis, such as simply printing more money. It is scary that some of these measures have been tried in Japan, but have failed to work. Could it be that we are now facing something even worse than deflation—debt-deflation?

Deflation is bad news for policy makers wanting to reflate the economy following a macroeconomic shock. Deflation is also bad news for debtors. Debt and deflation can interact in a downward spiral from which it is very difficult to escape.

deflation leads to debt....

Deflation is not just harmful in itself; it is also a major cause of indebtedness, particularly for households. If house prices rise by 25 per cent per year and real wages rise by only 2 per cent, people are forced to borrow heavily to secure a roof over their heads. Indeed, in a deflationary economic environment, consumers *must* get into debt just to keep the economy going. In general, people on lower incomes—wage earners—tend to consume a greater proportion of their incomes than the rich. When an increasing share of national income is going to wealthier households in the form of dividends and capital gains, consumption—and hence profits—is threatened. In the end, ordinary wage-earning consumers must get out there and spend, invariably on credit, just to keep a floor under demand.

.... and then to 'debt deflation'

Irving Fisher first coined the term 'debt-deflation' in 1932, at the height of the Great Depression. He observed that when prices are falling, the value of debts increases in real terms. As people try to save money to pay off their debts, demand falls further, causing further deflation, and a further increase in the real value of debt. Once an economy enters a debt-deflationary spiral, governments can be powerless to pull it out again.

Record levels of debt in many of the world's major economies and looming deflation means that the risks now are real. And this time could be worse because finance-led globalization has emasculated governments' ability to act with the appropriate policy instruments. Consumers have been forced into debt by creditor-imposed deflationary economic policies; those same policies will prevent them from getting out again.

slicing and dicing risk

joseph stiglitz

At one time, it was hoped that the New Economy would end the business cycle. That clearly has not happened. Indeed, it is now recognized that much of the deregulation that was associated with the 1990s actually made the economy more unstable, and that the cutting back of welfare systems and the reduction of progressivity reduced some of the 'automatic' stabilizers. Other reforms, such as the switch from defined-benefit to defined-contribution systems, and the partial privatization of social security in some countries, exposed workers to increased risk, and at the same time increased economic volatility.

One of the often-lauded innovations of the past two decades has been in financial engineering, the ability of the economy to slice and dice risk, to shift it to those most able to bear it. But in spite of all of these innovations, developing countries are still forced to bear the risk of interest rate and exchange rate fluctuations, at enormous costs to themselves and the stability of the global economy. When investor sentiment shifts against emerging markets, the interest rates that they face may soar, and even well-managed countries may be pushed to the brink of bankruptcy. In 2002, Brazil managed its way through such a looming crisis. But the likelihood of another crisis emerging in some other country remains extremely high.

Meanwhile, the IMF, the international economic institution responsible for promoting economic stability, continues with its fixation on inflation.

Not only has it done nothing to address the fundamental real problems of risk, the policies it has pushed, especially capital market liberalization, have actually increased global economic instability; and meanwhile, when countries face an economic downturn, the contractionary policies it imposed on the countries exacerbates their economic downturn. While it finally admitted that it had pursued excessively contractionary fiscal policies in East Asia, it seems to have repeated the same mistake in Latin America. And while it finally admitted that capital market liberalization may yield little benefits in terms of economic growth, but exposes developing countries to the risk of increased instability, it is not year clear whether the policies which it pushes, and in some cases almost forces, upon developing countries have yet to change fully. This instability has a high toll, especially on the poor within these developing countries.

While the good news is that there is growing recognition that something is wrong with the global financial system, even the IMF has begun to question the efficacy of the big bail-out strategies that dominated its policies in earlier years. The bad news is that it has yet to turn its attention to the central issue: what reforms are most likely to make the real global economy more stable, and especially promote growth and reduce poverty in the developing world?

loss of policy autonomy and poor macroeconomic management

The sacrifice of political autonomy by governments all over the world as the markets were crowned king has seriously weakened the efficacy of macroeconomic policy to tackle the world's mounting economic problems.

Developing countries have long been in the grip of the 'market' in the form of IMF diktats to follow 'creditor-friendly' macroeconomic policies, including cutting budget deficits, trade liberalization, privatization, and deregulation. What is new is that developed countries are now getting a taste of the medicine that the IMF has long imposed on others. Developed countries have given up their ability to control the supply of credit and they have given away their capacity to manage their exchange rates and hence their external balances.

During the 1930s, governments sat by and watched—and squabbled—while the world economy slid into depression. Hemmed in by the Gold Standard, they were unable to make the exchange rate adjustments that were needed to reflate their economies. Today, we have a mix of exchange rate regimes, some fixed like the Eurozone, others pegged to the dollar from Latin America to East Asia, others floating more freely. However, in contrast to the 1930s, today our exchange rates are determined by financial flows as opposed to the balance of trade. Rather than countries importing and exporting on the basis of their economic needs, and then borrowing from abroad to make up the shortfall, countries are instead receiving supply-led inflows of foreign capital and allowing the current account to adjust to whatever exchange rate is set by the capital markets. This is what allows some countries, most notably the United States, to maintain a chronically over-valued exchange rate and hence to import half as much again as they export, sucking in resources from the rest of the world.

In today's world, countries may run external deficits, but only for as long as the markets allow them to do so. Once the market decides a current account deficit is unsustainable, money pulls out, and fast. In a self-fulfilling prophecy, the crisis predicted by these unelected and unaccountable creditors will come true. The result is that we can no longer rely on a smooth and gradual adjustment process to restore external equilibrium, but instead face a rolling series of financial crises which governments can do little about.

The one defence a government can erect is to build up foreign exchange reserves to use as ammunition against speculators when they attack. The world's foreign exchange reserves, usually held in the form of US Treasury bills, are huge: China has around $309 billion in reserves, Taiwan a further $169 billion, and South Korea $124 billion.[28] This is an enormous waste of resources. In effect, a dollar held in reserves is a dollar that could otherwise have been invested in health, education, or transport. Dean Baker and Karl Walentin of the Center for Economic and Policy Research in the United States have quantified the cumulative cost of these reserves on developing countries over the ten years. The numbers are staggering: 24 per cent of GDP in East Asia and the Pacific; 16 per cent in Latin America and the Caribbean; and 9 per cent in Sub-Saharan Africa.[29] Conversely, the United States has benefited enormously from a seemingly infinite supply of low-interest loans.

Because governments can no longer use exchange rate adjustment to restore the balance of trade, protectionism is on the rise. This is why, in the 1940s, Keynes lobbied hard for capital controls to be a central pillar of the Bretton Woods Agreement. He argued—and gained broad agreement amongst policy-makers—that free movement of capital is simply not compatible with free trade.[30] We must now build a new consensus around this economic truth.

conclusion

The indictment of financial globalization can now be documented; the evidence is there. Growth is weaker, investment has fallen, inequality has risen, deflation looms, debt is becoming unsustainable; and governments' ability to tackle the serious problems we face has been fatally undermined.

references

[1] Economic and Social Research Institute, Japan: Annual Report on National Accounts of 2002, Stocks; IMF International Financial Statistics.

[2] UK Office of National Statistics, UK Economic Accounts; IMF International Financial Statistics.

[3] Again, it could be alleged that there is some double counting included in the stock of financial assets. However, the broad point still holds even if all the assets of the financial sector are excluded from the calculations.

[4] British Bankers Association, cited in *The Times*, 29 January 2003.

[5] M. Faber, 'The precarious position of the US consumer' Gloomboomdom.com, *Market Comment*, 15 January 2003 available at www.gloomboomdoom.com/marketcoms/mcarchive.htm.

[6] *The Economist*, 6 February 2003.

[7] N. Cohen, 'The hidden borrowings creep out' *Financial Times*, 10 February 2003.

[8] Non-performing loans are those that are not being paid back, and are not likely to be paid back.

[9] 'Survey of Asian Finance: The Weakest Link' *The Economist*, 6 February 2003.

[10] *Global Development Finance (Washington, DC:* World Bank, 2002).

[11] *Global Economics Prospects and the Developing Countries*, (Washington DC: World Bank, 2003).

[12] A. van Duyn, 'Pensions liabilities cut room for manoeuvre' *Financial Times*, 18 March 2003.

[13] P. Coggan, 'The £85bn question: what can be done to fill the gaping shortfall in Britain's corporate pension schemes?' *Financial Times*, 7 March 2003.

[14] Merrill Lynch/Cap Gemini Ernst & Young, *World Wealth Report 2002*, p. 1.

[15] UK Inland Revenue.

[16] Authors calculations from data provided in J. Banks, Z. Smith, and M. Wakefield 'The Distribution of Financial Wealth in the UK: Evidence from 2000 BHPS Data' Institute of Fiscal Studies WP 02/21.

[17] *Global Development Finance* (Washington DC: World Bank, 2003), p. 1.

[18] *Global Development Finance* (Washington DC: World Bank, 2002). Total debt service is equal to payment of principal plus debt service.

[19] *Global Development Finance* World Bank 2003, Table 1.1.

[20] B. Schneider, 'Issues in Capital Account Convertibility in Developing Countries' paper presented at an ODI Conference—Capital Account Liberalization: The Developing Country Perspective—London, 21 July 2000.

[21] Roland Baker, statement to the Senate Committee on Governmental Affairs in the US Permanent Subcommittee on Investigations, November 1999.

[22] 'Sustaining Global Growth and the Way Forward for Latin America'—Remarks by Horst Köhler Managing Director of the International Monetary Fund at the Bank of Spain, Madrid, 11 March 2003.

[23] D. Baker, 'Bull Market Keynesianism' *The American Prospect*, Vol 10, Issue 42, January/February 1999.

[24] 'Increases in business investment rates in OECD countries in the 1990s: how much can be explained by fundamentals?' OECD Economics Department Working Papers No. 327.

[25] D. Baker, 'Bull Market Keynesianism' op.cit.

[26] M. Hudson, 'Savings, Compound Interest and Asset-Price Inflation' International Working Group on Value Theory: Research on Political Economy. Eastern Economic Association, Annual Meeting, New York City 22 February 2003.

[27] *Handbook of Statistics* (Geneva: UNCTAD, 2002).

[28] *The Economist*, 26 April 2003.

[29] D. Baker and K. Walentin, *Money for Nothing: The Increasing Cost of Foreign Reserve Holdings to Developing Nations* Center for (Washington DC: Economic Policy Research, 2001).

[30] E. Helleiner, *States and the Re-Emergence of Global Finance* (Ithaca, NY: Cornell University Press: 1994).

real world economic outlook

romilly greenhill

In 0064—almost two thousand years ago—Nero famously sang to his lute and watched from the safety of a high tower while Rome burned. Today's Neros—the leaders of the G7, IMF officials, and economic forecasters—are not even shouting 'fire' as the world economy goes up in flames. They mutter strangled warnings about 'geopolitical uncertainties', 'financial imbalances', and 'structural weaknesses'. But, overall, they remain upbeat, saying, 'The global recovery is expected to continue during 2003.'[1] These words echo uncannily those of US President Hoover who, at the start of the worst depression of the 20th century in May 1930, said that he was convinced that US economic problems had 'passed the worst'.[2]

The reality is that the outlook for the global economy in 2003 is bleak. Financial globalization and the divergence of the superstructure of financial assets from the 'real' economy on which it is supposedly based, have led to one of the largest credit bubbles in history. Even recent stock market crashes have done little to dent the colossal stock of financial assets, now standing at almost ten times GDP in the G7 countries. At some point, the bubble must burst and that point is fast approaching.

As asset prices have ballooned, prices in the 'real' economy—wages and prices of goods and services—have sunk. Deflation may be good news for those looking to buy goods at lower prices, but it is bad news for debtors. The lethal combination of high levels of debt and falling prices was what characterized the Great Depression in 1929. There are now ominous signs of another debt-deflationary spiral.

the credit cycle collapse

Credit cycle collapses are not orderly or predictable but there are potential triggers—specifically to be found in the US economy—which suggest that the bubble will burst sooner rather than later.

As Dean Baker observes in Chapter 7, the US economy is currently running on three bubbles simultaneously: the dollar bubble, the asset price bubble, and the housing bubble. 'Bubbles' exist when things—including stocks, shares, and houses—are priced at a higher rate than is justified by their fundamental value. Often, assets are purchased not because of the promise of a future stream of income but simply because their prices are expected to rise over time. Belief that assets will continue rising is therefore crucial; and that belief, or confidence, is fragile. Just as it can maintain a system, it can also break a system and break it with astonishing speed. As Thailand, Mexico, Russia, Brazil, Indonesia, South Korea, and Argentina know all too well, once investors start to believe that prices of stocks, shares, or houses will fall, they rush for the exits very quickly.

what will trigger the collapse?

In our view, the United States, the world's largest economy, may well be the first to fall. There could be a number of triggers, the first of which is interest rates. There is a relationship between interest rates and the level of a government's budget deficit. When governments run deficits, they borrow from ordinary people to finance their spending. Individuals are given Treasury bills and bonds, which the government promises to redeem at a specified future date. The government pays interest on the loan and, if it wishes to increase its deficit, it has to persuade individuals to lend it the money—and so has to offer a higher rate.

In the United States, proposals to cut taxes by something between $350 billion and $726 billion over the next decade mean that the government deficit is sure to rise. Note that the US Government's spending plans do not at present take into account future liabilities under social security and medicare;[3] nor do they include the costs of homeland security or future military interventions internationally. The Bush Administration justifies tax cuts on the grounds that the economy needs a boost and argues that they will be revenue-neutral with faster growth boosting tax receipts back again. In our view, the tax cuts will do little to boost the economy because they are targeted on the rich—almost 80 per cent of the total benefit going to the wealthiest 20 per cent of households[4]—who are much more likely to save than spend the money. Moreover, even the additional spending undertaken by the Bush Administration as a result of the Iraqi War will not provide much of a stimulus to the economy, being concentrated in a few areas of the United States.[5] So the main effect of the tax cuts will be to push up the US deficit and therefore interest rates. That will lead to widespread debt defaults, bankruptcies, unemployment, and hardship.

The second possible trigger for US collapse is the dollar. By 2002, the US dollar was over-valued by something like 20 per cent. That is good for imports, which are 20 per cent cheaper than otherwise, but damaging for exports because US goods are over-priced. The result is that the United States is currently importing half as much again as it exports, and borrowing from abroad to make up the difference.[6] As Wynne Godley points out in Chapter 19, the primary balance-of-payments deficit had hit 5 per cent of GDP by the fourth quarter of 2002.[7] The total external US debt already stands at more than $2.3 trillion, more than the total foreign debt of all developing countries combined![8]

As in the case of the asset price bubble, the dollar only remains over-valued because people expect it to remain so. Demand for dollars is high because international investors, lacking other outlets for their money, are pouring funds into the United States. Funds have also been sucked into the United States from developing countries in the form of profit remittances, debt-service payments, capital flight, and the forced holdings of dollar reserves. So, US consumers have been able to live well beyond their means.

So far, the rest of the world has been happy to keep the dollar over-valued because it has helped them to export into the huge US market. But current geopolitical tensions mean that this may be changing—there are now signs that many countries are unhappy with the free ride that the United States has been given. Some countries in the Middle East are starting to hold euros rather than dollars as their reserve currency, and the Indonesian government announced in April 2003 that it might start to use the euro in export-import transactions.[9] Several OPEC countries are also considering quoting the price for oil in euros rather than dollars, creating an incentive for even more countries to hold euros as their reserve currency.[10]

If the US dollar does fall from favour as a reserve currency, that would mean less demand for dollars and a weaker dollar; conversely, it would mean a stronger euro. That is not good news for Eurozone exports, and therefore manufacturing jobs, at a time when growth is anaemic and unemployment is already rising sharply. However, in the longer-term, the Eurozone would, with the euro as a reserve currency, have the benefit of the kind of low interest loans from poor countries that the United States has long enjoyed. The European Commission recently calculated that a 10 per cent appreciation in the euro/dollar exchange rate due to increased demand for euro assets would increase Eurozone growth by some 0.2 per cent relative to baseline projections.[11] And of course, such a shift would also be good for the euro's prestige, undermining the global position of the United States.

A major shift into the euro may or may not happen; but it remains the case that the US dollar cannot remain over-valued forever. The United States is already starting to haemorrhage, with income from interest and dividends paid out to foreigners with US asset holdings sharply increasing in 2002, even at a time of low US interest rates.[12] Once foreigners start to lose confidence in the dollar it will fall and the United States—like Thailand and Mexico—will be forced to raise interest rates in an attempt to stop the flow. A falling dollar and rising US interest rates would not only be bad for the United States but also for the rest of the world.

the collapse of US financial markets

Higher US interest rates will spell disaster for US households and corporations that have record levels of debt. Personal and corporate bankruptcies will start to rise, as people can no longer afford to service loans that were taken out when rates were low and bankruptcies will further undermine already-fragile confidence in a system based on nothing more than a confidence trick. The US housing market will be increasingly unstable, as more and more homeowners find they are unable to afford their mortgage repayments. Even the IMF—an organization not known for doom mongering—has raised concerns about the state of the US housing market, cautioning that 'the chances of a bust are notable'.[13] Crashing house values will bring substantial hardship for the majority of the US population, which has been relying on high house prices to shore up its net worth.

As Peter Warburton explains in Chapter 17, the next crash will come more in debt defaults and bankruptcies rather than in further equity-price falls. 'In truth, the tolerance limits in the world financial system are very fine. Once annual defaults rates approach 1 per cent (of the value of the loans) across the whole lending spectrum, banks' profitability is called into question. If default rates reach 2 per cent, then the probability of financial crises rises appreciably. By my calculations, the first landmark has already been surpassed.' As *The Economist* notes, US bankruptcies are getting bigger. 'Of the ten biggest bankruptcies since the modern version of Chapter 11 bankruptcy law was introduced to the United States in 1978, seven were in the Courts at the time of writing, in September 2002.'[14]

Sceptics may argue that the recent stock price falls have already brought asset prices back to earth but actually the decline in the total stock of financial assets has not been large. Although the value of corporate equities fell by some 40 per cent, or $8 trillion, between 1999 and the end of 2002, this has been more or less offset by increasing credit market debt. Issuance of corporate and foreign bonds has surged by $1.6 trillion over the past three years while mortgages have increased by $2 trillion and US government securities have risen by $1.6 trillion. The credit superstructure is still very much in place.

the spread to other 'developed' countries

The US economy is the right place to look for the hardest crash because that is where the most extreme bubbles are located. But crashes will occur elsewhere in a knock-on reaction to the United States and an associated loss of confidence. Just as Malaysia and Indonesia found that they caught 'Asian flu' during the 1997 financial crisis when investors assumed that they *must* share the problems of nearby Thailand and South Korea, so there is a high chance of panic spreading from what appears to have been the world's best-performing economy.

The United Kingdom is vulnerable because it shares many of the US 'bubble' properties. There has not been a large fall in the total stock of UK financial assets despite recent falls in the stock market and UK consumer debt is also at record levels. The United Kingdom also has 'twin deficits'—a budget deficit forecast at £27 billion in 2003/04, and a widening current account deficit. The pound has already started to fall against the euro, and may fall further if there is a sharp decline in confidence, provoking a rise in interest rates both to stem the outflow of funds and also to prevent a build-up of inflation due to higher import costs.

Like the United States, too, the United Kingdom has a badly overheated housing market. Economist Andrew Oswald calculated in November 2002 that British house prices were at five times the average level of earnings, compared to a long-run average of about four times—and prices have risen even further since then. This in itself suggests that a correction will be necessary, and as Oswald points out, the decline in prices may 'overshoot' to below its long-run average as the market attempts to correct itself.[15] There are already signs that the UK housing market may be slowing, with house price rises at almost zero as at May 2003.[16] Once the housing boom cracks, consumer spending, which has been largely credit-financed, will slide, leading to lower demand, bankruptcies, and unemployment. The United Kingdom looks set to catch 'US flu'.

The Eurozone, which has had opprobrium heaped upon it because of low growth, rising unemployment, and difficulties of containing budget deficits within the limits of the Stability and Growth Pact, may, in one respect, be in a better position to insulate itself from financial crisis in the United States. The credit bubble is much more muted in continental Europe than in the Anglo-

Saxon economies. In Italy and Germany, the stock of financial assets is not that far out of line with the real economy, while consumer debt has not been rising at such record levels. In fact, although we do not have up-to-date figures, the losses on the stock markets in Italy and Germany over recent years may already be enough to bring financial markets back into line. Nobody expects the Eurozone to boom over the next few years—particularly when its major trading partners are stuck in recession—and Europe, as elsewhere is dangerously close to deflation. However, in the long-run, it may find itself in a better state of health than those economies currently boasting about their strong productivity growth and 'flexible' labour markets.

developing countries will be badly hit

Developing countries will be hard hit by any US financial crisis. As in the Great Depression in 1929, one of the 'transmission channels' from the United States to developing countries will be via lower demand for commodities and other major exports. This will further depress prices, which, as we have seen, are already at historic lows. As the past two decades demonstrate, adverse shifts in the 'terms of trade' (the price of developing country exports in relation to the price of their imports) have a very negative impact on output in poor countries.[17] Falling prices will hit poor people in developing countries particularly hard because they are so dependent on commodity exports.[18]

A falling US dollar will also increase competition from US exports in Third World country markets. Like Uganda, Thailand, Congo, or Mexico, the United States will find that it needs to start increasing exports to pay off external debt. Woe betide any country trying to compete with exports of the country with the largest economy on earth and the geopolitical power to match; unlike Uganda or the Congo, the United States will have the clout unilaterally to raise US tariff barriers to protect domestic industries.

The so-called 'emerging market' economies will be hard hit because new loans are likely to dry up. When a credit bubble bursts, funds that have appeared to be 'real' as a result of Ponzi-financed speculation will disappear as quickly as they came, leaving a reduced stock of capital flowing to developing countries. Poorer countries, most of which are dependent on aid rather than private finance, will also suffer. Aid flows are already in long-term decline, with recent commitments to additional resources unlikely to materialize once donor economies start to experience the kind of stress we are predicting. Even the aid budgets that remain intact are likely to be diverted towards the latest security hot spots, or countries of strategic interest to industrialized countries.

In the long run, this trend may be healthy for some developing countries, which have over-heated from the inflow and outflow of 'hot money' looking for high returns with little concern for the long-term effects on the host country. If this speculative money is no longer there in future, perhaps we will avoid the financial crises that so damaged Mexico, South Korea, Thailand, Malaysia, Indonesia, Argentina, Brazil, Uruguay, Russia, and Turkey. But in the short term, the reduction in flows will have a severe impact. Countries that rely upon a merry-go-round of new loans in order to repay old loans will find that the money no longer comes in while the debts continue to mount. As a result, the risks of financial crisis in heavily indebted emerging markets, many of which are already paying sky-high interest rates on their government debt, will increase sharply.

The outlook for developing-country debt could be even worse if US interest rates go up. Rates on developing-country debt are generally measured in terms of 'spreads' over the interest rates on US Treasury bonds so if US interest rates go up, all other things being equal, interest rates on emerging-market debt will also rise. This was one of the major factors behind the developing-country debt crisis of the 1980s, where the monetarist policies pursued by President Reagan pushed US interest rates to very high levels. Of course, all other things may not be equal; but it is likely that if there is a financial crisis in the United States, investors will seek a 'flight to quality'—they will want to put their money in as low-risk a place as possible. This means that they are likely to shy away from developing countries, which will put even further upward pressure on interest rates for these countries.

Add to this the fact that the collapse in the dollar will slash the value of the dollar reserves that developing countries have been so carefully squirreling away. Of course, the dollar value of debts will also fall, partly off-setting the loss of reserves but it will still leave countries more vulnerable to sharp falls in the value of their currencies as measured against the value of other world currencies.

Many of these trends will be accentuated by the impact of China's entry into the global economy. This is not directly related to the impact of the US/UK crash but it remains the case that China is tending to exacerbate global trends towards deflation, due to the impact of Chinese exports—which grew by as much as 22 per cent in 2002[19]—on global production. This is undermining the export potential of other parts of Asia, particularly in manufacturing. At the same time, China is also sucking in a steadily increasing proportion of the total flow of investment funds available to developing countries, becoming the world's leading destination for foreign direct investment in 2002.[20]

So, the outlook for the global economy is not rosy, and the chances of another bout of debt-deflation are high. What can governments do to respond to these worrying developments?

conclusion: what are the options open to governments?

In the Great Depression of the 1930s, governments *could* do little to reflate their economies and restore external balances. Moreover, the geopolitical tensions, which succeeded the First World War, and the failure of the United States to play an international leadership role, meant that governments *did* do little to get the global economy out of the abyss. Instead, they engaged in a pointless round of so-called 'tariff escalation' with each country trying to protect its own economy by imposing tariffs. All that was achieved was to reduce demand in other economies, further dragging the global economy down.[21]

What about governments today? To be sure, governments now have many more options in terms of 'policy instruments' that can be used to shore up falling prices and to prevent depression. In 1929, the Keynesian idea that governments should try to jump-start their economies by spending more or cutting taxes was still in its infancy. In those countries relatively free of excessive levels of government debt or stuck within the strictures of the Eurozone Stability and Growth Pact, increasing government spending remains an option. But, as the US experience has shown, they must take care to ensure that such fiscal stimuli serve to benefit the *whole* economy rather than certain narrow, privileged sectors.

In only a very limited number of countries, governments still have some scope to cut interest rates in order to provide a monetary stimulus. In the United States and the United Kingdom, however, we are likely to see interest rates go up; and many developing countries will fear that reducing interest rates will result in a substantial capital outflow. In Japan, short-term interest rates are already at zero.

Another option would be for governments to intervene by providing 'bail-outs'—that is, trying to prevent the financial collapse from happening in the first place. Bail-outs—of both companies and countries—are not a new idea. In 2002, the IMF made a $30 billion loan to Brazil, which helped to prevent investor panic over the new, potentially threatening left-wing government. In 1998, the US Federal Reserve organized a consortium of banks and finance houses to take over the failing Long Term Capital Management (LTCM) and to rescue the firm's portfolio.[22] But even the funds of powerful central banks such as the US Federal Reserve, or international institutions such as the IMF, will be limited by the willingness of global taxpayers to stump up the cash. It is unlikely that these institutions would be able to provide a bail-out of the level needed to prevent a credit collapse on the scale we are predicting.

We cannot be complacent, therefore, about the ability of our policy-makers to protect us from economic collapse. As we have seen, governments have already given away much of their ability to manage their economies: to prevent credit bubbles; control deflation; manipulate their exchange rate and so on. Indeed, this has been one of the defining features of the process we know as 'globalization'. Governments may find that, once the going gets tough, they wish they had not been so eager to meet the demands of finance capital.

references

[1] IMF *World Economic Outlook*, (Washington DC: IMF, 2003) also transcript of World Economic Outlook Press Conference, 9 April 2003.

[2] C. Kindleberger, 'The World in Depression: 1929–1939' in *The Pelican History of World Economy in the Twentieth Century.* (Middlesex: Penguin Books, 1987).

[3] P. Krugman, 'A Fiscal Train Wreck'—*New York Times*, 11 March 2003.

[4] Tax Policy Center, Urban Institute and Brookings Institution. Cited in E. Andres 'Bush team weighs a plan to dump the income tax' *New York Times*, 10 February 2003.

[5] J. D. McKinnon and A. Squeo, 'Shaking Economic Times Limit Bang of New Defense Spending' *Wall Street Journal*, 15 April 2003.

[6] *The Economist*, 14 February 2002.

[7] The primary balance of payments is defined as the overall balance less net payments abroad of interest, dividends and profits. It is equal to the balance of trade in goods and services plus net unilateral transfers.

[8] IMF International Financial Statistics.

[9] 'Indonesia considers switch from dollar to euro' *Asia Pulse*/Antara.

[10] R. Douthwaite, 'How to Stop the War: Boycott the dollars and bring peace to the world.' *Resurgence magazine*, forthcoming.

[11] European Commission, Quarterly Report on the Euro Area, No 1. 2003.

[12] 'US: Lest We Forget: No Economy Is An Island' *BusinessWeek Online*, Business Outlook, 7 April 2003.

[13] K. Rogoff, Transcript of World Economic Outlook Press Conference, 9 April 2003.

[14] 'The Firms that can't stop failing' *The Economist*, 5 September 2002.

[15] A. Oswald, 'The Great 2003–2005 Crash in Britain's Housing Market' *Warwick University*, 24 November 2002.

[16] 'A buyer's market as boom loses momentum' *Financial Times*, 3 May 2003.

[17] E. Mendoza, 'The Terms of Trade, the Real Exchange Rate, and Economic Fluctuations' *International Economic Review*, Vol 36 (1995), p. 101–137.

[18] IMF *World Economic Outlook*, (Washington DC: IMF, 2001).

[19] WTO cited in G. Duncan, 'China overtakes UK in League of Trading Nations' *Times Online*, 24 April 2003.

[20] Z. Peiyan, 'Report on the implementation of the 2002 plan for national economic and social development'—Minister of State, Development and Planning, Beijing, 21 March 2003.

[21] D. Aldcroft, 'From Versailles to Wall Street 1919–1929' in *The Pelican History of World Economy in the Twentieth Century*, (Middlesex: Penguin Books, 1987).

[22] J. Eatwell and L. Taylor, *Global Finance at Risk* (New York: The New Press, 2000).

real world environmental outlook

andrew simms

The global economy is dangerously addicted to fossil fuels, driving conflict, climate change, volatile energy costs, and unresolved confrontation over how to share the global commons of the atmosphere.

For a short time towards the end of 2002 and early in 2003, Hans Blix was one of the world's most famous men. Leading the UN's weapons inspection in Iraq, he was a daily feature in the global media. After diplomatic twists and turns, revelations and condemnations for all the protagonists in the looming conflict, Blix saved his most surprising words until after the war began and his job became effectively redundant, 'To me the question of the environment is more ominous than that of peace and war . . . I'm more worried about global warming than I am of any major military conflict.'[1]

This book is called the **Real** World <u>Economic</u> Outlook. But the economy is a 'wholly owned subsidiary' of the environment. To understand anything real about the world economy, therefore, we have to understand the condition of its owner, the earth, and its biosphere. We also have to understand the most critical relationships between the economy and the environment. Here, even the most pathologically optimistic observer creates a bleak picture.

These are the conservative predictions of a famously anti-environmentalist professor of statistics, Bjorn Lomborg.[2] As a result of humankind's impact on the environment through our economic activity, species are becoming extinct at a rate '1,500 times higher than . . . natural background extinction'. Elsewhere '20 per cent of tropical forests' has disappeared. In countries like Nigeria and Madagascar, that figure is 'well over half', and Central America may have lost 50-70 per cent. Over one third of fish caught in the world's oceans is taken from 'stocks showing declining yields'. Erosion of agricultural land has left 38 per cent degraded. Many other observers think things are much, much worse.

Stripped bare, economics is about meeting our basic needs. Yet the continuing blind spot of mainstream economics to environmental impact—so called 'externalities'—and the obsession with crude growth, means that the dogma of orthodox economics is undermining its primary purpose.

From the range of available plant and animal species we draw genetic and chemical information to improve crops, develop new medicines and countless other products, and understand the ecosystems that the economy ultimately depends on. But a consensus has emerged that the economic exploitation of natural resources is driving a mass extinction event. This, in turn, will have enormous, unpredictable economic impacts. Forest loss, for example, exacerbates climate change and species' extinction, and undermines the possibility for sustainable livelihoods linked to forest management. The food chain especially is vulnerable to environmental degradation. Soil loss leads to farming failure and hunger.

oil—the weakest link

The greatest common threat is the global economy's enduring addiction to fossil fuels and its resulting symptom, global warming. And the UN weapons' inspector Hans Blix almost certainly understated the links between the war on Iraq, the United States' strategic desire to secure Middle Eastern oil supplies to feed the US economy's addiction to cheap fuel, and the current administration's official contrarian policy toward climate change.

It was fashionable over the last decade to point to an increasingly 'weightless economy'. The information age and the old, 'new economy' were supposed to reduce our dependence on raw materials. But where one of the most fundamental raw materials, carbon from fossil fuels, is concerned, the global economy just keeps getting heavier. A decade after the UN Framework Convention on Climate Change (UNFCCC) was signed, ranging from the United States to Australia, Canada, and across Europe, countries are, per person, pumping out more carbon dioxide than they were at the time of the Earth Summit. To put that into perspective, beginning from the stroke of New Year, as they sit down to their evening meal on January 2, a US family will have already used, per person, the equivalent in fossil fuels that a family in Tanzania will depend on for the whole year.

Even with technological advances in energy efficiency, and the creeping introduction of renewable energy, there is still an incredibly close correlation between crude measures of economic wealth and the consumption of fossil fuels. Rich people pump more greenhouse gasses into the atmosphere. That is why there is no more fundamental issue than the distribution of wealth in a carbon-constrained world economy. Unfortunately, until renewable energy goes mainstream, access to economic opportunity and access to fossil fuels are, more or less, the same thing. This is a very big problem.

Estimates vary, but scientists suggest that to prevent dangerous climate change, 60–90 per cent cuts in greenhouse gas emissions will be necessary over the next century. Understandably, however, the majority world believes it has a right to become very much richer in the material things that the citizens of rich countries take for granted.

Without a radical change in how we manage the global commons of the atmosphere, that means one of three things. Either there has to be a massive reduction in rich country emissions, far beyond the scope of the current international agreement, the Kyoto Protocol, to give poor countries the environmental space to develop. Or, poor countries are to be simply denied the carbon-rich development path followed by industrialized countries. Or, finally, the engine of conventional development keeps running on carbon, as usual, and there is climate chaos. In this case radical or, perhaps, logical change, suddenly becomes an attractive option.

It's easy to forget how relatively new this predicament is. The global economy's oil addiction is little more than a century old. After early discoveries in Oil Creek, Titusville, Pennsylvania in the late 1850s, John D Rockefeller formed the Standard Oil Company of Ohio in 1870. No other event has bound the fate of economies as tightly to the fate of the environment. Anthony Sampson wrote his classic work on '*the great oil companies and the world they made*' in 1975.[3] If he were writing today with the benefit of hindsight and the knowledge of global warming, he might have said '*the great oil companies and the world they broke*'.

Almost all of humankind's fossil fuel emissions of carbon dioxide, the main global warming gas, have happened over the last century. Coal dominated first, followed by oil. The use of natural gas took off in the 1970s. All along there has been an almost exact correlation between greenhouse gas emissions and levels of economic activity—they rise and fall together. About 80 per cent of the world's total primary energy supply is accounted for by coal, oil, and gas.

The consequences for the climate are spelt out by an international scientific consensus in the reports of the Intergovernmental Panel on Climate Change (IPCC). According to the World Meteorological Organisation (WMO), 'Changes in climate are known to have occurred in the past. However, such changes were due to natural causes. Recent changes are largely attributable to human activities.'[4]

An increase in average global temperature of 0.6°C since detailed records began in the 1860s is linked to the rise in atmospheric greenhouse gas concen-

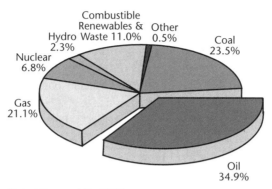

Figure 4.1 Global Energy Mix 2000
Source: International Energy Agency 2002

trations from about 280 parts per million by volume (ppmv) in 1750 to 370 ppmv at the end of 2001, an increase of over 32 per cent. Projecting forward against a huge range of scenarios, climate experts are unsure whether it will be possible to stabilize concentrations at any level ranging from 450 ppmv to 750 ppmv or beyond.

Yet even with current concentration levels, 1998 was the warmest year on record, with 2001 being the second. The 1990s was the warmest decade of the 20th century. Global average sea-level rise has been as much as ten times the average increase in the last 3000 years. Thinning sea ice and shrinking glaciers, droughts, floods, and storms are all driving natural disasters, the costs of which threaten to derail international efforts to reduce poverty in line with the Millennium Development Goals.[6] The scale of impacts is so great that it threatens the great reversal of human progress. With remarkable restraint, the Secretary General of the WMO said, 'The measures contemplated in mitigating climate change so far are inadequate to protect our future climate.'[7]

The problem is that global greenhouse gas emissions are set to keep rising for many years to come. There has been no move to agree a target for capping concentrations in the atmosphere at a level to prevent dangerous climate change. The International Energy Agency predicts that emissions will increase by 70 per cent by 2030.[8] This depends, however, on countless political, economic, and technological variables such as the will to switch to renewables, conservation measures, low-energy lifestyle choices, and rates of economic growth.

For many low-lying states such as the South Pacific islands, we already have dangerous climate change; any predictions of significantly rising emissions are nothing short of apocalyptic for their people as well as economies. Because of delayed reactions in the atmosphere, we will not even feel the full effects of today's energy-intensive lifestyles for many years.

Projecting forward the rising economic costs from mostly climate-driven natural disasters, global insurance giant CGNU predicted that, under a business-as-usual scenario, the costs of natural disasters would actually overtake the value of world economic output by around 2065.[9]

Another insurance-based estimate from the UNEP Financial Initiative suggests additional costs of $300 billion annually to the global economy by 2050. This is almost certainly an underestimate as many costs escape these types of calculations. Yet a single year's worth of such costs is equal to the entire amount of poor country debt that the international debt relief campaign Jubilee 2000 was attempting to get written off. Already the extent of economic 'value at risk' from climate change could be as much as 15 per cent of the total market capitalization of major companies[10]—that's equivalent to wiping some $262 billion off the market capitalization of companies on the FTSE All Share Index.[11]

Following calculations based on the work of the UN Advisory Group on Greenhouse Gases, and emissions rising at current levels, we will have burned as much fossil fuels as it is safe to do so in just over 30 years. Beyond that, temperature rises linked to increasing greenhouse gas concentrations imply *'rapid, unpredictable, and non-linear responses that could lead to extensive ecosystem damage'.*[12]

Abrupt, or runaway, global warming is a serious environmental possibility and the danger is that it sets in motion a process of oddly called 'positive feedback' processes (they are not positive at all), which means that warming would become beyond our ability to control.[13] Even environmental sceptics like Bjorn Lomborg believe that much more effort needs to go into addressing genuine catastrophe scenarios.

where next?

Even without the prospect of managing climate change, what we do with fossil fuels in general, and oil in particular, is sufficiently explosive. We go to war in the Middle East to control it (there was an immediate cost of $74 billion to the United States alone, even as it struggles with massive trade deficits and merely very large budget deficits). When the oil price lurches up and down, economies overheat or plunge into recession.

In the middle of all of that, we now have to work out how to use less of it. And, because the atmosphere it affects is a global commons and because poor countries are going to use more of it, we have to work out how to share our

collective fossil-fuel inheritance more equally—both within our own generation, and between this and future ones.

Exactly how difficult this is can be demonstrated by how easily even senior
civil servants can completely misunderstand the challenge. Take this graph
from the UK Government's environment department DEFRA.[14] Put briefly, its
projection for cutting emissions to 'stabilize' greenhouse gases at a certain level
shows that, by around 2070, there will be no fossil fuels at all for countries outside the First World club—not a barrel of oil, heap of coal, or canister of gas to
burn. Explaining that logic to India, China, Brazil, or Ethiopia will make for an
interesting ministerial meeting.

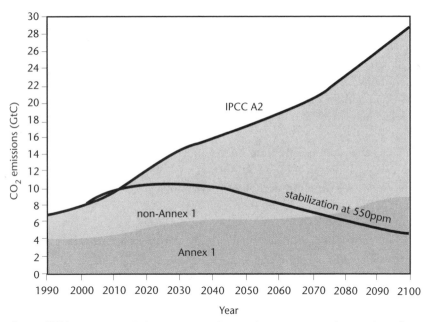

Figure 4.2 Projected global emissions under one business-as-usual scenario and a
possible pathway to stabilization at 550ppm that leaves non-Annex 1 (less
industrialized) countries no emissions entitlements

Source: DEFRA

This is politically explosive for another reason. Latest estimates show oil production in the high-consuming, advanced industrialized economies is set to
tail-off dramatically over the next few decades. They will be left increasingly
dependent on the Middle East, Russia, and other poorer producers for their oil.
A gap between demand and supply is set to open up.[15] At one of two extremes

it will be filled in rich countries by either military aggression to secure supply, or greatly reduced domestic demand, within the context of a new constitutional settlement to share the oil and the environmental space it takes.

It is never likely that everyone in the world will use identical amounts of fossil fuels. However, any future settlement will have to be based on the principle that, in a carbon-constrained world, everyone should have equal entitlements to their share of the atmosphere's ability to safely absorb pollution. Under that agreement, those people and nations that take the economic benefits by polluting more than their fair share will have to somehow pay compensation to the 'under-polluters' by purchasing their spare entitlements. Otherwise they run up a huge ecological debt.[16] The process will have to involve capping total emissions, progressively reducing them, and sharing entitlements using a formula that will, over an agreed timeframe, mean they converge to be equal per person. If chaos is to be avoided, this process—given the name 'Contraction and Convergence' by the London-based Global Commons Institute—is unavoidable. In essence, the world has a limited carbon cake and the only way to begin negotiations on how to cut the cake is to start with the principle of equal access rights. What we do with them is another matter.

This has enormous, and from a development perspective, very positive consequences. Based on IPCC assumptions in 1995, to stabilize atmospheric greenhouse gas concentrations at 1990 levels implied a global, equal, per-capita entitlement of about 0.43 tons of carbon. Typical US per-capita carbon use in 1995 was 5.3 tons.[17] The UK Government estimates that the damage cost of carbon emissions (not including their much larger economic value) is in the range of $56 to $223 per t/C.

That means that, just to account for the damage cost of their unsustainable carbon use, each US citizen would have been liable to pay between $273 and $1086 each year for the privilege to pollute more than their fair share.[18] For the United States as a whole, that is a bill of between $73 billion and $290 billion— imagine the impact of that money being channeled into sustainable development and the Millennium Development Goals. And, this money would not be aid, but entitlement. Such calculations reveal that huge proportions of the G7 countries' economic output are built on the foundations of unsustainable per-capita carbon use.[19]

Action to combat global warming cannot be delayed because, over time, emissions grow, populations rise, and the sustainable size of a carbon cake slice will get smaller and smaller. There has to be a rapid, managed retreat from fossil fuel addiction because there is no other way to escape impending climate chaos.

Alberto di Fazio[20] has noted that, to make the planet fit for human life, carbon dioxide in the atmosphere was converted by natural processes into fossil fuel reserves over the course of 180 million years. According to di Fazio, humanity is converting fossil fuels back into the atmosphere 'a million times faster'. The correlation between the growing size of the global economy, which doubles roughly every 17 years, measured by 'world industrial product', and carbon dioxide emissions is, he says, 'astoundingly high . . . practically total correlation'.

Mainstream economists and policy-makers seem to assume that efficiency can grow indefinitely. This gives them the excuse to believe that carbon dioxide emissions can be cut without either renouncing fossil fuels or limiting conventional economic growth. However, even under the most impossibly optimistic scenario, bringing us close to the limits of the laws of thermodynamics, the best technology can do is not very much. Maximum efficiency gains in the best-case scenario would only postpone higher greenhouse gas levels by 24 years. A more realistic assessment of global best efforts, taking account of the difficulty of collective political action, is that the delay would be 'negligible'.

Trusting to efficiency will not allow 'any significant or appreciable control of the coming climate crisis', di Fazio concludes. From a strictly technical perspective, 'either we switch to non-fossil fuel sources of energy [which because of an implementation time-lag will take several decades to meet demand] or we limit the world industrial product, or both in some proportion'.[21]

conclusion

The magazine *Shares: the investors champion* ran a front page at the height of the Iraq War. It said, 'Oil, the burning issue: which stocks to buy.' They recommended buying one company's shares because it had '*got rid of interests in renewable energy . . . to focus on oil drilling*'.[22]

The global economy is run by a carbon aristocracy, holed-up in a handful of the richest countries, still wilfully oblivious of the real problem. But, presiding over extreme poverty and injustice like other aristocracies before them, they are fragile and ultimately unsupportable. At the time of writing, the oil-rich Middle East is riven with instability, recovering from one war and threatened with another. There is mutiny in Nigeria's offshore oil fields and violent protests in the oil producing areas on land. Other major producers like Venezuela are in turmoil. US economic hegemony is challenged by the rise of the euro against the dollar as a potential global reserve currency, possibly aided by a move to denominate more oil trades in euros.[23] With fabulous irony, the shares of oil giant BP are hit repeatedly when production is disrupted by climate-driven extreme weather events in the Gulf of Mexico. And, all the time, the climate keeps warming.

We have to live within our environmental budget because we cannot survive without the life-supporting properties provided by the atmosphere—a bank of natural capital. The international community must agree to cap and reduce its carbon emissions, using a formula that equitably distributes entitlements to the carbon cake. Without that, the real world economic outlook is for an inextricably entwined economic and environmental crash, not a 'correction', as the complacent jargon has it, but a potentially irreversible collapse.

references

[1] 'Hans Blix's Greatest Fear', New York Times, 16 March 2003.

[2] B. Lomborg, The Skeptical Environmentalist—measuring the real state of the world: (Cambridge: Cambridge University Press, 2001).

[3] A. Sampson, The Seven Sisters: the great oil companies and the world they made, (New York: Viking Press 1975).

[4] Our Future Climate, World Meteorological Day, WMO 23 March 2003.

[5] International Energy Agency 2000.

[6] The End of Development? Global warming, disasters and the great reversal of human progress, (London: NEF & BCAS, 2002).

[7] Our Future Climate, World Meteorological Day, WMO 23 March 2003.

[8] World Energy Outlook 2002, (Paris: International Energy Agency, 2002).

[9] Environmental Finance, Vol 1, No 7, May 2000.

[10] Estimate by Innovest Strategic Value Advisors Inc. See: www.innovestgroup.com/pdfs/NYT_081802.pdf.

[11] Total market Capitalization of the FTSE All Share index at 12—12—2002 was £1,100.351 billion.

[12] B. Hare (Climate Policy Director, Greenpeace International) Fossil Fuels and Climate Protection: The Carbon Logic, September 1997.

[13] Abrupt Climate Change, Science, Vol 299, 28 March 2003.

[14] The Scientific Case For Setting A Long-Term Emission Reduction Target, (London: DEFRA, 2003).

[15] Graphs available at www.gci.org.uk.

[16] Balancing the Other Budget: proposals for solving the greater debt crisis—(London: NEF, 2002).

[17] R. Engleman, Profiles in Carbon: An Update on Population, Consumption and Carbon Dioxide Emissions, (Washington DC: Population Action International, 1998).

[18] Energy White Paper: Our Energy Future—Creating A Low Carbon Economy, (London: DTI, February 2003).

[19] *Who Owes Who? Climate change, debt, equity and survival*, (London: Christian Aid, 1999).

[20] Senior Scientist, National Institute of Astrophysics Gianfranco Bologna.

[21] A. Simms, *An Environmental War Economy*, (London: NEF, 2001).

[22] *Shares*, Vol 5 Issue 14, 3-9 April 2003.

[23] 'When will we buy oil in euros?' *The Observer*, 23 February 2003. A former US ambassador to Saudi Arabia speaking to the US congress, said, 'The US treasury can print money and buy oil, which is an advantage no other country has . . .' Saudi Arabia has historically insisted on pricing oil in dollars but questions could be raised within Saudi about why 'they should be so kind to the United States'.

real outlook for the world's regions

introduction

Part 02 focuses on different regions of the global economy, and provides more detailed analyses and outlooks for the Middle East, Latin America, North America, South Asia, East Asia, Europe, and Africa. This Part is written by our distinguished partners, renowned economists embedded within these regions.

Their perspectives are rooted in the 'homes and hearths' of their communities; and are very different from standard reviews of their economies, written from within the ivory towers of Washington, Geneva, and London.

While there has been some editing of texts to meet space limits, there has been no attempt to achieve uniformity of presentation or voice. The result is a rich and illuminating *tour d'horizon* of the global economy.

CHAPTER 5

outlook for the middle east: unfulfilled promises and devastation

erinc yeldan

The Middle East, North Africa, and Central Asia, a region of almost 600 million people, is a land of devastation, war, and unfulfilled promises. This region, known as the birthplace of civilization, is host to the three major religions of the world and encompasses a diverse cultural and historical heritage, which has been a source of mutual respect and peaceful coexistence for centuries. Yet, the strategic interests of the neoliberal 'Petro Core' have ignored these riches, focusing only on one aspect: oil.

It is oil that finally triggered the war in Iraq, which holds some 11 per cent of the world's oil reserves. This, in my view, was the strategic climax of the converging interests of the so-called 'Petro Core'—currently consisting of British Petroleum, Royal Dutch/Shell, Exxon-Mobil, and Texaco-Chevron, the world's four biggest private oil companies, which want the open flow of oil resources at 'administered' (read oligopolistic) prices to the detriment of the supplying Arab nations, and the arms industry, whose interests have been under pressure as the aggregate military budgets of the world have fallen by over 30 per cent and trade in weapons has dwindled. This alliance is one of the most fearsome facets of the new collective imperialism which will profit from a permanent state of war in the world and which sees our planet merely as merchandise for sale. There is little doubt that the conflict in Iraq—and its repercussions in the region—will have long-lasting effects and will serve to exacerbate the already deep economic problems of the Middle East and Central Asian nations.

two decades of stagnation

It is no exaggeration to say that the economic performance of the region has been a complete failure. After the bonanza of economic expansion of the 1970s due to surging oil prices, the 1980s and 1990s have seen virtual stagnation for the economies of the Middle East and North Africa (MENA). In the 1980s, the annual per capita average income fell by 1 per cent; in the 1990s, it grew by a mere 1 per cent, better only than Sub-Saharan Africa. Growth rates have been erratic, often following the zigzags of oil prices in the international markets. The real rate of growth of per capita GNP has been very low in comparison to the rest of the developing world (see Figure 5.1). As of 2000, average per capita GNP was $2060, less than half of the world average (see Table 5.1). There are large differences in income levels from country to country with per capita GNP as high as $23,500 in Qatar and $19,710 in Israel but as low as $370, $970, and $976 in Yemen, Syria, and Iraq respectively.

In Central Asia, economies have suffered from 'transition', with established institutions being dismantled and regions being left open to the assault of neoliberal globalization. Between 1990 and 1999, growth has been falling, in some cases dramatically—by 9 per cent in Azerbaijan, 5.9 per cent in Kazakhstan, and 3.5 per cent in Turkmenistan (see Table 5.1).

Table 5.1 Structure of the economy in selected Middle East and Central Asian countries

	GNP per capita (Dollars)	GNP per capita (PPP Dollars)	GDP Average Growth 90–99	Structure of GDP, 1999(%)						
				Private Consump-tion	Public Consump-tion	Total Invest-ment	Domestic Savings	Current Account Balance	Exports	Imports
Qatar	23,500		5.7	21.4	26.6	21.4	–	18.0	–	–
Saudi Arabia	6,874		3.2	38.9	29.8	20.3	31.5	–1.2	36.0	31.0
Syria	970	2.761	2.1	69.5	11.4	18.8	18.2	1.3	29.0	40.0
Turkey	2,900	6,126	4.1	68.0	11.0	24.0	19.6	–0.7	26.0	31.0
Yemen	370	1,755	–2.8	72.4	14.8	20.9	11.8	1.5	37.0	45.0
Azerbaijan	550	2.322	–9.0	84.0	11.0	34.0	5.0	–29.5	29.0	58.0
Kazakhstan	1.230	4,408	·–5.9	68.0	17.0	15.0	15.0	–3.1	43.0	43.0
Krgyz Rep.	300	2,223	–7.4	93.0	17.0	10.0	–11.0	–18.7	37.0	58.0
Tajikstan	290	981	–9.8	–	–	20.0	–	–5.5	81.0	85.0
Turkmenistan	660	3,099	–3.5	–	–	40.0			63.0	53.0
Uzbekistan	720	2,092	–2.0	–	–	11.0	–	–	25.0	22.0
Middle East and North Africa	2,060	4,600	3.0	60.0	21.0	22.0	19.0	–2.0	25.0	28.0
World	4,890	6,490	2.5	62.0	15.0	22.0	23.0	–0.2	22.0	22.0

Sources: ERF, *Economic Trends in the MENA Region,* (Cairo: American University in Cairo Press, 2003); World Bank, *World Development Indicators,* (Washington DC: World Bank, 2001); AFESD, *United Arab Economic Report,* (Kuwait: AFESD, 2000).

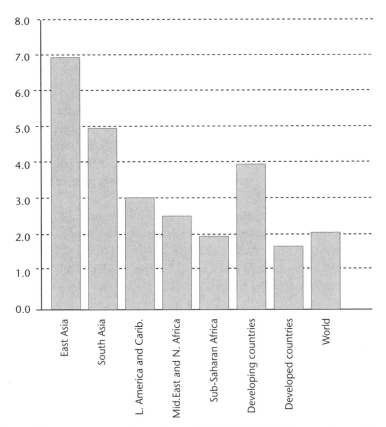

Figure 5.1 Average annual rate of growth of GDP, 1990–99 across the world

Sources: UNCTAD, *Trade and Development Report,* (Geneva: UNCTAD, 2003); World Bank, *World Development Indicators,* (Washington DC: World Bank, 2001).

The World Bank estimates that the transition economies will grow by 3.3 per cent and 3.4 per cent respectively over 2003 and 2004 and that the non-oil exporting MENA region will be growing at rates of 2.7 per cent and 3.6 per cent respectively. These growth rates are significantly lower than those of developing countries, which are expected to see average growth of 3.9 per cent in 2003 and 4.7 per cent in 2004.

a crisis in savings and investment

The MENA region suffers, in particular, from low savings generation and consequently a dismal investment performance. Savings-to-GNP ratios average 19 per cent compared with the world average of 23 per cent. Saudi Arabia has the highest savings rate and Bahrain has an exceptionally high investment rate. Yet overall, spending on fixed investments in the Arab countries grew by only 1.1 per cent between 1999 and 2000. This is largely because of cuts in public investment as part of government austerity measures.[1]

This meagre savings performance has a number of causes, one of which is the region's high proportion of young and dependant people who find it hard to save out of scarce incomes. Another reason is the fragile and mostly shallow state of the region's financial systems, which fail to provide the necessary intermediary role between savers and investors. Publicly controlled banks, with an excessive exposure to government debt, outdated or poor regulations, and weak management predominate.

Within this context, premature liberalization of weak financial systems has been disastrous, in most cases diverting savings into short-term speculative ventures rather than to productive activities in the real economy. Turkey, with the fresh memories of the severe financial crises of 2000/2001 is a prime example. After the complete liberalization of its foreign capital regime, Turkey suffered a fall in the credit available to investors. As credit-to-GDP ratios fell, banks took on the role of financial *rentiers* and became prime movers in diverting priorities towards speculative finance.

Adding to the region's problems, it has failed to attract more than a fraction of the foreign direct investment going to the developing world, despite severe competition between countries that have offered an array of incentives including tax holidays, long-term leases, greater foreign ownership rights, and generous entry rules.

International trade has been weak too, despite the signing of trade agreements between the EU and Israel, Tunisia, Morocco, Jordan, Egypt, and Lebanon over the past few years and Turkey's formation of a full customs union with the EU in 1995. Export performance has varied across countries but, in general, volumes have fallen catastrophically. Overall, MENA-countries' share of the world exports market has fallen by more than half over the last two decades. Consequently, many countries in the region had to rely on workers' remittances as a source of foreign exchange earnings. Yet, coupled with the increased debt-servicing costs, the region has built up sizeable current account deficits averaging 2 per cent of GNP in comparison with the world average of –0.2 per cent in 1999 (see Table 5.1).

labour markets under pressure

The region's economic weaknesses are being exacerbated by the fact that its rate of population growth is one of the fastest in the world. MENA's population was nearly 300 million in 1999. Between 1980 and 1998, it grew by an average of 2.8 per cent. During the 1990s, the number of people of working age rose by 3.1 per cent, far exceeding the world average of 1.7 per cent (see Table 5.2). Estimates suggest that employment in the MENA region has to grow by more

Table 5.2 Population and the structure of labor force

	Total Population (1999, Millions)	Labor Force Growth rate (90–99, %)	Participation Rate (%)		Illiteracy Rate (%)		Public Exp on Education (1997, % of GNP)
			Male	Female	Male	Female	
Bahrain	0.7	3.6a	62.8	21.9	9.8	18.8	
Egypt	62.4	2.9	52.3	23.5	34.5	58.2	4.8
Iran	63.0	2.4	44.3	17.0	18.3	32.6	4.0
Iraq	12.5	3.0a	43.9	11.1	36.1	56.6	
Jordan	4.7	5.2	43.9	15.0	5.8	17.4	6.8
Kuwait	1.9	−1.6	52.9	26.7	16.8	21.5	5.0
Lebanon	4.3	3.1	42.4	20.3	8.5	20.9	2.5
Oman	2.3	2.0a	41.6	9.6	22.0	42.5	
Qatar	0.7	1.4a	71.0	23.3	20.2	18.3	
Saudi Arabia	21.4	3.1	49.9	11.9	17.2	35.6	7.5
Syria	15.7	4.0	46.1	17.4	12.8	41.9	3.1
Turkey	64.4	2.8	59.2	36.4	7.1	25.0	2.2
Yemen	17.0	4.7	45.0	17.9	34.3	77.3	7.0
Azerbaijan	8.0	1.7					3.0
Kazakhstan	15.4	−0.2					4.4
Kyrgyz Rep.	4.7	1.4					5.3
Tajikistan	6.2	2.7				1.0	2.2
Turkmenistan	4.8	3.5					
Uzbekistan	24.5	3.0				1.0	7.7
Middle East and N. Africa	291.0	3.1					5.2
World	5947.7	1.7					4.8

a. Av. Population growth rate for 1980–98

Sources: ERF, *Economic Trends in the MENA Region 2002*, (Cairo: American University in Cairo Press, 2003); World Bank, *World Development Indicators*, (Washington DC: World Bank, 2001).

than 4 per cent per year just to absorb the new additional workforce, leaving aside provision of new jobs for the existing army of unemployed.[2] Given the lack of investment, this seems an impossible task.

With high unemployment giving employers the whip hand, workers' wages and conditions are under constant threat. In Egypt, workers are faced with a new law that allows employers to terminate contracts without compensation. In Turkey, new labour legislation aimed at raising standards to EU levels has been postponed for a third time under pressure from powerful business associations that are arguing that the change would 'inhibit flexibility in the Turkish labour market'.

Across the region, there is a process of working conditions being marginalized. Widespread privatization and de-unionization are undermining basic workers' rights (see Table 5.2 for a survey of MENA labour markets, which share low participation rates, deep gender inequalities, and high illiteracy rates, leading to low productivity, together with low shares of public investment in education). On average, the number of adult females who can read and write reaches only two-thirds of that of men in MENA countries. The equivalent numbers are 98 per cent in Latin America, 76 per cent in Sub-Saharan Africa, and 86 per cent in East Asia. The underlying cause of illiteracy is low public investment in education. Only Saudi Arabia (7.5 per cent), Jordan (6.8 per cent), Yemen (7 per cent), and Kuwait (5 per cent) have spending-to-GNP ratios higher than the world average of 4.8 per cent. Formerly part of socialist economies with generous social welfare programs, the economies of Central Asia tend to have higher investment in education but this will not last as these countries face up to the scourge of servicing large debts, a phenomenon to which I now turn.

debt and the assault on welfare

External debt and the need to service this debt are a huge drain on the region's resources and are contributing to a painful assault on welfare and social spending. Although there has been a gradual decline in the total external debt position (to $202.1 billion in 2001 from $216 billion in 1995), many countries in the region are still classified as 'severely indebted'. And, despite improvements in the ratio of total external debt to GNP (from 37.3 per cent in 1995 to 31.2 per cent in 2000) and that to total exports of goods and services (from 112.5 per cent in 1995 to 94 per cent in 2000), the pressure to service debt continues to exert a dangerous deflationary force onto the region.

The size of the region's short-term debt—$47.4 billion in 2001 or about a fifth of total debt—is a significant concern (see Table 5.3 for individual countries).

It is deeply damaging that indebted countries are often being forced to meet their short-term repayment obligations by incurring even further debt. For example, Turkey and Qatar had to borrow more in 2001, while Morocco was forced to liquidate its privatization revenues. In 2001 and 2002, Turkey, to comply with IMF targets, was forced to reduce its short-term external debt to less than $15 billion in 2002 from $26 billion in mid-2000. Yet total foreign debt rose to $125.9 billion in the second quarter of 2002 from $102.9 billion in 1999 and debt-servicing costs increased to 16.8 per cent of the GNP in 2000–2001 from 11 per cent previously and to 70.1 per cent of its export earnings from 69.3 per cent. Interest costs as a ratio to GDP has reached 19 per cent—higher

Table 5.3 External indebtedness in the Middle East and Central Asia, averages for 1999–2001

	Total External Debt (Billions US$)	Short Term Debt (Billions US$)	Total External Debt/ GDP (%)	Total Debt Service/Exports (%)
Egypt	29.0	4.1	23.2	9.0
Iran	7.4	3.7	7.3	29.0
Jordan	7.6	0.7	89.0	11.0
Lebanon	12.5	2.5	71.0	27.0
Oman	5.9	1.3	–	7.0
Syria	21.3	5.7	136.0	5.0
Turkey	115.0	20.1	78.6	70.0
Yemen	4.2	0.7	61.0	5.0
Azerbaijan	0.9	0.2	18.8	8.0
Kazakhstan	6.7	0.5	36.6	17.0
Kyrgyz Rep.	1.4	0.1	102.9	29.0
Tajikistan	0.9	0.6	94.9	11.0
Turkmenistan	–	0.5[a]	–	32.0[a]
Uzbekistan	4.2	0.3	30.4	26.0
Middle East and N. Africa	202.1	47.4	31.2	94.0
World	2,375.1[a]			

a. Data for 1998

Sources: ERF, *Economic Trends in the MENA Region 2002*, (Cairo: American University in Cairo Press, 2003); World Bank, *World Development Indicators*, (Washington DC: World Bank, 2001).

Table 5.4 Fiscal balances and indicators

	Fiscal Balance as % of GDP (1999)	Tax Revenues as % of GDP (1998)	Ratio of Net New Financing to Debt Stock (%, 1998)	Interest Costs to GDP (%, 1999)	Social Expenditures[a] as % of Total Fiscal Expenditures
Egypt	−4.2	16.6		6.0	23.6
Iran	−5.7	11.2		0.1	41.8
Israel	−1.2	35.8	3.7	3.8	57.6
Jordan	−4.2	19.8	2.7	3.7	44.6
Kuwait	−13.8	1.5		1.7	
Lebanon	−14.4	12.7	11.9	12.9	19.4
Oman	−7.8	23.9			
Syria	−4.2	16.4			16.4
Turkey[b]	−14.4	22.0	70.2[c]	19.1	25.7
Yemen	−0.1	13.7		3.6	22.4
Azerbaijan[c]	−1.0	18.2		0.1	37.6
Kazakhstan[d]	−0.1	12.0	2.2	1.4	26.4
Kyrgyz Rep.	−3.3	14.9	1.9	1.5	40.7
Tajikistan	−1.0				
World	−1.5				

a. Social expenditures refer to education, health, social security, welfare, housing and community amenities. (1998)
b. Data refers to 2002; c. Data refers to 2001; d. Data refers to 2000
Sources: IMF, *Government Finance Statistics Yearbook,* (Washington DC: IMF, 2002); World Bank, *World Development Indicators,* (Washington DC: World Bank, 2001).

than the aggregate value added of agriculture, which employs nearly 40 per cent of the labour force.

So, for the sake, as the IMF would put it, of 'gaining credibility and trust in the foreign financial markets', Turkey has been forced to repay short-term debts to foreign creditors at the considerable and damaging price of increasing its debt to the IMF and crippling its economy even more with debt service (see Table 5.4 for other country examples where new borrowing has led to higher ratios of net new finance to existing debt stock).

As a result of low growth, high unemployment, and crippling debt service, public finances, particularly in the MENA region—Central Asian countries also have widening deficits but not to the same extent—are in crisis and social welfare provision is facing draconian cuts. In 1999, the combined budget deficit of the Arab countries was over $30 billion—that is 5.7 per cent of their combined GNP (see Table 5.4 for individual countries). To meet debt-service obligations, social investment in education, health, social security, and other amenities is being slashed.

the years ahead

The economic fate of the Middle East is, in the near future, very much dependent on how the post-war social and political dynamics will evolve. Even without these political uncertainties, however, the region faces a darkening economic future, not least because of the formidable pressure of debt service. In heavily indebted countries such as Turkey and Lebanon, interest costs of debt servicing will necessitate further cuts in social welfare programs, worsening poverty. In the years ahead, the new transition economies of Central Asia also look destined to be forced into their own debt trap. The outlook is grim.

further reading

Boratav K., E. Yeldan, and A. Köse, 'Globalization, Distribution, and Social Policy: Turkey, 1980–1998' in L. Taylor (ed.) *External Liberalization and Social Policy* (London and New York: Oxford University Press, 2002).

Economic Research Forum, *Economic Trends in the MENA Region, 2002*, (Cairo: The American University in Cairo Press, 2003).

World Bank, *World Development Indicators* (Washington DC: World Bank, 2001).

World Bank, *Global Development Finance* (Washington DC: World Bank, 2003).

Yeldan, E. 'On the IMF-Directed Disinflation Program in Turkey: A Program for Stabilization and Austerity or a Recipe for Impoverishment and Financial Chaos?' in N. Balkan (ed.) *The Ravages of Neo-Liberalism: Economy, Society and Gender in Turkey* (New York: Nova Science Pub., 2002).

references

[1] European Research Forum (ERF) (2003).

[2] ERF (2003), p.6.

outlook for south and central america: economic stagnation and state decline

franklin serrano

The economic, political, and social situation in South and Central America is currently very poor and the outlook is gloomy. Latin American growth was only an average of 0.4 per cent in 2001 and the regional economy actually contracted by 1.1 per cent in 2002. To put this in perspective, this was an even weaker performance than Africa, which grew by 4.3 per cent in 2001 and a projected 3.4 per cent in 2002.[1]

The next few years promise no improvement. A decade of financial liberalization has bequeathed the region weakened governance, large public and private external debts, an eroded industrial base, and a pattern of trade specialization that is increasingly reliant on exporting standardized natural-resource-based commodities. From the environmental point of view, this makes a number of economies, particularly those west of the Andes, even more vulnerable to phenomena like El Niño, while those of Central America and the Caribbean are more exposed to hurricanes. Global warming (whether man-made or not) will doubtless be costly in these areas. The highly-indebted economies of the region are now facing the current marked slowdown of growth of the world economy and fierce competition from the dynamic Asian developing economies for industrial markets. The pressure is piling up.

the social cost of low growth

Slow and unstable pattern growth in the region has led to social devastation. According to the ILO, the region is facing the worst crisis in terms of employment of the last 30 years. The bargaining power of the working classes has rarely looked weaker. The Latin American average open rate of urban unemployment reached 9.1 per cent in 2002. Among the highest rates in the region were 21 per cent in Argentina, 17 per cent in Uruguay, 17.6 per cent in Colombia, 15.8 per cent in Venezuela, 12.9 per cent in Nicaragua, and 16.1 per cent in Panama. During the 1990s, the proportion of the urban, economically-active population with jobs without any legal labour (or social security) rights has grown from 45 per cent in 1990 to 50.5 per cent in 2002 across Latin America. The proportion of the population classified as poor in the continent was 40.5 per cent at the beginning of the 1980s. By 1990, it had risen to 48.3 per cent. Slightly improved economic growth in the 1990s saw the figure fall but it was back to 44 per cent by 2002. In the last few years, as most countries of the region had to devalue their exchange rates to deal with their balance-of-payments difficulties (which I survey later), inflation has picked up and substantially eroded real wages. In the past year, formal sector real wages have fallen by 15.4 per cent in Argentina, 9 per cent in Uruguay, 7.6 per cent in Venezuela, and 4.9 per cent in Paraguay.

This has contributed to a drastic increase in violent crime across the region. In the *favelas* in Rio and São Paulo in Brazil and in whole regions of Colombia, drug lords totally control and terrorize whole territories inhabited largely by poor people. The weakening of the social bargaining power of the working classes has resulted in increasing insensitivity to popular needs among politicians who continue to impose recessive and anti-social policies and reforms across the region. In most countries, a sense of exclusion from the political process is leading to lower election turnouts and civic demobilization. In Argentina, Ecuador, Peru, Paraguay, and Bolivia, street riots are becoming the norm. In Venezuela, popular revolt led to the election of left-wing President Chavez who, so far, has survived two US-supported coup attempts from the oil elites. In Brazil last year, although Lula (Brazil's great working class leader) was elected despite international financial blackmail organized by the Cardoso Government in the run-up to the election, he has still capitulated to pressure from the international financial community and has guaranteed that his administration will continue the neoliberal macroeconomic policies and reforms of the previous government.

the contradictions of financial liberalization

How have we come to this state of affairs? To answer that question, we must analyze the impact of financial liberalization, which in this region perhaps more than in any other, was imposed in its extreme form. There is a fundamental contradiction in external financial liberalization.[2] It leads to a spectacular increase in the propensity of the local private and public sector to get into various forms of debt in foreign currency (overwhelmingly US dollars). Yet this process is not accompanied by a proportional increase in the ability of the developing country to earn the dollars necessary to service these liabilities. In fact, more often the opposite has been the truth—most 'reforms' that usually come with financial liberalization make it increasingly difficult for these economies to generate the required foreign exchange.

Lessons have not been learned. Major external financial liberalization was tried in Argentina and Chile in the late 1970s with literally disastrous results. Yet the same prescriptions still reappeared in the 1990s (including, again, in Argentina) as the Brady Plan encouraged the rescheduling or rolling over of old external debt and new financial regulations in the United States made US pension funds and other institutional investors eligible and interested in putting new money in 'emerging' markets.[3]

With a lot of new money flowing to the region, governments, which for years had been in a straitjacket of drastic import restrictions and low growth caused by the debt crises of the 1980s, saw an opportunity temporarily to remove these balance-of-payments constraints. Many countries used the foreign capital to tackle high or even hyperinflation by stabilizing nominal exchange rates.[4] In all countries, the dollars paid for the imports associated with the modest economic recovery in the first half of the 1990s. The aggregate growth rate for Latin America between 1991 and 1997 was only 3.5 per cent. Many countries also embarked on sweeping privatization programmes prescribed by the IMF and the World Bank.

All these policies had deeply negative effects on the ability of these economies to meet their new external liabilities. The nominal exchange rate stabilization plans invariably led to an over-valuation of the real exchange rate and this reduced the profitability of export industries and discouraged investment. Over-valuation, coupled with unilateral import liberalization, naturally led to an import boom; a large number of domestic producers of similar goods were wiped out and millions of industrial jobs were lost.

The privatization mainly of public utilities that were sold to foreign corporations (including, ironically, European state-owned enterprises) created a new layer of commitments to pay in foreign currency to the new, foreign owners in areas such as electricity, utilities, or toll roads that could not possibly generate a return in hard currency. In the vast majority of cases (an exception was mobile and cell phones where there was a little more competition), the promised efficiency gains failed to materialize for the rather obvious reason that public monopolies became private monopolies, insulated from competition. In general, Latin American privatization has tended to increase infrastructure costs and so reduce the international competitiveness of the other goods produced in the economy.

So, imports grew much faster than exports.[5] Worse still, because the interest rates on foreign capital were very high, most countries found themselves with dramatic growth in their current account deficits. The ground was laid for a series of external crises that then erupted. In late 1994, the Mexican peso crisis provided a warning that the policy prescriptions I have described were unsustainable. Most countries in the region started adopting restrictive fiscal and monetary policies to slow down growth and so stem the tide of imports and current account deterioration. The flow of new capital started to dry up and then massive capital flight developed, leaving governments with a huge external debt problem.

yet another latin american debt crisis

The problem of debt was hidden for some time in larger countries such as Brazil and Argentina because foreign direct investment attracted by privatization and mergers and acquisitions, more than made up for the decline in other financial inflows, so helping to finance deteriorating current accounts. But, in the end, even Greenfield FDI is not a gift but an external liability (with, of course, considerably lower liquidity than debt), which has to be paid off through profit remittances into the indefinite future. Those remittances can often be large since the profit margins of multinational corporations are usually much higher than the interest rate. An additional drain on the Latin American economies was the fact that most FDI went to sectors that did not generate hard currency. Moreover, multinational enterprises tend to import a large proportion of their supplies, parts, and components, which, far from boosting exports, actually further significantly increased imports.

latin america's submerging markets

The lesson from South and Central America is clear—external financial liberalization generates fundamentally unsustainable external liabilities. It is no accident that the international financial agents involved in this process (both residents and non-residents) make such a point of being short-term and demand maximum liquidity. They know that, since the debts are unsustainable, it is a matter of *when* not *if* a crisis is going to develop and they need to get out of their positions in emerging markets quickly. Foreign investors even make money speculating on when the country is likely to default on its external debt. And, once they have made their profits and left, the economies of Latin America are left crippled.

It is no wonder that one of the most hotly discussed topics in the region, after the Argentinean default, is the possibility of new rules for orderly debt defaults and restructuring for the bigger and richer countries[6] and debt-reduction strategies for the smaller and poorer countries. Bolivia, Guyana, Honduras, and Nicaragua have already become eligible as HIPCs for debt-reduction schemes. In the current decade we are seeing a new phenomenon in the region: submerging markets.

Yet, international institutions still fail to understand the real reasons for the region's manifest failure. The UN's Economic Commission for Latin America (ECLAC) admits that there has been a disastrous 'Lost Half Decade' with Latin American GDP growing by only 1.1 per cent per year in the years from 1997 to 2002. It blames this on the short-term mentality and irrationality of the international financial markets and investors who, stung by the 1997 Asian crisis, scaled back the flow of new capital to Latin America. FDI has fallen drastically in the last couple of years.[7] The Asian crisis apart, it is only common sense that FDI flows based on privatization and M&A cannot last forever—you eventually run out of things to privatize and mergers and acquisitions are, by their nature, a once-and-for-all affair.

ECLAC's analysis is based on the premise that the South and Central American debts were sustainable. They clearly were not as the Argentinean default, the biggest in history, demonstrated. And ECLAC has missed another point. Capital started flowing back to Asian economies because they quickly adjusted their economies to export more by adopting helpful exchange- and interest-rate policies.

I believe that UNCTAD's view of Latin America is more accurate. It acknowledges that the region relied too much on capital flows and failed to set policies to boost exports. So, the fall in the terms of trade of non-oil commodities since 1998, the current slowdown in the world economy, and worsening financial conditions have simply laid bare the vulnerability of Latin America's pattern of integration into the global economy.[8]

the destructive aim of liberalization realized

After years of economic instability, low growth, and budget cuts, we are witnessing, in most countries of the region, a political and social crisis. The capacity of the State to control the economy has progressively shrunk, the environment can no longer be controlled, and the effective citizenship rights of the majority of the population can no longer be guaranteed. Financial liberalization has thus achieved its real political agenda—to weaken, as much as possible, the region's governance and ability to develop, leaving it vulnerable to the power of the United States, of international capital, and financial interests.

further reading

Akyuz, Y., *Some reflections on SDRM*, (2003) available at www.networkideas. org.

Jomo K. S., G. Epstein, and I. Grabel, 'Capital Management Techniques in Developing Countries: an assessment of experiences from the 90's and lessons for the future' (2003) available at www.networkideas.org.

Medeiros, C. and F. Serrano, 'Capital Flows to Emerging Markets under the Floating Dollar Standard: a critical view based on the Brazilian experience', *Kalamazoo Conference on Dollarisation* (Michigan: Kalamazoo College, 2001).

Ocampo, J. 'A Lost Half-Decade in Latin America', *Wider Angle, No. 2* (2003)

UNCTAD, *Trade and Development Report* (Geneva: UNCTAD, 2003) *forthcoming*.

references

[1] Economic Commission for Africa, *Economic Report on Africa, 2002*, (Ethiopia: UNECA, 2002).

[2] C. Medeiros and F. Serrano, 'Capital Flows to Emerging Markets under the Floating Dollar Standard: a critical view based on the Brazilian experience', *Kalamazoo Conference on Dollarisation* (Michigan: Kalamazoo College, 2001).

[3] The main exceptions this time being Chile and to a lesser extent Colombia, which introduced capital controls and prevented overvaluation of their currencies. Needless to say these countries had much better performance than the others [see K. S. Jomo, G. Epstein, and I. Grabel, *Capital Management Techniques in Developing Countries: an assessment of experiences from the 90's and lessons for the future* (2003) available at www.networkideas.org].

[4] For the most radical of these attempts see Chapter 21 on dollarization.

[5] In fact export growth in the region was not very impressive. The exceptions were Chile throughout the 1990s and Argentina before 1998 as it took advantage of Brazil's big over-valuation. The only country where exports grew really fast in Latin America in the 1990s was Mexico because of NAFTA. The inclusion of Mexico in Latin American averages gives a totally distorted picture in terms of export dynamism of the region.

[6] See Y. Akyuz, *Some reflections on SDRM*, (2003) available at www.networkideas.org.

[7] For this interpretation see J. Ocampo, 'A Lost Half-Decade in Latin America', *Wider Angle*, No 2 (2003).

[8] UNCTAD, *Trade and Development Report*, (Geneva: UNCTAD, 2003).

outlook for north america: the three-bubble economy

dean baker

The mid-term prospects for the US economy, and therefore the economy of North America, will be largely determined by the course of three bubbles: the stock market bubble, the dollar bubble, and the housing bubble. While these bubbles fed the prosperity of the late 1990s, they have also led to enormous economic distortions that will impede economic growth on the continent for the foreseeable future. The failure to recognize these bubbles, and to take steps to deflate them early on, was an enormous public policy mistake, the consequences of which will be felt across the continent and the world for many years to come.

The economies of North America, which have become more heavily integrated since the United States, Canada, and Mexico joined the free-trade area, NAFTA, are likely to face serious obstacles in the next several years, as the US economy attempts to recover from the imbalances that developed in the 1990s boom. While the stock bubble has largely deflated, neither firms nor households have adjusted to this decline. Many firms built up considerable debt as a result of over-investment or badly chosen acquisitions during the boom. The collapse of the bubble also deflated pension funds leaving large, un-funded liabilities for many corporations and state and local governments. In addition, the rash of accounting scandals has undermined confidence in the integrity of financial markets.

Households have yet to adjust their spending to take account of the declining value of their stock portfolios. The ratio of consumer debt to disposable income is at a record level, more than 3 percentage points above its peak before the 1990 recession. The growth of indebtedness would be even larger had car leasing not substituted for many purchases on new cars with borrowing. In addition, the ratio of mortgage debt to home equity stands at a record high, even though equity values have been inflated by a housing bubble. This run up in debt has taken place at a time when the demographics of the population are extremely favourable to saving. The savings rate will have to increase substantially in the very near future, if the baby boomers are to have any hope of a decent living standard in their retirement.

The dollar bubble has reached a level that cannot be sustained for long, with the current account deficit in the United States now approaching 5.5 per cent of GDP. Although the dollar has depreciated substantially in the last two years against the euro, this has yet to arrest growth in the trade deficit. With investors already taking large losses by holding dollar assets, it is difficult to envision that they will continue to add to these holdings at the rate needed to sustain the US current account deficit. A sharper fall in the dollar, leading to rising import prices and therefore higher inflation, seems a likely near-term prospect.

If the Federal Reserve Board tries to stem this inflation by raising interest rates, then the US economy will face a prolonged period of stagflation. Higher interest rates will quickly burst the housing bubble and leave millions of older homeowners desperate to try to rebuild their savings before retirement. The fiscal problems of state and local governments, with the resulting increases in taxes and cuts in spending, will worsen the slump.

united states

At the peak of the US stock market bubble in March 2000, the price-to-earnings ratio for all US corporate equity exceeded 30 to 1, more than twice its historic average.[1] While the market in general was over-valued, the over-valuation in the tech sector was the most extreme, with price-to-earnings ratios often exceeding 100 to 1. As a result, an enormous amount of capital was diverted to investment in the tech sector. When the bubble collapsed beginning in 2000, tech investment plunged, throwing the US economy into a recession.

The stock bubble also had three other important negative effects on the US economy. In an era in which stock prices lost any relationship to reality, as did projections for future revenue and profit growth, it was inevitable that some corporate executives would take advantage of this situation and deliberately defraud the public. The accounting scandals that came to light in Enron, Global Crossing, WorldCom, and many other major corporations were entirely predictable (and predicted) outcomes of the stock bubble.[2] As a result of these scandals, many otherwise healthy companies have been forced into bankruptcy, and will find it difficult to obtain the capital needed to maintain normal operation. Many of the shareholders in these companies, including many of their own workers, saw much of their savings disappear in a matter of weeks, as the scandals were uncovered.

The bubble also led to a consumption boom, as stockholders increased their spending in step with the rise in the value of their portfolio. This 'wealth effect' is conventionally estimated at 3.5 to 4 cents on the dollar.[3] With households owning close to $7 trillion worth of 'bubble wealth' at the peak of the market, this translated into $245 to $280 billion in additional consumption spending. As a result of this consumption boom, the savings rate in the United States hit a record low of 2.3 per cent in 2001, a year in which the demographics of the population were highly favourable to saving.

Finally, the bubble led to a surge in tax revenue at all levels of government as households earned large capital gains as a result of bubble-inflated stock prices. While the collapse of the bubble was an entirely predictable event, budget fore-casters made revenue projections that implicitly assumed that the bubble would continue to inflate. These projections are now recognized as having been wildly over-optimistic. In the case of the federal budget, more realistic projec-tions of capital gains revenues translate into much larger projected deficits. In the case of state governments, the overly optimistic projections are forcing large cutbacks in spending and tax increases, since most states are required to run balanced budgets. This will seriously dampen growth over the next two years.

While the stock bubble has largely dissipated, the other two bubbles have yet to be deflated. The over-valuation of the dollar is leading to record current account deficits. In the fourth quarter of 2002, the current account deficit was running at an annual rate of almost $550 billion, or 5.3 per cent of GDP. This deficit has contributed to a loss of more than two million manufacturing jobs in the last five years. When the dollar eventually falls to a more sustainable level, it will raise the core rate of inflation by between 1 and 3 percentage points. If the Federal Reserve Board refuses to accommodate this inflation, the drop in the dollar may be associated with a long period of slow growth and high unemployment.

The housing bubble is the third bubble that has driven the US economy. The rise in the price of houses has exceeded the overall inflation rate by more than 30 percentage points over the last seven years,[4] creating more than $3 trillion in bubble-driven housing wealth. This has helped to maintain high levels of consumption, even as the stock market plunged. A combination of soaring house prices and near record-low mortgage interest rates has led to a surge in borrowing against home equity. As a result, the ratio of equity to value stood at just over 55 per cent at the end of 2002, a near-record low. By contrast, this ratio averaged more than 67 per cent through the 1960s, 1970s, and 1980s. This ratio is even more striking considering bubble-inflated prices directly raise equity.

Also, the population was far older in 2002 than in prior decades, a factor that should be associated with a higher equity-to-value ratio.

The combination of weak investment, slowing consumption, and a rising trade deficit led to relatively slow growth of 2.9 per cent in the US economy in 2002. The housing sector was the one clear source of strength, although this will end with the collapse of the bubble. A surge in military spending at the federal level is acting to largely offset cutbacks being made by state and local governments. Even the slow growth of 2002 will be difficult to maintain once the housing bubble collapses. This will happen with even a modest upturn in interest rates (possibly induced by a falling dollar). Alternatively, overbuilding and record rental vacancy rates indicate that the bubble is likely reaching its limits even if interest rates stay low.

The downturn in the US economy threatens to reverse positive developments for much of the US labour force in the late 1990s boom. For the first time since the 1960s, most of the labour force was experiencing healthy real-wage growth, as the unemployment rate averaged 4 per cent in 2000, a 30-year low. Throughout the 1980s and the first half of the 1990s, increasing wage inequality meant that real wages were declining for most of the work force, even as average wages were more or less keeping up with the modest productivity growth of the period. In the late 1990s, a 0.5 percentage point increase in the rate of productivity growth, coupled with low unemployment, allowed workers at all levels of the wage distribution to achieve real-wage gains.[5] Real wages for most workers were rising at close to a 1.5 per cent annual rate in the late 1990s.[6] However, with the unemployment rate hovering near 6 per cent by the second half of 2002, real wages were stagnating for much of the labour force.

Interestingly, the low unemployment rates of the boom seemed to offer more benefit for men than women. While the gender pay gap continued to narrow, the rate slowed. From 1989 to 1995 the hourly wage for a typical woman worker went from 73.1 per cent of typical male worker's wage to 76.7 per cent. In the next six years, the gap closed by only 1.4 percentage points, rising to 78.1 per cent.

The higher unemployment rate disproportionately hit disadvantaged segments of the labour force, with the unemployment rate for African Americans rising from a year-round average of 7.6 per cent in 2000 to close to 11 per cent at the beginning of 2003. The unemployment rate for African-American teens rose from 25 per cent in 2000 to well over 30 per cent in the first months of 2003.

canada

As a result of extensive integration with the US economy, the Canadian economy to a large extent shared in the boom of the late 1990s, with GDP growth averaging 3.7 per cent annually from 1995 to 2000.[7] The unemployment rate fell from 8.6 per cent in 1995 to 6.1 per cent in 2000. However, following the onset of the recession in the United States, the unemployment rate in Canada has moved back up near 7 per cent in 2002.

The growth of the 1990s did not lead to widespread gains in living standards. For most of the range of income distribution, after-tax family income was stagnant between 1989 and 1998.[8] There was a rise in the percentage of people with low incomes over this period, with the percentage of men with low incomes rising from 9.7 per cent in 1990 to 11.4 per cent in 1998. The increase among women was somewhat smaller, with the percentage of women with low incomes rising from 12.4 per cent in 1990 to 13 per cent in 1990.

mexico

Mexico has been even more directly affected by the weakness of the US economy. After suffering a 6.2 per cent drop in output as a result of the 1994 peso crisis, Mexico sustained a modest recovery fuelled by the boom in the United States with GDP growth averaging 5 per cent annually from 1995 to 2000.[9] In spite of respectable growth in the second half of the decade, per capita GDP growth for the whole decade averaged less than 1 per cent annually. Even after the growth of the late 1990s, real wages are still more than 10 per cent below the pre-crisis level. There has been some reduction in gender-based inequality in the decade, with women's wages rising to 82.6 per cent of men's wages in 2001, compared to 76 per cent in 1993.[10]

While the US boom of the late 1990s produced modest gains for Mexico, the current recession is leading to large losses. After the passage of NAFTA, US direct investment did rise substantially, peaking at just under $6 billion (an amount that exceeded 1 per cent of Mexico's GDP) in 1999. However this investment flow has collapsed in the last two years, with US direct investment in *all* of Latin America running at less than a $2 billion annual rate in the first three quarters of 2002.[11] In addition to the recession in the United States, it is likely that the admission of China to the World Trade Organization has also had a negative impact on US investment in Mexico. With wages considerably lower in China than Mexico, many US firms are choosing to move their operations to China. In some cases, US firms have relocated factories from Mexico to China. Mexico grew just 1.7 per cent in 2002, after shrinking by 0.3 per cent in 2001. The ongoing weakness of the US economy, coupled with increased competition will pose major obstacles to Mexico's growth for the next several years.

conclusion

Mexico and Canada's economies are likely to be dragged down with the US economy, as slumping demand in the United States will constrain growth in both nations. In short, the North American economy seems likely to pay a high price for the excesses of the United States in the late 1990s. Huge foreign policy uncertainty after the war in Iraq, and the associated financial costs, makes the economic future for the region look even bleaker.

further reading

Baker, D. 'The Costs of the Stock Market Bubble', (Washington DC: The Center for Economic and Policy Research, 2000).

Baker, D. 'The New Economy Goes Bust', (Washington DC: The Center for Economic and Policy Research, 2000).

Baker, D. 'The New Economy: A Millennial Myth', *Dollars and Sense*, March/April (2000).

Bernstein, J. and D. Baker, *The Benefits of Full Employment: When markets work for people* (Washington, DC: The Economic Policy Institute, 2003).

Dynan, K. and D. Maki, 'Does Stock Market Wealth Matter for Consumption?' *Finance and Economics Discussion Series 2001-23*. (Washington, DC: Federal Reserve Board, 2001).

Maki, D. and M. Palumbo, 'Disentangling the Wealth Effect: A Cohort Analysis of Household Saving in the 1990s', *Finance and Economics Discussion Series 2001–21* (Washington, DC: Board of Governors of the Federal Reserve Board, 2001).

references

[1] At end of March of 2000, after it had fallen back somewhat from its peak level, the value of outstanding equity was $17,850.8 billion (Federal Reserve Board, Flow of Funds, Table I.213, line 20). After-tax corporate profits for 1999 were $558 billion (National Income Product Accounts, Table 1.14, line 30).

[2] D. Baker, 'The New Economy: A Millennial Myth', *Dollars and Sense*, March/April (2000). D. Baker, 'The Costs of the Stock Market Bubble', (Washington DC: The Center for Economic and Policy Research, 2000).

[3] K. Dynan and D. Maki, 'Does Stock Market Wealth Matter for Consumption?' *Finance and Economics Discussion Series 2001–23.* (Washington, DC: Federal Reserve Board, 2001). D. Maki and M. Palumbo, 'Disentangling the Wealth Effect: A Cohort Analysis of Household Saving in the 1990s', *Finance and Economics Discussion Series 2001–21* (Washington, DC: Federal Reserve Board, 2001).

[4] D. Baker, 'The New Economy Goes Bust', (Washington DC: The Center for Economic and Policy Research, 2000).

[5] The upturn in productivity growth in the late 1990s is usually estimated as close to 1 percentage point, rising from 1.5 per cent in the period from 1973 to 1995, and 2.5 per cent since 1995. This overstates the actual gains to the economy. There has been a sharp divergence between the growth rate of gross output and net output in the late 1990s, as the depreciation of equipment and software takes up a growing share of GDP (see Endnote 4). Wages and profits must be paid out of net output, which means that the net measure of productivity growth in the late 1990s, approximately 2 per cent, is the more relevant measure.

[6] J. Bernstein and D. Baker, *The Benefits of Full Employment: When markets work for people* (Washington, DC: The Economic Policy Institute, 2003)

[7] GDP data for Canada was taken from the website of the OECD's Washington office available at www.oecdwash.org. The unemployment rate data is from the United States Bureau of Labor Statistics available at ftp://ftp.bls.gov/pub/special.requests/ForeignLabor/flsjec.txt .

[8] The data on income distribution in Canada comes from the Canadian Centre for Policy Alternatives 2000 'Overview of Current Economic Conditions in Canada', available at http://www.gpn.org.

[9] This data comes from Risel, 2002.

[10] This data is taken from the International Labour Organization available at http://laborsta.ilo.org/cgi-bin/brokerv8.exe.

[11] The 2002 data can be found at http://www.bea.gov/bea/international/bp_web/simple.cfm?anon=288&table_id=10&area_id=10 (data for Mexico alone is not available. Data on direct investment in Mexico for years up to 2000 can be found at http://www.bea.gov/bea/international/bp_web/simple.cfm?anon=288&table_id=11&area_id=22).

outlook for south asia: capital flows, deflation, and the persistence of poverty

jayati ghosh

The economies of South Asia—and especially India—are often portrayed among the 'success stories' of the developing world since the early 1990s. But India has been a comparative star simply because the performance in the rest of the developing world has been so much more depressing and chaotic, with the spectacular financial crises in several of the most important and hitherto dynamic late industrializers in East Asia and Latin America, and the continuing stagnation or even decline in much of the rest of the South. At least India, along with the smaller economies in the region, has been relatively stable by comparison.

It remains the case that both India and the entire South Asian region have experienced far less impressive growth recently than in the preceding decade. Further, that growth has not been an effective job-creator; there is greater income inequality and persistent poverty. In other words, despite some apparent successes in certain sectors, overall the process of global economic integration has done little to cause a dramatic improvement in the material conditions of most of the population; indeed, it has added to the greater vulnerability and insecurity of the economies in the region.

india—growth but not many jobs

India has achieved growth of between 5.5 per cent and 5.8 per cent in each five-year period since 1980 but average GDP growth rates have declined in recent years and employment growth has been anaemic. Between 1993 and 2000, rural employment has grown at an annual rate of less than 0.6 per cent, lower than any previous period in post-Independence history, and well below (only one-third) the rate of growth of rural population. For the past two years, there has been a severe crisis in the agricultural sector, as producers have struggled to compete with cheap, highly-subsidized imports that have coincided with cuts in domestic input subsidies.

Urban employment growth, at 2.3 per cent per year, was also well below that of earlier periods, and employment in the formal sector stagnated.[1]

Other indicators point to disturbing changes in patterns of consumption. Per capita foodgrain consumption declined from 476 grams per day in 1990 to only 418 grams per day in 2001.[2] The National Sample Survey data also suggests that even aggregate calorific consumption per capita declined from just over 2200 calories per day in 1987–88 to around 2150 in 1999–2000. Given the aggregate growth rates and the evidence of improved lifestyles among a minority, this clearly shows a widening income inequality, confirmed by national survey data.[3] Meanwhile, declining capital expenditure by the government has led to more infrastructure bottlenecks and worsening provision of basic public services. All this—decelerating employment growth, declining access to food for ordinary people, and worsening coverage and quality of public services—has had particular impact upon the condition of ordinary women.

One positive feature of the Indian economic landscape has been the relative overall stability of growth compared to the boom-and-bust cycles in other emerging markets. This reflects the relatively limited extent of capital account liberalization over much of the period, and the fact that India was never really chosen as a favourite of international financial markets and so did not receive large inflows—and subsequently outflows—of speculative capital. At the same time, the balance of payments was helped by substantial inflows of workers' remittances from temporary migrant workers in the Gulf and other regions, amounting to more than all other forms of capital inflow put together.

While it is true that India has escaped the worst instabilities of large capital flows experienced by other economies, it is still the case that an official desire to attract such flows has led to constraints on policy. For example, there has been a self-imposed limit on fiscal expansion (designed to impress foreign investors) which means that, over the past two years, there has been hardly any increase in state spending despite domestic recession, unemployment, the crisis in agriculture, and clear signs of slack in the form of high surplus holdings of foodgrain and large foreign exchange reserves.

bad politics and bad economics combine

In other countries of the South Asian region, growth has been even less impressive. In Pakistan, average annual growth rates plunged in the 1990s to only about one-third of typical rates in the previous decade. A prime reason was a historically-low rate of investment, as private investment failed to compensate for declining public spending. Industrial growth rates almost halved from 8.2

per cent to 4.8 per cent per year. The earlier success at reducing poverty was reversed in the 1990s, as the proportion of households living in absolute poverty increased from 21.4 per cent in 1990–91 to 40.1 per cent in 2000–01. Since the military government took over, roughly 15.4 million more individuals have been pushed below the official poverty line to a total of 56.3 million by June 2001. Unemployment rose, real wages fell, income distribution worsened, and human development indicators, poor to start with, deteriorated further. Several analysts have blamed this on the single-minded pursuit by the government of stabilization targets *a la* the IMF, which has been at the cost of growth and poverty alleviation.

The past two years have involved even more economic volatility, with military instability in the region, including the US-led war on Afghanistan and the build-up of troops along the border with India, playing a role. Politics have exerted opposing influences on Pakistan. On one hand, the desire of the United States to keep Pakistan as an ally has meant the waiver or rescheduling of some external debt, which provides short-term relief but implies future problems. On the other, uncertainty and instability in the region have also meant falling domestic and external investment.

In Bangladesh, while growth over the 1990s was marginally higher than in the earlier decade, the overall incidence of poverty (at around 45 per cent of the population) has been stubbornly resistant to change. Indeed, the rate of poverty reduction slowed down in the mid-1990s because of lower growth of production and weaker employment generation. All the productive sectors in Bangladesh have been adversely affected by trade liberalization in India which, given the porous border, has meant substantial smuggling. Import penetration has adversely affected production and employment in both agriculture and in most manufacturing, and even sectors of rural economic diversification such as livestock and poultry rearing. Income distribution worsened during the 1990s.

The economy of Nepal has been similarly affected by Indian trade liberalization because of its open border with India. Growth in the productive sectors has been weak, especially in agriculture where the removal of subsidies was not accompanied by public investment in rural infrastructure. In Sri Lanka, relatively low growth in the 1990s (especially in the agricultural sector) was associated with high macroeconomic imbalances, high trade deficits, and reduced employment generation. Domestic political strife and the state of war in the North were only partly responsible for this; an important role was played by the decline in value of agricultural exports, the mainstay of Sri Lanka's economy.

liberal agenda leaves region vulnerable

Throughout the region, therefore, the process of increased integration with the global economy failed to produce higher growth, more jobs, and a reduction in poverty. Instead, employment became more fragile and inequality increased. Attempts to impose 'fiscal discipline' by cutting public expenditure undermined the quality and quantity of physical infrastructure and basic public services. The loss of revenues from import tariffs, the associated declines in domestic duties, and the need to provide incentives to capital through tax concessions, all led to declines in tax-to-GDP ratios across the region, further reducing the spending capacity of the governments. In short, the material circumstances of a large proportion of the peoples of the region declined.

So why did governments pursue neoliberal economic strategies? Obviously, the political economy processes involved are complex and vary from country to country. But some idea may be had from a more detailed consideration of the Indian experience. In India, liberalizing economic reform was the policy of choice for various elements of the capitalist class, which had proliferated and diversified during the years of import-substituting growth. New products and markets developed and new players were able to challenge the traditional bases of monopolistic groups in areas such as trade, finance, and some service industries. As competition became tougher, even established large capital found it had to look for new avenues, including expansion abroad, to maintain its profitability and, even in this group, state controls became less of a bonus and deregulation became more acceptable.

Another key driver of deregulation was the globalization of Indian society through the growth of its post-war diaspora—the phenomenon of non-resident Indian groups especially middle class professionals. This contributed to demands within Indian society to open up the economy since the middle classes increasingly welcomed deregulation and the opportunity to benefit from international quality consumer goods.

And, finally, of course, liberalization was supported by the top echelons of the Indian bureaucracy, which had close links with the IMF and the World Bank, either as ex-employees who might return any time to Washington DC, or through being engaged in dollar projects of various kinds. This element of the bureaucracy had been growing rapidly, and its inclination naturally was in the direction of the Washington-consensus-style policy regime. Quite apart from the growing leverage exercised by the international agencies in their capacity as 'donors', liberalization had been good for India's economic elites. It should be remembered that while the liberalizing reforms failed to better conditions for the majority, there was a definite improvement in the wealth of a substantial section of the upper and middle classes. Since these groups had a political voice that was far greater than their share of population, they were able to influence economic strategy to their own material advantage. It is in this sense that local elites and middle classes were not only complicit in the process of integration with the global economy, but active proponents of the process.

capitalism for the few

The neoliberal economic reform programme involved a different relationship between government and the economy, not a 'withdrawal of the state'. It is true that the state effectively reneged on many of its basic obligations in terms of providing its citizens access to minimum food, housing, health, and education. However, the state remained crucial to the way in which markets functioned and the ability of capital to pursue its different goals—indeed, after a decade of reforms, the upshot was an overall centralization of economic and financial power. Many had believed that a 'retreat of the state' and the exposure of the economy to the discipline of the market would cut out arbitrariness of decision-making and the corruption that is inevitably associated with it. Instead, corruption, cronyism, and arbitrariness rose to unprecedented levels, the privatization process being an excellent vehicle for the primitive accumulation of private capital as public assets were acquired on the cheap. Precious natural resources, hitherto kept inside the public sector, were handed over for a pittance. The 'discipline of the market' proved to be a chimera.

These concomitant trends of greater economic and financial centralization and increased income inequality in turn aggravated the various regional, fissiparous, and community-based tensions that have become such a defining feature of South Asian societies. The region has seen an increase in the degree of instability and the growing absence of security. This has been reflected not only in greater cross-border tensions, as in the case of India and Pakistan, but also in civil and communally inspired clashes within national boundaries. Unrest is often caused by bad economics and, in turn, contributes to further economic deterioration—cynically, these skirmishes also play the useful role of diverting attention from the policy failures of government.

Obviously, not all such tension can be attributed to economic problems in the region. Nevertheless, the combination of greater economic insecurity in terms of lower real incomes and more precarious employment opportunities for a very large section of the population, together with the explosion of conspicuous consumption on the part of a relatively small but highly visible minority, can be explosive. Too often, the frustration is vented against weak targets such as minority groups. The inability to confront those who are responsible for the system, or actually benefiting from it, or even the lack of desire to confront these much more powerful elements, given that they still have the power to distribute some amount of material largesse, has too often meant that they escape scrutiny and accountability.

the breakdown of society

The rise of finance capital and the hugely powerful role played by speculative capital in determining the fortunes of even large industrial countries has contributed hugely to divisiveness and the breakdown of social consensus. Increasingly, governments point to the threat of capital flight by foreign investors who have no stake in the well-being of the developing countries in which they temporarily place their money as the reason why they cannot undertake basic measures for the welfare of most of the citizens. Anything that involves more expenditure for the people is inherently viewed with disfavour by international capital. Those elite groups who actually benefit from international capital find it easy to argue that 'there is no alternative'. So, we have the spectacle of local elites and governments not just advocating, but also able to continue to push through policies that are likely to be to the detriment of most of the people.

further reading

Chandrasekhar, C.P. and J. Ghosh, *The market that failed: A decade of neoliberal economic reforms in India* (New Delhi: Leftword Books, 2002).

Delhi Science Forum, *Alternate Economic Survey 2001–02*.

Easterly, W. *The political economy of growth without development: A case study of Pakistan*, (Washington, DC: The World Bank, 2001).

Ghosh, J. *Women in India: A status report* (2002) available at www.macro scan.org.

Mahbub-ul-Haq Development Centre, *South Asia Human Development Report 2001–02*, (Lahore, Pakistan).

Muqtada, M. *Promotion of employment and decent work in Bangladesh: Macroeconomic and labour policy considerations*, (Geneva: ILO, 2003).

Patnaik, P. *The retreat to unfreedom: essays on the emerging world order*, (New Delhi: Tulika Books, 2003).

Patnaik, P. *Whatever happened to imperialism and other essays* (New Delhi: Tulika Books, 1995).

Ramachandran, V. K. and M. Swaminathan, (eds) *Agrarian Studies* (New Delhi:Tulika Books, 2002).

references

[1] The only positive feature in employment patterns was the decline in educated unemployment, largely related to the expansion of IT-enabled services in metropolitan and other urban areas. However, while this feature, along with that of software development, has received much international attention, it is still too insignificant in the aggregate economy to make much of a dent.

[2] Of course, it has been argued that this can represent a positive diversification of consumption away from foodgrain that is associated with higher living standards. But it is usually the case that aggregate foodgrain consumption does not decline because of indirect consumption of grain (for example, through meat and poultry products that require feed). In any case, the overall decline in calorific consumption (covering all food products) suggests that the optimistic conclusion may not be valid.

[3] While the evidence on poverty has been muddied by changes in the procedure of data collection, which have made the recent survey data non-comparable with earlier estimates, overall indicators suggest that while the incidence of head-count poverty had been declining from the mid-1970s to 1990, subsequently that decline has been slowed or halted.

outlook for east asia: US dependency and deflation

jomo k.s.

east asia and the united states

More than any other region, the fortunes of the East Asian economies over the next few years will be greatly affected by the outlook for the United States, in particular the dollar. East Asia is dependent on the fortunes of the United States to maintain the value of its enormous foreign currency reserves, overwhelmingly held in dollars; for export performance; and even for the levels of its own currencies. And there are worrying signs from the United States, with a probability of a double-dip recession, exacerbated by the US-led war in Iraq. This would spell disaster for the rest of the US-centric world economy, particularly the economies of East Asia.

In recent decades, the value of the dollar has been increasingly propped up by vast imports of capital from East Asia, rather than the strength of US exports (indeed, 'intellectual property rights' are the largest and fastest growing major export earner for the United States). East Asian exporters have been earning US dollars, which have been used by their governments to buy US Treasury bonds. Almost half of all US Treasury bonds are held as reserves by foreign central banks, principally in East Asia. By early 2003, East Asia—mainly Japan, China, Taiwan, Korea, Hong Kong, and Singapore—accounted for about a trillion dollars-worth of US Treasury bonds. In recent years, China was responsible for well over half the export growth from developing countries. Last year, it added $60 billion to its reserves, with most of its huge trade surplus with the United States converted into American assets. Such generous East Asian lending at relatively low interest rates has allowed the US economy to circumvent the constraints that might otherwise be imposed by the massive US current account deficit.

At the time of writing in spring 2003, there is great concern in East Asia about the likelihood of US dollar depreciation. The dollar lost more than 10 per cent against the yen during 2002, and has fallen further to $1.12 against the euro in late April. Any decline in the dollar will have an equivalent impact on the value of dollar reserves held by East Asian countries, particularly in relation to debts held in other currencies. Although a weaker dollar might bolster East Asian stock and bond markets, it would also adversely affect the region's exports, usually denominated in US dollars, especially to the United States. Most of East Asia has not yet begun to wean itself away from excessive reliance on the US market.

Before the 1997–98 East Asian currency and financial crises, most currencies in South East Asia were pegged, in various ways, to the US dollar. Hence, the region experienced a decade-long boom from the late 1980s after the region's monetary authorities depreciated their currencies against the US dollar and then followed it south after the Plaza accord. However, when this situation was reversed from mid-1995, South East Asia continued to peg to the appreciating greenback, thus reducing its attractiveness for Japanese, Taiwanese, and Korean capital relocating production overseas, until its currencies and stock markets collapse from July 1997.

Since the 1997–98 crises, the region's currencies have massively depreciated, while the economic recoveries in 1999 and 2000 were uneven and not sustained outside Korea. However, there was optimism in those East Asian economies still pegged to the dollar, most notably China. The falling dollar is supposed to boost their exports.

But macroeconomic policy in the region remains deeply flawed. East Asian economies remain hopelessly dependent on the US economy and most national authorities seem reluctant to reduce this reliance by pursuing domestic growth-led policies, including stimulating growth through fiscal and monetary policy.

deflation in east asia

Deflation is now rampant in East Asia. As *Asia Week* commented as far back as 1999, 'The region's deflationary trend began with East Asia's crushing devaluations from mid-1997 to mid-1998, which helped lower the dollar prices of many Asian exports. Even before the Crisis, commodity prices had been southbound for years, hammered by anti-inflation policies pushed by the West and the IMF.'[1]

The most seriously affected economy is Japan, which has been mired in a deflationary morass for four years now. China is also experiencing deflation, although for different reasons: much of this is related to increased productivity rather than collapsing demand. Consumer prices fell by 0.8 per cent in 2002. Although prices did rise towards the beginning of 2002, in part due to higher oil prices, the country is still saddled with substantial excess capacity due to a recent spate of corporate investments leading to over-supply.

The price deflation in China has not dented its growth, but instead seems likely to further enhance its international price competitiveness, exacerbating problems for other economies in the region competing in the same markets. China is, in effect, exporting deflation to other countries in the region, through a combination of cheap export prices and low-cost plants for Asian firms, which have depressed wages and property prices elsewhere. Hong Kong has seen prices drop by 3 per cent, Singapore by 0.4 per cent, and Taiwan by 0.2 per cent. Only Indonesia, Malaysia, and South Korea appear to be free from the deflation disease.[2]

The continued priority given to deflationary monetary policy in the region despite the demise of inflation is an additional blow to efforts to reflate East Asian economies, and means that counter-cyclical fiscal policy efforts are largely ineffectual. Although price inflation has been largely contained (except in Indonesia), most monetary authorities, which had been conservative even before the crises, have since explicitly adopted inflation targeting as the principal monetary policy instrument. It is claimed that inflation targeting may be used as a monetary instrument to reflate the Japanese economy but elsewhere, it is simply exerting a deflationary bias.

Moreover, financial, especially capital account, liberalization also continues to limit efforts to promote more growth in the East Asian economies. At the same time, further trade liberalization is likely to exacerbate the de-industrialization of South East Asia, consigning it to colonial-style primary commodity production for export.

false optimism?

According to the Asian Development Bank, GDP growth in East Asia should average 5.6 per cent in 2003 and 6.2 per cent in 2004.[3] However, this apparently rosy scenario depends fundamentally on the strength of the US economy, and on a new willingness—not evident as of now—by the economic authorities of the region to actively fight deflation. And now the region has a new problem as the SARS virus sweeps through, destroying confidence. The virus has already had a devastating effect on many of the region's economies, particularly China. Forecasts for a return to rapid growth in the years ahead seem fragile, given a combination of a falling dollar, which will hit most of the region hard; collapsing exports; deflation; and the negative effects of a runaway virus.

further reading

Asian Development Bank, *Asian Development Outlook 2003*, (Oxford: Oxford University Press, 2003).

US—China Economic and Security Review Commission, *The National Security Implications of the Economic Relationship between the United States and China* (Washington DC: USCC, 2002).

references

[1] A. Reyes, 'Asia's deflation threat. From oil to gold to microchips, prices are falling across the region. Asians are smiling—and hurting', *Asia Week*, 29 January 1999.

[2] 'Deflation spreading across Asia due to China', *Agence France Press*, 2 March 2003.

[3] Asian Development Bank, *Asian Development Outlook 2003* (Oxford: Oxford University Press, 2003).

CHAPTER 10

outlook for europe: the neoliberal stranglehold on growth

janet bush

Since the 1980s, the European economy, in the 1950s and 1960s an engine for world growth and an area of growing prosperity, has faltered, posting years of low growth and very high levels of unemployment. Now, although it is particularly perilous to forecast economic developments in a period of unusual economic and political turbulence, there seems little prospect of an end to Europe's economic underperformance. Worse still for the continent's prospects is the fact that the relatively dynamic economies of Central and Eastern Europe, ten of which are due to join the European Union in 2004, are also now faltering. For example, Poland was growing by between 6 and 7 per cent a year in the mid-1990s. But, by the end of the decade, growth had faltered badly to only 0.5 per cent in 2002. Far from being a growth locomotive for the world, it is hard to see where growth within Europe can be generated.

europe's growth downgraded

The world's leading forecasting institutions have been forced repeatedly to downgrade their forecasts for Europe. In autumn 2002, the IMF forecast growth in that year of 0.9 per cent and 2.3 per cent in 2003 for the 12 Eurozone economies, 0.5 per cent weaker in both years than it had estimated six months earlier. The OECD was looking for 2.2 per cent growth in 2003. This was then lowered to 1.8 per cent and in April that was revised down to only 1 per cent.

Germany is a particular black spot, which is worrying for the European economy as a whole because it accounts for a third of output. In April, Germany's top six economic think tanks slashed their 2003 growth forecast to only 0.5 per cent—only one third of their forecast in October 2002. The institutes still expressed hope of some kind of rebound in 2004 but this may prove as ill-founded as their forecasts for this year, given the fact that the euro has been rising sharply since late 2002 as funds poured out of the United States in the wake of a wave of high-profile corporate scandals and nervousness about the war in Iraq. In the first two years after the launch of the single currency in 12 countries in January 1999, the euro was extremely weak, dropping some 20 to 25 per cent against the dollar, the Japanese yen, and sterling. This helped boost exports and the average Eurozone unemployment rate fell from 9.8 per cent at the euro's start to 8 per cent through most of 2000. Then, courtesy of anaemic growth, it started to rise again, reaching 8.7 per cent in March 2003. With the euro rising, it is hard to see anything but a further rise in unemployment. In May, a survey in Germany found that 45 per cent of companies were planning to lay off workers this year.

the threat of a rising euro

Economists at Dresdner Kleinwort Benson calculate that a 10 per cent rise in the euro would take 1.5 per cent off GDP over a two-year period, leaving a very real possibility of outright deflation and recession in Germany. By 2003, German unemployment had reached 4.5 million, one in nine of the population and the third highest figure since the institution of the Republic after the Second World War. Germany's Institute for Labour Market Research said in March that, taking account of the 'hidden unemployed' not counted by official statistics; unemployment could be as high as 7.2 million.

The prospect of more years of sub-par growth and rising unemployment coincides, as elsewhere in the industrialized world, with high government and personal debt levels and leaves European households deeply vulnerable. A 1996 study carried out for the European Commission found that there were approximately 53 million over-indebted individuals in the EU, 18 per cent of the total population over 18 years old. More recent data is hard to come by but the study concluded that unemployment (that year at an average 10 per cent in the EU) was a major contributory factor to over-indebtedness.

monetarist orthodoxy to blame

The failures of Europe—and now the Eurozone—predate the current world economic slowdown. So what has gone wrong? An important part of the answer is that, since the oil shocks of the 1970s, the European economic establishment has embraced a classic monetarist orthodox approach, centred on bearing down on prices by reining in growth and cutting budget deficits. In the 1970s, the Bundesbank reacted with extraordinary zealousness to the threat of higher inflation from rising oil prices and, because of the high degree of integration in continental Europe other central banks were forced to follow the

German central bank's restrictive policies throughout the 1980s. Inflation came down but so did growth.

This obsession with inflation and disregard of growth continued in the 1990s after the European establishment decided to formalize its commitment to orthodoxy in plans for Economic and Monetary Union, enshrined in the 1992 Maastricht Treaty. Centre-stage was a set of convergence criteria, aimed at making it more sustainable for different economies to live with a single interest rate. The criteria were highly conservative, ordering reductions in inflation through swinging cuts in budget deficits and public debt levels for applicant countries. By 1999, when the euro was launched, the orthodox economic establishment was congratulating itself on a cut in EU inflation from an average of 4.9 per cent in 1986–90 to 3.9 per cent in 1991–95. Budget deficits fell sharply. But the result of this restrictive programme was an exponential rise in unemployment. Between 1992 and 1999, national income in the economies that joined the EMU rose by only an average of 1.7 per cent a year. From 1994 to late 1998, the average rate of unemployment never dropped below 10 per cent (about twice the rate in the United States over the same period).

Attributing these economic developments substantially to the Maastricht convergence programme may seem controversial but compare what happened in those European economies that did not set policy to join the euro in the first wave. The United Kingdom, which saw unemployment double between 1990 and 1992 when it briefly locked the pound to European currencies in the Exchange Rate Mechanism, then saw unemployment fall from 9.3 per cent to 6.1 per cent in 1999. Able to pursue monetary and fiscal policies unfettered by Maastricht and then by the discipline of the euro itself, unemployment fell further to 5.1 per cent by the end of 2002. Denmark, which also negotiated an opt-out from the euro, saw unemployment drop from 8.2 per cent to 4.7 per cent at the end of 2002. A measure of how restrictive policies were for euro candidates comes from Brian Burkitt of the University of Bradford who estimated that, had Britain joined the euro in 1999, it would have had to cut public spending by £42 billion to meet the Treaty's 3 per cent deficit limit.

the assault on public spending and welfare

Inside the EMU, the squeeze has continued. The European Central Bank (ECB) was modelled on the Bundesbank with a sole mandate to bear down on inflation. Unlike the US Federal Reserve, it has no mandate to promote growth and employment and the ECB has been far slower than central banks in the United States or in Britain to cut rates in response to the world slowdown since

2001. Compounding this ultra-conservatism on interest rates has been the continuing squeeze on public spending in the Eurozone under the 3 per cent deficit limit imposed by the Stability and Growth Pact. Even as growth stagnates and unemployment rises, Eurozone economies are being obliged to cut spending or raise taxes in order to comply. A counter-cyclical boost to demand, as Keynes classically prescribed, is outlawed. Indeed, the opposite has been occurring—fiscal policy is being tightened even as growth slows.

Germany is planning to cut the equivalent of £35.8 billion off spending in the period to 2006. France announced early in 2003 that it was 'freezing' €4 billion of the French budget. According to *Le Figaro* newspaper, €615 million will be frozen from education, €258 million from health, €333 million from the economic ministry, and €335 million from the employment office. Portugal has been forced to raise VAT from 17 per cent to 19 per cent and has had to postpone a promised cut in corporate taxes, designed to give the economy a boost. Britain, an EU member but outside the Eurozone, was advised to cut public spending by £10 billion up to 2006 to meet the Pact's requirements, advice that has been rejected. Instead, the UK Chancellor announced increases in borrowing, preserving investment plans and boosting the economy while it is turning down, the classic Keynesian response to the threat of recession.

Despite a general consensus at the start of 2003 that the rigidity of the Pact was exacerbating the Eurozone economic slowdown, the orthodox architects of the rules stayed firm. In March, the European Parliament adopted a resolution in favour of enshrining the Pact into the new EU constitutional treaty to avoid any backsliding on fiscal discipline. The Parliament even stipulated that 'factors such as public investment in services' should not be taken into account in calculating deficits. And the neoliberals are unrepentant on the euro exchange rate too. Nicholas Garganas, a member of the ECB's Council and Governor of the Greek Central Bank, welcomed the euro appreciation because this would help counteract any inflationary impact of higher oil prices during turmoil in the Middle East. In May, the ECB's monthly report concluded that Eurozone governments would no longer be able to afford publicly-funded national health services.

Even the IMF, the world's cheerleader of neoliberal economics, takes a more flexible view. In its *World Economic Outlook* in 2002, it called for further action to bring Eurozone deficits down despite evidence of tepid growth. By the spring of 2003, it was so alarmed that it called on the EU to relax its budget rules. 'Automatic stabilisers should be allowed their full impact, even if that were to lead to a breach of the three per cent limit of the Stability Pact in 2003,' the

Financial Times reported in advance of formal publication of the IMF's spring outlook.

now neoliberalism spreads east

Worse still for European economic prospects in the years ahead is the fact that the neoliberal approach is now being applied to the ten Central and Eastern European economies due to join the EU in 2004 and which have provided most of the rare growth hot-spots of recent years. There is the obsession with inflation at the expense of jobs. In March, Tommaso Padoa Schioppa, a member of the ECB Board, told applicant countries that 'they must strive for price stability right from the beginning of the preparation process' and ensure that they institute independence for their central banks, so that the fight against inflation is put at the centre of policy. Applicant countries are also under intense pressure to cut budget deficits, potentially devastating for their already-high unemployment levels.

Poland, the largest of the accession countries, is a case study in how monetarism is being imposed as the price of membership and unemployment and growth are being forcibly neglected. While unemployment peaked at over 18 per cent in 2002, inflation had fallen to an all-time low of 1.9 per cent as interest rates were kept above 8 per cent. Clearly, the economy has been suffering from a lack of demand and monetary policy is too restrictive. Two small coalition partners in Poland's left-wing government drafted a controversial bill in 2002, demanding that the independent National Bank of Poland's mandate should be made to include the promotion of employment and growth in addition to ensuring price stability. Poland's president rejected the bill, proposing an alternative measure that would comply with EU requirements for central bank independence.

Low growth has seen Poland's budget deficit soar and, as the country struggles to shape up to meet the Maastricht criteria for euro entry, it is under pressure to cut its deficit—a policy that will only exacerbate Poland's lack of growth and mass unemployment. In 2002, Poland's parliament proposed a programme that would limit the annual growth of public spending to only 1 per cent in real terms. Days after Hungarians voted overwhelmingly to join the EU, their Prime Minister revealed a substantial programme of public-spending cuts, including on health are. In 2002, Hungary's deficit ballooned to 9.4 per cent of GDP. To meet the euro entry criteria, it has to fall to no more than 3 per cent of GDP. There is no escape from a chronic slowdown ahead, led by fiscal retrenchment.

In its end-2000 survey of the region, the European Bank of Reconstruction and Development (EBRD) identified the impossible circle that Central and Eastern European economies are being forced to square if they are to comply with the membership rules for the EU and Economic and Monetary Union. It acknowledged that 'rapid growth over a sustained period is necessary for the accession countries to catch up with the EU average for productivity and living standards'. In 2001, the average income per head in the ten accession countries was only 40 per cent of the EU average. However, the EBRD said, 'at the same time they will be subject to the demands of the Stability and Growth Pact and, for those countries striving for early adoption of the euro, the Maastricht criteria'. It noted that the 'looming requirement of a general government budget that is close to balance or in surplus in the medium term further points to the need for early fiscal consolidation in many of the accession candidates'. Fiscal consolidation is economist-speak for cutting budget deficits either through lower public spending or higher taxes.

As in Western Europe, Eastern Europe is coming under pressure to cut unemployment not through the pursuit of higher growth but through 'free market reform'. Rather than respond to rising unemployment by boosting growth through a combination of higher public spending or lower taxes and through lower interest rates, the neoliberal establishment wants deregulation of labour markets and dismantling social protection, so making it easier and cheaper for employers to hire and fire. Quite simply, workers in high unemployment areas will be expected to see their wages and conditions slashed until they 'price themselves back into the market'. Poland, for example, is planning to make its Labour Code more flexible. In Germany, on the same day as the Institute for Labour Market Research issued its estimate of 7.2 million unemployed, the Government announced cuts in unemployment benefit entitlement.

free market agenda or bust

This free market agenda is given succour by the absence of a European redistribution mechanism, an alternative to screwing down wages and conditions in regions that find themselves stuck with chronic levels of unemployment and poverty. The EU budget accounts for 1.27 per cent of EU GDP and half of that goes on agricultural subsidies under the Common Agricultural Policy. In comparison, in the United States, 25 per cent of GDP is available for redistribution—for every $1 lost by a state experiencing an economic downturn, it gets 40 cents to compensate from the federal budget.

And the disparities in Europe are dramatic compared with those of the United States, making the rigidities of the euro system and the lack of a mechanism for fiscal redistribution even more worrying. In the United States, unemployment ranges between 2 per cent and 6 per cent. In 2001, Eurostat figures showed a range in unemployment rates in the EU of 1.2 per cent to 33.3 per cent. In the ten accession countries, the range was similar, between 2 per cent and 32.8 per cent. One quarter of EU regions and nine out of ten of the ten accession countries had GDP below 75 per cent of the EU average. And the average woman in the EU earns a quarter less than a man.

conclusion

In both Western and Eastern Europe, there is little room for optimism as long as policy remains in the grip of anti-inflation zealots. Well-meaning reports on boosting employment have come and gone and have, in any case, focussed on the need to deregulate markets, not on boosting demand. There have been challenges to the macroeconomic straitjacket that has squeezed European growth but they have been swatted aside. Heavily indebted households will find worsening balance sheets as unemployment rises. And without a redistribution mechanism for the European economy, there is no realistic prospect of relieving income inequalities and the political tensions that will surely follow.

further reading

Arestis, P., A. Brown, and M. Sawyer, *The Euro: Evolution and Prospects* (Cheltenham: Edward Elgar Publishing, 2001).

Arestis, P., K. McCauley, and M. Sawyer, 'An Alternative Stability Pact for the European Union', *Cambridge Journal of Economics, Vol. 25*, (2001).

Begg, I. and D. Hodson, *Is Keynes Alive, Dead, or in need of Re-incarnation in the EU?* (London: South Bank University, 2000).

European Economists for an Alternative Economic Policy in Europe, *Better Institutions, Rules and Tools for Full Employment and Social Welfare in Europe*, Memorandum (2002).

Moss, B.H. and J. Michie, (eds) *The Single European Currency in National Perspective, A Community in Crisis?* (London: Macmillan Press, 1998).

Tsakalotos, E. 'European Employment Policies: A New Social Democratic Model for Europe' in P. Arestis and M. Sawyer, (eds) *The Economics of the Third Way: Experience from around the world* (Cheltenham: Edward Elgar Publishing, 2001).

references

[1] *The problem of Consumer Indebtedness*, OCR Macro International Social Research for DG Health and Consumer Protection (1996). http://europa.eu.int/comm/consumers/ policy/developments/fina serv/fina serv06 en.pdf".

[2] A number of relevant critiques by Philip Arestis and Malcolm Sawyer for the Levy Economics Institute are available at http://www.levy.org/.

[3] B. Burkitt, M. Bainbridge, and P Whyman, *EMU A Critical Perspective*, Department of Social and Economic Studies, University of Bradford. Available at http://www.bullen. demon.co.uk/cibbb4.htm.

[4] EBRD Transition Report, 31 December 2002 available at http://www.ebrd.com/ pubs/index.htm.

[5] Bank of Finland, Institute for Economies in Transition (BOFIT) available at http://www. bof.fi/bofit (2002).

CHAPTER 11

outlook for africa: debt, AIDS, and the feminization of poverty

zo randriamaro

Real GDP growth in Africa over the past few years has been relatively strong according to the UN's Economic Commission for Africa (ECA). In 2001, Africa is reported to have grown by 4.3 per cent 'faster than any other developing region'.[1] The ECA attributes this higher-than-expected level of economic growth to 'better macroeconomic management; strong agricultural production; higher than expected exports; currency depreciation in the largest economy (South Africa); and the cessation of conflicts in several countries'.[2]

However, this assessment should not make us complacent about Africa's prospects, not least because it is clear that the growth that has been generated by Africa's economic policies has not been pro-poor. Nor has it been people-centred and equitable. Indeed, Africa is now the second most unequal region in the world, with 51 per cent of total expenditure accruing to the richest 20 per cent of the population in 1998 compared to only 5 per cent accruing to the poorest 20 per cent. For the mass of the population, therefore, chronic poverty remains a daily reality, with 59 per cent of the rural population and 43 per cent of the urban population earning less than the internationally agreed poverty line of $1 per day.[3]

an uncertain future

The outlook for African economies over the next three to five years will be influenced to a large extent by the performance of the continent's largest economies, notably South Africa and Nigeria. The processes and mechanisms related to economic governance in the New Partnership for Africa's Development (NEPAD) that have been adopted by African Heads of State and the international donor community as the blueprint for Africa's development in the new millennium will also be determining factors. In March 2002, a peer review mechanism was established to ensure 'mutual accountability' and compliance with the agreed economic performance targets and standards. Whether this process succeeds in promoting 'good governance' in the continent remains to be seen.

While the 'high performers' in terms of GDP growth (for instance Egypt, Morocco, Tunisia, and Equatorial Guinea) offer the best prospects in the face of the global economic slowdown, increased uncertainties shade the future of countries like Nigeria due to considerable downside risks linked to both external factors and internal policy issues.

Nigeria is struggling to deliver a 'democracy dividend' which the ECA anticipated in 2001 would include faster economic growth and higher standards of living. The burden of debt is a major cause of its problems. In 2002, the country was unable to pay $3.4 billion in debt service. At the same time, the over-reliance of the economy on oil for foreign exchange and public revenue makes it particularly vulnerable to price volatility, while putting increased pressure on the environment and undercutting economic opportunities for the 3.5 million young Nigerians who enter the labour market every year.

Another cause for major concern is the enormous and unchecked power of multinational oil companies, and the devastating impacts of their activities on the environment and people's livelihoods. As reported by the GERA research project in the Niger Delta region—'the nerve centre of Nigeria's oil industry', producing over 90 per cent of national exports earnings—these include heavy pollution of water bodies and land, deforestation, loss of land and biodiversity, destruction of farmlands and fishing grounds, and weakening in social cohesion with increased social conflicts. These, in turn, have led to increased vulnerability and poverty as a result of changing strategies and declining incomes, especially among women who have been forced out of their livelihood activities and suffer from lower incomes and joblessness, according to the GERA Programme in 2003.

The case of 'globalizer' countries like Ghana, praised by the Bretton Woods institutions and the donor community alike for its mid-term growth prospects and for its good governance, is still worrying. Some analysts have expressed concern that the monetary policy implemented under the IMF Poverty Reduction and Growth Facility (PRGF) is seen only 'as an essential tool in the achievement of macroeconomic stability'[4] and that this has become an end in itself, rather than a means to the achievement of poverty reduction and growth. These analysts point to the need for 'a delicate balance of the options and weighing of the trade-offs'[5] in order to prevent a tough monetary policy being counterproductive on growth.

The absence of any serious attempt to address the instability of the international financial architecture entails important risks for many African countries where rapid financial liberalization is coupled with an open-door policy towards foreign investment. This is especially true since the continent's emerging markets are reported to have experienced a sharp increase in private capital flows, mainly due to large-scale deals in net equity investment in South Africa and Morocco (from $5.2 billion in 2000 to $9.5 billion in 2001) and an increase in net portfolio equity flows (from $1.7 billion in 2000 to $4.5 billion in 2001).[6] Decreasing the volatility of private capital flows, together with ensuring sufficient policy space for African governments to regulate the entry and conditions of operations of investors in order to support their national development goals, will be key strategies for mitigating the financial risks in the mid-term.

For all African countries, growing social inequalities will remain an outstanding issue, likely to be exacerbated by the neoliberal framework that continues to be imposed externally by the international financial and trade institutions, and internally through initiatives such as NEPAD. The trend towards a shrinking policy space for African nation states is matched by an expanding power of global economic institutions and MNCs. The impoverishment and exclusion of an increasing majority of African peoples create a climate of frustration and national disillusionment. Against this background, history tells us that the rise of fundamentalism in different parts of the continent—notably in Nigeria—is a strong signal that should be taken very seriously.

Paradoxically, because of the challenges that it poses for Africa's autonomous development strategies, NEPAD points to the central role of economic regional integration in the mid- and long term. In light of the trends that have been described above, it is necessary for African countries to overcome the fragmentation of their markets and to unite around a homegrown, people-centred, equitable, and sustainable development paradigm. This is a major task, given the continuing imposition of neoliberal policies designed in Washington.

the washington consensus in africa

Africa's development over the past two decades has taken place against the background of World Bank- and IMF-style 'structural adjustment policies'. These policies, which remain largely unchanged since they were first imposed in the 1980s, contain all the elements of the 'Washington Consensus': tight fiscal and monetary policies; restructuring of financial markets, industrial relations, and legal systems; trade liberalization; deepening of customs and tax reforms; and strengthening of fiscal discipline. Social and environmental issues have remained secondary to the control of inflation and macroeconomic stability. Over the past few years, these structural adjustment policies have been enforced through the process of 'Poverty Reduction Strategy Papers' linked to debt relief under the World Bank and IMF's HIPC initiative.

Macroeconomic policies in Africa since the 1980s have provided a typical illustration of the 'deflationary bias' that has been criticized by feminist economists. The hallmark of these policies has been an over-emphasis on austerity measures such as cutting public expenditure and inflation rates, and raising interest rates. These negative effects have been disproportionately borne by women. According to feminist economists, 'Using deflation to deal with problems caused by inappropriate financial liberalization has made the position of poor people, and poor women in particular, worse—as the financial crises in South East Asia have shown.'[7] Cuts in public spending, particularly in the social sectors, have resulted in a shift in the cost burden onto communities, households, and individuals, while tight monetary policies have brought about a decline in access to credit and productive resources amongst small farmers and micro-entrepreneurs.[8]

Structural adjustment policies have also had a substantially negative impact on agriculture, a key strategic sector for Africa's development, accounting for 70 per cent of its employment. In 2000, 431 million people, a majority of them women, depended on agriculture for their livelihoods.[9] Liberalization policies have ignored the non-market functions of agriculture, notably natural resource management, environmental protection, social cohesion and stability, and cultural continuity and heritage. As recognized by one of the promoters of free market policies in the region, 'Recent agricultural policies have placed too much reliance on market forces, neglecting more fundamental structural issues such as technology and extension services, marketing infrastructure, and civil conflicts over land and pasture.'[10]

trade and investment policies

Trade liberalization in Africa has continued apace under the influence of structural adjustment conditionalities. In particular, import regimes have been rationalized, including the elimination of import quotas; the reduction and unification of tariffs; and the removal of special tariff concessions and exemptions. However, these policies have tended to ignore the supply-capacity constraints faced by many African economies. This means that export growth has failed to keep up with the expansion of imports, meaning that the majority of non-oil exporting African countries has experienced chronic balance-of-payments problems over the past two decades. Most importantly, as the Structural Adjustment Participatory Review Initiative has pointed out, 'A political economy analysis of the impact of trade liberalisation measures under adjustment reveals that the most disadvantaged segments of the society had to disproportionately share the burden of adjustment.'[11]

Trade policy reforms have also had a critical gender bias. This is because policy-makers ignored the basic fact that trade policies affect men and women differently and generate different responses due to pre-existing gender inequalities. Studies on the impact of trade liberalization and intensification in Africa have found that these policies have exacerbated inequalities along class and gender lines, and undermined women's rights and livelihoods.[12]

African countries have also continued to be obsessed with providing an 'enabling environment' for FDI. One consequence of this has been a marked reduction in taxes on corporations and a concomitant increase in consumption taxes. Consumption taxes impact disproportionately on the poor, as they increase the costs of basic items. This has led to popular protests in countries like Ghana. From a gender perspective, it has also increased the so-called 'reproduction tax' on women—in other words, the burden of providing unpaid care to sustain their families and communities.

growth of external debt

Sub-Saharan Africa continues to be weighed down by its colossal debt burden. In 2001, total external debt amounted to $209 billion, or roughly 70 per cent of the region's gross national income. Debt service in the same year was $14.5 billion, representing 12 per cent of exports. Despite the impact of recent debt-relief initiatives in Africa, debt service has continued to grow year-on-year, increasing from $13.6 billion in 1999 and $12.3 billion in 2000.[13] While the continued implementation of the HIPC initiative in Africa should bring debt-service burdens down, research by Eurodad has suggested that such debt service could start to rise again from 2006 and in some cases from as early as 2002. Eurodad has pointed out that in ten countries—Sao Tome and Principe, Guinea-Bissau, Malawi, Madagascar, Mozambique, Cameroon, Mali, Burkina Faso, Zambia and Niger—'average debt servicing will **increase** by one-third between 2001–2003 and 2007–2009'.[14]

exports

As already noted, export growth in Africa over the past few years has been slow, particularly in relation to the growth of imports. The financial crises in emerging markets and recession in the so-called 'developed' world have served to depress prices for the entire range of African exports, particularly oil. The September 11 attacks had mixed effects on African markets. Some countries experienced an increase in some exports under bilateral trade agreements; but at the same time the attacks accentuated weak demand while the dollar—the currency in which most commodities are traded—remained strong. As a result, average commodity prices in 2001 were 17 per cent below their level in 2000.

For Africa as a whole, average annual export growth for 2000–01, the latest year for which data is available, fell by 2.4 per cent. Within the region, Sub-Saharan Africa saw a slightly lower fall than North Africa, at 1.9 per cent against 2.9 per cent. In general, Africa has seen a steadily falling share of world exports, down from 4.6 per cent in 1980 to 1.9 per cent in 2001.[15] Falling export values as a result of lower commodity prices have served to reduce the income of agricultural communities as well as further undermining the ability of African countries to import crucial consumer goods and inputs for the industrial sector.[16]

the economic impact of AIDS

The impact of the AIDS pandemic continues to affect Africa's growth, its social institutions, as well as human and investment capital. In South Africa, where the incidence of HIV/AIDS is among the highest in the region, studies on the likely impact of AIDS forecast a 1 per cent decrease of GDP by 2010. In total, between $112 million and $180 million in resources is needed by South Africa for AIDS-related treatment and prevention on an annual basis. In Botswana, AIDS is expected to bring about an average 8 per cent reduction in household income, and a 13 per cent fall for the poorest. In Burkina Faso, due to the negative impact of AIDS on agricultural output and productivity, farmers' real income fell by between 25 per cent and 50 per cent in 1997.

The devastating impact of AIDS will continue to exacerbate the assault on the poor, particularly women, in Africa that has for too long been the result of the imposition of neoliberal policies in the Continent.

further reading

Elson, D. 'International Financial Architecture: A View from the Kitchen', paper for *International Studies Association Annual Conference in Chicago* (2001).

Kerr, J and D. Tsikata (eds), *Demanding Dignity: Women Confronting Economic Reforms in Africa* GERA Programme (Africa: NSI/TWN, 2000).

Mbilinyi, M. (ed) *Gender Patterns in Micro and Small Enterprises of Tanzania*, MCDWAC Tanzania/Women's Research and Documentation Project, (Rome: AIDOS, 2001).

Randriamaro, Z. *The NEPAD, Gender and the Poverty Trap* (2002).

references

1 ECA, *Economic Report on Africa* (2002), (Ethiopia: UNECA, 2003).

2 ibid, p. 13.

3 ECA, *Economic Report on Africa* (1999), (Ethiopia: UNECA, 2000).

4 CEPA (2002): 161.

5 CEPA (2002): 161.

6 ECA, *Economic Report on Africa*: 23 (2002), (Ethiopia: UNECA, 2003).

7 D. Elson and N. Cagatay, 'The Social Content of Macroeconomic Policies', *World Development*, Vol 28. No.7.

8 J. Kerr, and D. Tsikata, (eds) '*Demanding Dignity: Women Confronting Economic Reforms in Africa*', GERA programme (Africa, NSI/TWN, 2000).

9 Op. Cit. ECA 2002.

10 Op. Cit. ECA 2002.

11 Structural Adjustment Participatory Review Initiative (Washington DC: SAPRIN, 2002).

12 Op. Cit. Kerr et al.

13 World Bank, *Global Development Finance* (Washington DC: World Bank 2003).

14 Eurodad, Debt and HIPC Initiative Spring Meetings Update, April (2001).

15 UNCTAD, *Handbook of Statistics* (2002), (Geneva: UNCTAD, 2003).

16 ECA, *Economic Report on Africa*, (2001), (Ethiopia: UNECA, 2002).

PART 03

---

globalization and its inconsistencies

introduction

Part 03 challenges some of the myths of globalization. Herman Daly discusses a major inconsistency in the economic framework that *was* globalization, contrasting the unrestricted flow of goods, services, and capital across boundaries, with the highly restricted migration of people. He notes that the logic of globalization 'is the erasure of national borders for economic purposes' and by implication the elimination of national economic policy as well and questions the viability of this approach.

Gita Sen argues with great clarity that globalization led to the forceful expropriation of resources and wealth, and the separation of people from their means of production, consumption, and survival. At the same time, there were significant increases in wealth and income inequality. She reminds us of Marx's key concept of 'primitive accumulation'—and notes that this powerful insight helps us understand our world.

Nic Marks of the New Economics Foundation explores the new discipline of 'subjective well-being research' and notes that output as measured by GDP is flawed as an indicator of quality of life.

Alan Freeman and Robert Hunter Wade challenge the assertion by Washington-based economists like Surjit Bhalla that there is a 'steady convergence between the richer and poorer segments of the global family'.[1] On the contrary, Wade and Freeman both conclusively demonstrate that globalization has led to economic stagnation and divergence between rich and poor. First, Alan Freeman demonstrates that the period 1980–2000 was a period of economic stagnation and also of divergence as industrialized and other 'advanced' economies pulled away from the rest of the world. Robert Hunter Wade highlights in particular the statistical sleights of hand that have been used by the neoliberal establishment in assessing economic growth and poverty reduction in China and India and challenges the World Bank's dominant role in producing development knowledge.

reference

[1] S. Bhalla, *Imagine there's no country: Poverty, Inequality and Growth in the Era of Globalization* (Washington DC: Institute for International Economics, 2002).

CHAPTER 12

globalization and its inconsistencies

herman e daly

Advocates of globalization want goods, services, and capital to flow without restriction across national boundaries. But where is the campaign for free migration of people? The same economic logic of global gains from trade that is used to justify free movement of goods, services, and capital applies with equal force to free movement of labour (or human capital). Yet I have seen no advocacy of free migration by the WTO, the IBRD, or the IMF. Why should people not enjoy the same rights and privileges that are extended to goods, services, and capital? If the WTO wants foreign capital to be able to go anywhere in the world, and once there to have the same rights as domestic capital, why do people not have the right to go anywhere in the world, and once there, have the same rights as the indigenous people?

This inconsistency may have something to do with the fact that the least mobile factor of production is at a competitive disadvantage in the distributive struggle. Clearly, the WTO, the IBRD, and the IMF are friendlier to capital than to labour and so they promote the international mobility of the former but not the latter. Surprisingly The *Wall Street Journal*, a special friend of capital, consistently favours free migration of labour—or is it just free immigration of cheap labour into the United States that it favours?

why not free migration of labour?

Go more deeply and perhaps free traders instinctively recoil from free migration because they can see the problems of 'tragedy of the commons' and destruction of existing local community that free migration would entail. How could any national community maintain a minimum wage, a welfare programme, subsidized medical care, or a public school system in the face of unlimited immigration? How could a nation punish its criminals and tax evaders if they were free to emigrate? Indeed, would it not be a lot cheaper to encourage emigration of your poor and your sick and your criminals, than to run welfare programmes, charity hospitals, and prisons? Or how could a country reap the benefit of educational investments made in its own citizens if they were free to emigrate? Would nations continue to make such investments in the face of free migration and a continuing 'brain drain'? Would any country any longer try to limit its birth rate? With free migration, it could never control its numbers anyway.

Few would deny that some migration is a very good thing—but we are speaking here about free migration, where 'free' means 'deregulated, uncontrolled, unlimited', as in free trade or free capital mobility. Some cosmopolitans think that it is immoral to make any policy distinction between citizen and non-citizen, and therefore favour free migration. They also suggest that free migration is the shortest route to their vision of the *summum bonum*, the equality of wages worldwide. Fair enough—let them then answer the questions in the preceding paragraph! In my view, a more workable moral guide is that our obligation to non-citizens is to do them no harm, while our obligation to fellow citizens is first to do no harm, and then to try to do positive good. Consequences of globalization, such as over-specialization on a few volatile export commodities, crushing debt burdens, exchange rate risks, foreign corporate control of national markets, and unnecessary monopolization of 'trade-related intellectual property rights'—all of these mean that the 'do no harm' criterion is still far from being met.

even markets need borders

If globalization advocates refuse to follow their own logic to embrace free migration, maybe they should question whether their misgivings about the free flow of people might also apply to the free flow of things that are vital to people, namely goods, services, and capital. Markets hate boundaries, but public policy, in the interest of community, requires them. Markets need policy and laws for their functioning; so indirectly, even markets ultimately require boundaries.

Since globalization is the erasure of national borders for economic purposes, it also comes close to being the elimination of national economic policy as well. In addition, it implies the eradication of international economic policy. Suppose all nations agreed to the Kyoto Accord. Then try to imagine how these nations could enforce domestically what they had agreed to internationally, when they have no control over their borders. Institutions of control would have to be global because the unit being controlled would be global—and not global in the federated sense of cooperation among individual nations that control their borders, but global in the cosmopolitan sense of the integration of formerly separate economies into a single borderless world economy. International interdependence is to global integration as friendship is to marriage. All nations must be friends, but should not attempt multilateral marriage.

the end of the nation?

The opposite of 'free trade' is not 'no trade'. It is 'regulated trade'. Free trade is a rhetorically persuasive label for deregulated trade. No one is against freedom, or against trade, but many are against the total deregulation of international commerce. Was deregulation of the savings and loan banks such a good idea? Has deregulation of financial markets, stock markets, and energy markets been such a success? Why has the traditional regulation of international commerce in the national interest become an anathema to most economists? Do they want to abolish the nation and institute a world government? Or turn it all into a global commons for corporations to plunder?

further reading

Daly, H. E. and J.B. Cobb Jr. *For the Common Good: Redirecting the Economy toward Community, the Environment and a Sustainable Future.* (Boston: Beacon Press, 1989).

Goodland, R., H.E. Daly, and S. El Serafy (eds) *Population, Technology, and Lifestyle: the transition to sustainability* (Washington DC: Island Press, 1992).

CHAPTER 13

primitive accumulation revisited

gita sen

One of the most powerful insights that political economy provides for our understanding of the world is the concept of 'primitive accumulation'—the forceful expropriation of resources and wealth and the separation of people from their means of production, consumption, and survival. Marx analyzed this in depth in the lead-up to the industrial revolution in Europe. The making of the industrial working class involved the forcible breaking over centuries of older entitlements to land and other resources, of long-held claims on subsistence, older guarantees of livelihood, and security provided by feudal relations. This was done to the advantage of the wealthy and politically powerful, and rendering large sections of people partially or through creating relations of private property where none existed before, reordering established property relations wholly destitute. It was often the insecurity created by the breaking of older relations that coerced ordinary people to submit to the travails of industrial discipline.

primitive accumulation goes global

As we look at the global economy as it has evolved during the past three decades, it becomes clear that primitive accumulation is not some once-and-for-all, long-forgotten happening buried in the mists of early capitalism. Primitive accumulation recurs every time the resources of a new region of the world are eyed by the greedy, or when a new group of people is seen as a barrier preventing free access to such resources. The colonial period was one such time, when primitive accumulation went global. Today, with the promise of a major biotechnology revolution, and the multinational race to capture and privatize the rich biodiversity that has been the traditional common property of people in many parts of the South, we are seeing primitive accumulation occurring once again on a global scale. Seeds, plants, fauna, water are all being privatized by both domestic and multinational firms and prospectors on a scale never witnessed before.

As in previous times, the two main mechanisms through which primitive accumulation occurs are force and debt. Force comes into play if the prospective victim is seen as unlikely to go into debt—if you want her oil, roll in with tanks and depleted uranium bombs, and grab control. But debt is a marvelous mechanism because it usually makes the use of force unnecessary. If countries and people can be bribed, bullied, cajoled, or confused into borrowing beyond their means to repay, and if the terms of repayment can be 'managed' so that repayment becomes an ever more distant dream, then countries and people can become like the Red Queen in *Alice in Wonderland*—running harder and harder to stay in the same spot. Their resources, their control over their means of livelihood, the security of their old age, their children's futures, and their ability to make decisions based on their own assessments of their needs and realities all become forfeit to the moneylender.

the corrosive power of the moneylenders

Traditional moneylenders always make sure that they retain control over four things: the size of the initial loan (the larger the better!), the rules of repayment (conditionalities of different kinds), the back up of economic sanctions, and, if these don't work, physical force. It requires no great feat of imagination to see how remarkably similar is the functioning of the modern-day global moneylenders.

Periods of primitive accumulation are always accompanied by significant increases in wealth and income inequality of the kind we are now witnessing both between and within countries. I do not claim that all of the recent increase in inequality is the result of primitive accumulation. However, take India as an example, a country whose experiments with economic liberalization and privatization over the last decade have been lauded by the economic elite but which has also seen increasing destitution, deaths from starvation, suicides by debt-ridden farmers and traditional artisans, and a growing struggle for control over common property resources, biodiversity, and water.

women take the brunt

Such periods hit hardest at the most vulnerable, and in particular at women who bear primary responsibility for the daily care and survival of families. The double whammy of the gender division of labour on the one hand, and of male bias and violence on the other, becomes particularly acute in such times. As common resources get privatized and commercialized, women's ability to care for families is stretched to breaking point. And their inability to 'manage' often becomes the excuse for violence against them.

Ironically, it is the last three decades that have seen the clearest public articulation and recognition of women's household work (the so-called 'care economy') and its dependence in much of the world on women's access to resources such as water and traditional common lands for food, fodder, fuel, medicines, and seeds. There has also been a growing understanding of how gender relations of power not only constrain women's traditional role as 'carers', but also impact harmfully on their own lives and health, their control over childbearing, their ability to experience and express their sexuality, their right to live free of fear and violence. Unfortunately, the same agencies and governments that have helped to promote this understanding often turn a Nelson's eye to the worsening condition of women's livelihoods, and certainly refuse to acknowledge this to be a consequence of policies they espouse. This in turn provides an easy excuse for those countries and organizations that are opposed to the idea of gender equality or women's human rights.

Primitive accumulation has, however, another side that we are also witnessing today. While recognizing the destitution and misery it brings about, it is important not to romanticize the traditional relations that primitive accumulation tears asunder. Feudal and other pre-capitalist relations are often oppressive, coercive, exploitative, and violent. While their breaking brings greater insecurity to livelihoods, it also holds forth the promise of newer, more equal relationships. Nowhere in the present time is this more clearly visible than in the transformation of gender, caste, and ethnic/race-based relationships. Such changes can be and often are, difficult, paradoxical, and contradictory for women and other traditionally subordinate groups. Addressing the paradoxes honestly and effectively provides the greatest challenge today for organizations wishing to work for a more just and equitable world.

further reading

Francisco, J. and G. Sen, 'The Asian Crisis: Globalisation and Patriarchy in Symbiosis' *Social Watch* and *DAWN Informs* (2000) available at www.dawn.org.fj.

Sen, G. and S. Correa, 'Gender Justice and Economic Justice: Reflections on the Five Year Reviews of the UN Conferences of the 1980s' *DAWN Informs* (2000) available at www.dawn.org.fj.

Francisco, J. 'Gender Dimensions and Dynamics in International Lobbying on Trade and Development' *DAWN Informs* (2000) available at www.dawn.org.fj.

CHAPTER 14

the well-being of nations

nic marks

Adam Smith wrote the *Wealth of Nations* in 1776. In this seminal book, he proposed ways of measuring financial wealth and thereby paved the way for comparisons to be made between nations. Today, league tables of the poorest and wealthiest nations are commonplace, but how do these financial figures relate to people's *real* quality of life in these countries? It is widely accepted that output, as measured by GDP, is flawed as an indicator of quality of life. It is less well known that a great deal of research has been done over the past 30 years in order to improve measurement of quality of life and we must bring this research to bear on economic policy-making if we are to fulfil its ultimate aim of improving our well-being.

Research using 'objective' indicators of quality of life to build a more textured picture of the standard of living in different countries, such as the UN's Human Development Index, is increasingly well understood. However, in the last few decades, new research has emerged from psychologists and sociologists using surveys to explore and measure people's subjective feelings of happiness (or 'subjective well-being'). This work is still relatively unknown by economists and policy-makers. Different questions are used in different surveys, but a typical one would be: 'If you consider your life as a whole, how happy (or satisfied) would you say you are?' The responses to this type of question have been found to be very robust. They compare well to physical observations of happiness such as smiling and laughing, to electrical activity in parts of the brain, as well as other people's assessment of how happy the respondent is. The questions have also been tested on bilingual people and within bilingual nations and found to translate well into other languages. Subjective well-being research is still a relatively 'young' discipline and there is a great deal of exploration still to be done. Nevertheless, interesting patterns have already emerged which can add a new dimension of thinking to economic policy-making.

It is possible to make international comparisons with subjective well-being data. Figure 14.1 is based on data for 65 nations (although there are very few African and Arabic countries included and it is difficult to assess how representative data is in some countries). A plot of GDP against average happiness is still illuminating, as can be seen in Figure 14.1.

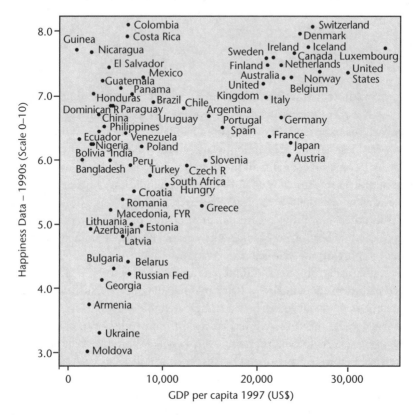

Figure 14.1 An international comparison of the happiness and GDP of nations

Source: R. Veenhoven, *World Database of Happiness, Catalog of Happiness Queries.*
www.eur.nl/fsw/research/happiness *(2003)*

Figure 14.1 shows roughly three groups of countries.

1. Low GDP—Low Happiness. These countries are typically from the former Soviet block.

2. Low GDP—High Happiness. These countries are typically from Latin America, although this group also includes China, Nigeria, and Guinea.

3. High GDP—High Happiness. This group is made up of 'economically developed' nations.

It is very telling that there are no High GDP—Low Happiness nations so we can only conclude that wealthy nations are usually happy nations. There are debates about how the wealth of a country raises happiness. Several authors argue that a high GDP ensures that society provides safety nets through social policies to prevent misery, thus raising the overall average for the country.[1]

It is also clear that happy nations are not always wealthy nations. The divergence in happiness between nations with low GDP suggests that cultural and social systems play a large role in determining happiness. Indeed Amartya Sen, the Nobel Prize-winning economist, argues very elegantly for the central importance of 'freedom' for human development. He points out, in his book *Development as Freedom*, that there has never been a famine in a functioning democracy. Other research suggests that factors such as health, education, judicial systems, equality, absence of corruption, and respect for human rights as well as prevalent personality groups (optimists are by definition happier than pessimists, so perhaps some nations are typified by 'sunnier' personalities) are influential in explaining differences in national happiness.

To gain a rounded picture, international comparisons need to be supplemented with national data. For instance, Figure 14.2 shows the levels of life satisfaction in the United Kingdom from 1973 to 2001. It is striking that (apart from one survey in 1988, which must be considered a statistical aberration) the level of life satisfaction in the United Kingdom has been remarkably flat—averaging 6.9 on a scale of 0–10. So, despite GDP increasing by over 66 per cent in real terms from nearly £8500 per person to over £14,500 (figures in 1995 pounds) in those years, people's satisfaction with their lives has not really changed at all in 30 years.

These results and other research suggest that, up to a point, increases in output push up happiness in a nation. But beyond this, as demonstrated by the case of the United Kingdom, the relationship is extremely weak. The reason for this is still being explored. Theories vary—that people adapt quickly to new levels of wealth, or that their expectations rise just as quickly; or that growth gives rise to externalities which push down well-being; or because there is a hierarchy of needs and that once material needs are fulfilled, more money does not necessarily help fulfil other needs. There is also some evidence to suggest that people who prioritize material values in their lives are actually less likely to be happy. Perhaps the wanting (and the not having) suppresses happiness.

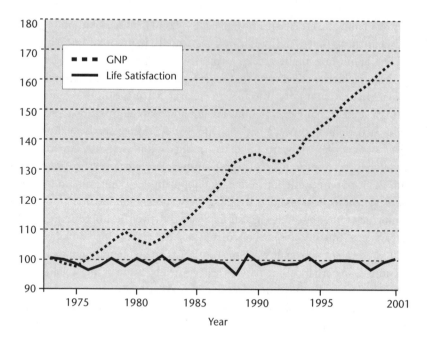

Figure 14.2 Life satisfaction and GNP growth in the UK 1973–2001

Source: R Veenhoven, *World Database of Happiness, Catalog of Happiness Queries.*
www.eur.nl/fsw/research/happiness (2003)

conclusion

Measuring quality of life is inherently subjective—different measures that claim objectivity tell different stories. So if we are to understand people's quality of life, then probably a fruitful route is to use methodologies that ask them about their subjective perceptions. Data on subjective well-being exists in many countries although there are also many regions for which there is little or unreliable data. Subjective well-being research is still in its infancy but is likely to be a fruitful source for economists.

Some interesting patterns have already emerged. Happiness in developed countries is fairly insensitive to rises in GDP. But, taking a broader range of economies, higher output does seem to correlate with higher happiness. This is suggestive of a 'threshold effect'—that happiness rises with output up to a point, with the relationship then breaking down. If this is correct, the existing research around subjective well-being provides an argument for redistribution towards poorer countries as this could lead to substantial increases in total well-being. It also provides a challenge for richer countries. If more output fails to make people in developed countries happier, what does this mean for policy?

further reading

Kahneman, D., E. Diener, and N. Schwarz (eds) *Well-Being: The Foundations of Hedonic Psychology* (New York: Russell Sage, 1999).

Lane; R.E. *Loss of Happiness in Market Democracies* (New York: Yale University Press, 2000).

Sen, A. *Development as Freedom* (Oxford: Oxford University Press, 1999).

Veenhoven, R. *World Database of Happiness, Catalogue of Happiness Queries,* (2003) available at www.eur.nl/fsw/research/happiness.

reference

[1] See, for example, Diener and Suh's paper in D. Kahneman, E. Diener, and N. Schwarz (eds) *Well-Being, The Foundations of Hedonic Psychology* (New York: Russell Sage, 1999).

poverty and income distribution: what is the evidence?

robert hunter wade

Neoliberals claim that world poverty and income inequality have both fallen over the past two decades or so, for the first time in more than a century and a half. This gratifying result, they argue, is due in large part to the rising density of economic integration between countries, usually described as globalization. So the solution for regions that are lagging behind is more of the same. Opponents of globalization, it is claimed, have no serious empirical evidence to back up their view. In the words of Martin Wolf of the *Financial Times*,[1] they are preaching 'the big lie' and their favoured policies would cause more poverty and inequality.

In this essay, I summarize my conclusions on what is happening to poverty and income distribution on a world scale. I emphasize how sensitive the statistics are to methodological choices, and the scope for flattering them in order to confirm that globalization is good news. I discuss the drawbacks of having the World Bank as the main international generator of knowledge about development.

poverty

The World Bank—effectively the sole producer of the world poverty head-count—says, in the words of President James Wolfensohn, that 'over the past 20 years, the number of people living on less than $1 a day has fallen by 200 million, after rising steadily for 200 years'.[2] The opening sentence of the Bank's *World Development Indicators 2001* says: 'Of the world's 6 billion people, 1.2 billion live on less than $1 a day', the same number in both 1987 and 1998.[3]

A statistic about the world total of just about anything inevitably is subject to a large margin of error. But the poverty numbers are particularly problematic and error-prone and the errors probably bias the trend in a favourable direction.[4]

large margin of error

The Bank's poverty headcount comes from household surveys, which have serious limitations, adding up to a large margin of error in national poverty numbers and so also in the world totals. Some are well known; such as the exclusion of most of the benefits that people receive from publicly provided goods and services. Others are less well known; such as the sensitivity of the poverty headcount to the design of the surveys. For example, the shorter the recall period, the more expenditure is reported. A recent study in India suggests that a switch from the standard 30-day reporting period to a seven-day reporting period itself lifts 175 million people from poverty (using the Indian official poverty line). This is a difference of nearly 50 per cent. Using the $1 per day international poverty benchmark, which is higher, the fall in recorded poverty would be even greater.[5]

Another important point is that the poverty headcount is very sensitive to the precise level of the national and global poverty lines because income distribution in the vicinity of developing country poverty lines is typically fairly flat. Even a small change in the line brings a large change in the number of people below it.

In addition, the Bank's often-cited comparison between 1980 and 1998—1.4 billion in extreme poverty in 1980, 1.2 billion in 1998—is not legitimate. The Bank introduced a new methodology in the late 1990s, and has recalculated the poverty numbers with the new methodology only back to 1987 so there is no 1980 figure under the new method. The new method a) changed the way the international poverty line was calculated from the official poverty lines of a sample of low- and middle-income countries; b) reset the international poverty line from $PPP 1 per day to $PPP 1.08 per day; and c) altered the procedure for aggregating, country by country, the relative price changes between 1985 and 1993 (the dates of the two major international price surveys for a standard bundle of goods and services).

What we do know is that this new method caused a huge change in the poverty count even for the same country in the same year using the same survey data.[6] Table 15.1 shows the methodology-induced changes by regions for 1993. Angus Deaton,[7] who knows as much about world poverty statistics as anyone, comments that 'changes of this size risk swamping real changes' and that 'it seems impossible to make statements about changes in world poverty when the ground underneath one's feet is changing in this way'.[8]

Table 15.1 1993 poverty rate using old and new World Bank methodology

	Old Poverty Rate (%)	New Poverty Rate (%)
Sub-Saharan Africa	39.1	49.7
Latin America	23.5	15.3
Middle East/N Africa	4.1	1.9

Source: A. Deaton, 'Counting the World's Poor: Problems and Possible Solutions', *The World Bank Research Observer* (2001)
Note: *The poverty rate is the proportion of the population living on less than $1 per day*

direction of bias

There are further sources of error which seem to bias the results in a downwards direction. The first of these is that both the old and the new methods use a misleading notion of the poverty line. The problem is that the Bank's poverty line refers to a 'general consumption' bundle, not to a basket of goods and services that makes sense for measuring poverty, such as food, clothing, and shelter (though '$1 per day' does have intuitive appeal to a Western audience being asked to support aid). We have no way of knowing what proportion of food, clothing, and shelter needs the Bank's poverty line captures. If the Bank used a basic-needs poverty line rather than its present artificial one, the number of absolute poor would probably rise. This is because the national poverty lines, equivalent to a global, basic-needs poverty line expressed in US dollars, would probably rise (maybe by as much as 25 to 50 per cent). They would increase because the general consumption bundle used for calculating purchasing power parities in different countries includes many services that are very cheap in developing countries (for example, massages) but irrelevant to the poor and this gives a misleadingly high measure of the purchasing power of the incomes of the poor. Food and shelter are relatively expensive. If they alone were included in the PPP exchange rate used to express the incomes of the poor in US dollars, national poverty lines would go up. Indeed, the rates of 'extreme poverty' for Latin American countries using poverty lines based on *calorific* and *demographic* characteristics are roughly *twice* as high as those based on the World Bank's $1 per day line.[9]

Moreover, the new international poverty line of $PPP 1.08 translates into *lower* national poverty lines in 77 per cent of the 94 countries for which data is available, containing 82 per cent of their population. The new international line lowers the old national line for China by 14 per cent, for India by 9 per cent, and for the whole sample by an average of 13 per cent.[10] It is likely that future 'updating' of the international poverty line will continue to artificially lower the true numbers, because worldwide average consumption patterns (on which the international poverty line is based) are shifting toward services whose relative prices are much lower in poor than in rich countries. This will give the false impression that the increase in the cost of the basic consumption goods required by the poor is lower than it is. And as I have noted, even a small upwards shift in the poverty line would substantially raise the number of people recorded as being in extreme poverty.

the politicization of statistics

All these problems have to be resolved in one way or another in any estimate of world poverty, whoever makes it. But the fact that the World Bank is effectively the monopoly provider introduces a further complication. The number of absolute poor is politically sensitive. For example, The *World Development Report 2000/2001: Attacking Poverty* says that the number of people living on less than $1 per day *increased* by 20 million from 1.18 billion in 1987 to 1.20 billion in 1998. When it was being written in the late 1990s, the key ideas-controlling positions in the Bank were held by Joe Stiglitz and Ravi Kanbur (respectively, chief economist and director of the *World Development Report 2000/2001*), not noted champions of the Washington Consensus.[11] And at that time the Bank was trying to mobilize support for making the Comprehensive Development Framework the new template for all its work, and *lack* of progress in development helped to justify the new approach. Then the majority report of the Meltzer Commission, for the US Congress, was published, which said that the Bank was failing at its central task of poverty reduction and therefore should be sharply cut back. It cited as proof of failure the 'fact' that the number of people in absolute poverty remained constant at 1.2 billion between 1987 and 1998[12] (a spurious argument if ever there was one). Now the Bank needed to emphasize progress. Out came a major Bank publication called *Globalization, Growth, and Poverty: Building an Inclusive World Economy* which claimed that the number of people living in poverty *decreased* by 200 million in the 18 years from 1980 to 1998.[13] By this time both Stiglitz and Kanbur were gone and David Dollar, a prominent Bank economist, was ascendant. He was chief author of *Globalization, Growth, and Poverty*. The comparison between the two reports suggests that the data and the choice of methodologies may change with the people and the organization's tactical objectives.

In short, we should be cautious about accepting the World Bank's poverty headcount as approximately correct. We do not know for sure whether the late 1990s' revisions to the methodology and the PPP numbers have the effect of raising or lowering the poverty headcount, and whether they alter the direction of the trend over the 1980s and 1990s. But it is likely that the Bank has under-estimated the true magnitude of poverty.

inequality

Many analysts claim world income inequality fell sharply in the second half of the 20th century, especially in the final quarter.[14] But in the past several years, world income distribution has become a hot topic of debate and there is now less agreement about income distribution than about poverty. While we *could* get better data on the poor, which would command general agreement, there are no easy solutions to measuring inequality.

There are numerous studies of world income distribution, which come up with very different trends. Results depend on a) alternative measurements of income (GNP per capita converted to US dollars using market exchange rates or GNP per capita adjusted for differences in purchasing power across countries); b) alternative samples of countries and alternative weightings of countries (each country weighted as one unit or by population); c) alternative measures of distribution (the Gini or other average coefficient of inequality or ratios of the income of the richer deciles of world population to that of poorer deciles or average income of a set of developed countries to that of a set of developing countries); and d) national income accounts or household income and expenditure surveys. These choices make a big difference to the results, and *there is no single best measure.*[15]

market exchange rates vs. PPP

If incomes of different countries and of all the world's people are converted into a common *numeraire* (the US dollar) by market exchange rates, the results are unambiguous. World income distribution is becoming rapidly more *unequal.* Everyone accepts this. The dispute is about what the figures mean. Most economists say that exchange-rate-based income measures are irrelevant and that GNP incomes should always be adjusted by purchasing power parity exchange rates to take account of differences in purchasing power. Since the market prices of goods and services sold only locally are significantly cheaper in poor countries relative to those facing international competition, the adjust-ment generally raises the income of poor countries and lowers income of rich countries, making world income distribution more equal.

It is true that market-exchange-rate-based income comparisons suffer from distortions in official exchange rates and from sudden changes in the official exchange rate. Nevertheless, we shouldn't therefore accept the argument that incomes converted via PPP exchange rates should always be used instead. For one thing the PPP incomes of China, India, and countries of the former Soviet Union are of very uncertain reliability. For another, if we are interested in questions about the impact of one country or region on the rest of the world—including the capacity of developing countries to repay debts, import capital goods, and represent themselves in international trade negotiations—then relative incomes converted via market exchange rates are more relevant than PPP incomes.

At the end of the day we can be confident of three propositions about the distribution of PPP income. Comparing the richest decile of the world's population with the median decile and the poorest decile against the median, PPP-adjusted income distribution has become *much more unequal* over the past two decades. Secondly, if we use a measurement of the average distribution and weight countries equally (China = Uganda), inequality between countries' average PPP-adjusted income has also *increased* since at least 1980. Using the dispersion of per capita GDP across the world's (equally weighted) countries also shows a rise in inequality between 1950 and 1998, an increase which accelerated in the 1990s. One study using these dispersion measures concludes that there is 'no doubt as to the existence of a definite trend towards distributive inequality worldwide, both across and within countries'.[16] A third method which measures average distribution but weights countries by population finds that inequality between countries has been *constant or falling* since around 1980. This is the result that Martin Wolf, *The Economist*, and many others celebrate. But it comes entirely from fast average growth in China and India and, if they are excluded, even this measure of inequality shows inequality widening since 1980. The fact is that this measure is the *only* one that supports the liberal argument on inequality.

china and india: statistical sleights of hand?

With 38 per cent of world population, China and India shape world trends. According to official statistics, they have grown very quickly over the past decade in the case of India and two decades in the case of China. China's average purchasing power parity income rose from 30 per cent of the world average in 1990 to 45 per cent in 1998, or 15 percentage points in only eight years. The performance of these two huge economies, if the statistics are accurate, may well have contributed to world poverty and inequality being less than they would otherwise have been. But can we rely on the official numbers? I believe we must be very cautious.

Purchasing power parity-adjusted income figures for China and India—the two most important countries for the world trends in poverty and inequality—contain an even bigger component of guesswork than for most other significant countries. The main sources of PPP income figures (the Penn World Tables[17] and the International Comparison Project) are based on two, large-scale international price benchmarking exercises for calculating PPP exchange rates, one conducted in 1985 in 60 countries, the other in 1993 in 110 countries. The government of China declined to participate in both. The PPP exchange rate for China is based on guesstimates from small, ad hoc price surveys in a few cities, adjusted by rules of thumb to take account of the huge price differences between urban and rural areas and between Eastern and Western regions. The government of India declined to participate in the 1993 exercise. The price comparisons for India are extrapolations from 1985, qualified by small, ad hoc price surveys in later years. The lack of reliable price comparisons for China and India—and hence the lack of reliable evidence on the purchasing power of even average incomes, let alone incomes of the poor—compromises any claim about levels and trends in world poverty.[18]

China's growth is probably substantially overstated. Many analysts have recently been revising China's growth statistics downwards by large amounts. While government figures show annual real GDP growth of 7–8 per cent in 1998 and 1999, one authority on Chinese statistics estimates that the economy may not have grown at all, putting the real figure at between –2 and +2 per cent.[19]

Even the Chinese government says that the World Bank has been *overstating* China's average income, and the Bank has recently revised its numbers down. Look at Table 15.2. It shows the Bank's estimates for China's average GNP in US dollars for 1997–99 and the corresponding growth rates. The level of average (exchange rate-converted) income *fell* sharply between 1997 and 1998, while the corresponding growth rate between 1997 and 1998 was 6.4 per cent! Behind this inconsistency is a tale of the

Chinese government's arm-twisting of the World Bank (especially after the allegedly accidental US bombing of the Chinese embassy in Belgrade in May 1999) to lower China's average income below the threshold of eligibility for concessional IDA lending from the Bank. China wanted to be eligible not so much for the cheap IDA loans as the privilege extended to companies of IDA-eligible countries to add 7.5 per cent uplift on bids for World Bank projects.[20]

Table 15.2 China's GNPPC and growth rate, 1997–99

	1997	1998	1999
GNPPC/PPP (US$)	3,070	3,050	3,550
GNPPC (US$)	860	750	780
Annual growth rate of GNPPC	7.40%	6.40%	6.10%

Source: World Bank World Development Indicators 1999, 2000, 2001, (Washington DC: World Bank, 1999–2001)
Note: each volume gives figures for one year only so that the discrepancy can be seen only by compiling one's own table

Over the 1990s, China's annual growth rate is more likely to have been around 5–6 per cent than the 8–10 per cent that the official statistics show. This one change (assuming constant internal distribution) lowers the probability that world interpersonal distribution has become more equal. In addition, taking account of even just the obviously big and roughly-measurable environmental costs lowers China's official GDP by roughly 8 per cent; India's, by 5 per cent.[21]

Not only are China's growth rates and income level probably overstated but the rise in inequality within the two giants partly offsets the reduction in world income inequality that comes from relatively fast growth—although careful calculations of the relative strength of the two contrary effects have not yet been made.[22] China's surging inequality is now greater than before the Communists won the civil war in 1949, and the inequality between regions is probably higher than in any other sizable country. The ratio of the average income of the richest to poorest province (Guangdong to Guizhou) rose from around 3 to 1 in the early 1990s, to 5 to 1 in the late 1990s. The corresponding figure for India in the late 1990s was 4.2 and in the United States, 1.9.

> The large margins of error in Chinese and Indian figures of income distribution and the number of people in extreme poverty mean that we cannot have a lot of confidence that the poverty and inequality numbers for the world as a whole have been declining over the past 20 years.

More comprehensive studies, using a range of different measurements, show inequality rising. One makes an approximation to the distribution of income among all the world's people by combining between-country inequality in PPP-adjusted average incomes with within-country inequality weighting countries by population. It finds that world inequality *widened* between 1980 and 1993 using all of four common measures of inequality over the whole distribution.[23] Another recent study used comprehensive data drawn only from household income-and-expenditure surveys (it does not mix data from these surveys with data from national income accounts). It finds a sharp *rise* in world inequality over as short a time as 1988 to 1993 (see Table 15.3).[24]

Table 15.3 World income distribution by households, 1988 and 1993

	1988	1993	% change
Gini	0.63	0.67	6
Richest decile/median	7.28	8.98	23
Poorest decile/median	0.31	0.28	−10

Source: Branko Milanovic, 'True World Income Distribution, 1988 and 1993: first calculations based on household surveys alone' *Economic Journal* (2002)

the united states and other anglo political economies

All the countries of English settlement, led by the United States, have experienced big increases in income inequality over the past 20 to 30 years. In the United States, the top 1 per cent of families enjoyed growth of after-tax income of almost 160 per cent between 1979 and 1997, while families in the middle of the distribution had a 10 per cent increase.[25] Within the top 1 per cent most of the gains have been concentrated in the top 0.1 per cent. This is not a matter of reward to education. Inequality has expanded hugely among the college-educated.

conclusion

My strong conclusion on measuring poverty is that we must be agnostic because our current statistics are not good enough to yield a confident answer. It is plausible that the *proportion* of the world's population in extreme poverty has fallen in the past two decades. But it can also be concluded that poverty numbers are probably higher than the Bank says, and have probably been rising over the past two decades.

On income distribution, the strong conclusion is that world inequality has risen since the early 1980s when income is expressed in terms of market exchange rates; and the same is true for PPP incomes when a top-to-bottom ratio is used (rather than an average). A rising share of the world's income is going to those at the top.[26] Moreover the absolute size of the income gap between countries is widening rapidly.

These trends should be better known. The problem is that the World Bank tends to set the agenda of international development debate, and has an Official View that globalization has been effecting improvements in economic performance, as seen in falls in poverty and inequality. It needs its own statistics and development research to confirm this argument, in order to sustain its legitimacy. Other regional development banks and aid agencies have largely given up on statistics and research, ceding the ground to the World Bank. Alternative views come only from a few 'urban guerrillas' in pockets of academia and the UN system. Such intellectual monopolization can have huge impact.

Some would argue that the Bank's poverty and inequality statistics are produced by mid-level professionals exercising their best judgment in the face of difficulties that have no optimal solutions and who are managerially insulated from the tactical goals of the organization. Others take a different view—that staff cannot be 'kept pure' and inevitably have to engage in data manipulation beyond the limits of professional integrity (or else quit). The truth is somewhere in between. The Bank is exposed to arm-twisting by the G7 member states and international NGOs; it must secure their support and defend itself against criticism. It seeks to advance its broad, market-opening agenda not through coercion but mainly by establishing a sense, via its statistics and its economics research, that the agenda is right and fitting. Without this it would lose the support of the G7 states, Wall Street, and fractions of some developing country elites. The units of the Bank that produce the statistics are partly insulated from the resulting pressures, but not wholly. Perhaps that the Bank should appoint an independent auditor to verify its main development statistics or cede the work to an independent agency, perhaps under UN auspices.

further reading

Babu, P. and P. Khanna, 'Environmental Evaluation of Economic Growth: An Agenda for Change', *Yojana* 13–18 (1997).

Hommann, K. and C. Brandon, 'The cost of inaction: valuing the economy-wide cost of environmental degradation in India', presented at the *Modelling Global Sustainability Conference*, United Nations University, Tokyo (1995).

Jha, R. 'Reducing poverty and inequality in India: has liberalization helped?' *World Institute for Development Economics Research—Paper 204* (2000).

Kynge, J. 'Pyramid of power behind numbers game', *Financial Times*, 27 February (2002).

Reddy, S. and T. Pogge, 'How not to count the poor' (2002) available at www.socialanalysis.com.

Waldron, A. 'China's disguised failure: statistics can no longer hide the need for Beijing to instigate painful structural reforms', Personal View, *Financial Times*, 4 July (2002).

references

[1] M. Wolf, 'The big lie of global inequality', *Financial Times*, 8 February, 2000.

[2] World Bank, *World Development Indicators 2002*, Foreword, (Washington DC World Bank, 2002). Also, World Bank, *Global Economic Prospects and the Developing Countries 2002: Making Trade Work for the World's Poor*, (Washington DC: World Bank, 2002) p.30.

[3] See *World Development Indicators 2001*, The World Bank, p.3. The $1 per day is measured in purchasing power parity. See also *Globalization, Growth, and Poverty: Building an Inclusive World Economy* (The World Bank and Oxford University Press 2002), and A. Deaton, 'Is world poverty falling?' *Finance and Development* Vol. 39 No. 2 (2002).

[4] I am indebted to Sanjay Reddy for discussions about the problems with the Bank's poverty numbers. See S. Reddy and T. Pogge, 'How not to count the poor' at www.social analysis.org. Also, M. Karshenas, 'Measurement and nature of absolute poverty in least developed countries', SOAS, University of London Economics Working Paper Series No. 129 (2001).

[5] Reported in A. Deaton, 'Counting the world's poor'.

[6] The new results were published in *World Development Report 2000/01*.

[7] Angus Deaton is the Dwight D. Eisenhower Professor of International Affairs and Professor of Economics and International Affairs at the Woodrow Wilson School of Public and International Affairs and the Economics Department at Princeton University.

[8] A. Deaton, 'Counting the world's poor: problems and possible solutions', *The World Bank Research Observer*, 16 (2), 125-47, (2001) p.128.

[9] For example, Brazil's extreme poverty rate according to the CEPAL line was 14 per cent, according to the World Bank for roughly the same recent year, 5 per cent; Bolivia, 23 per

cent, 11 per cent; Chile, 8 per cent, 4 per cent; Colombia, 24 per cent, 11 per cent, Mexico, 21 per cent, 18 per cent. *Panorama Social de America Latina 2000–01*, CEPAL, September 2001, p.51.

[10] See S. Reddy and T. Pogge, 'How not to count the poor' available at www.social-analysis.org (2002).

[11] See R. Wade, 'US hegemony and the World Bank: The fight over people and ideas', *Review of International Political Economy*, May 2002. This uses Stiglitz's firing and Kanbur's resignation to illuminate the US role in the Bank's generation of knowledge.

[12] United States Congressional Advisory Commission on International Financial Institutions (Meltzer Commission), *Report to the U.S. Congress on the International Financial Institutions*, 2000 available at www.house/gov/jec/imf/ifiac. Meltzer later described the fall in the proportion of the world's population in poverty from 28 per cent in 1987 to 24 per cent in 1998 as a 'modest' decline, the better to hammer the Bank (A. Meltzer) 'The World Bank one year after the Commission's report to Congress', hearings before the Joint Economic Committee, US Congress, 8 March, 2001).

[13] World Bank *Globalization, Growth, and Poverty: Building an Inclusive World Economy*, (2002) and A. Deaton, 'Is world poverty falling?' *Finance and Development* Vol. 39 No. 2 (2002).

[14] Martin Wolf of the *Financial Times* champions the idea that globalization improves global income distribution. He says, 'Evidence suggests the 1980s and 1990s were decades of declining global inequality and reductions in the proportion of the world's population in extreme poverty.' (M. Wolf, 'Doing more harm than good', *Financial Times*, 8 May (2002). [See also M. Wolf, 'Growth makes the poor richer: reversing the effects of globalization might increase equality as the critics claim, but it would be an equality of destitution', *Financial Times*, 24 January (2001); 'A stepping stone from poverty', *Financial Times*, 19 December (2001); and 'The big lie of global inequality', *Financial Times*, 8 February (2000)]. Anthony Giddens, described by some as the leading social theorist of his generation, agrees but pushes the turning point back two decades. He says, 'World inequalities did rise over a period of a century from the middle of the nineteenth century up to the early 1960s. But since that time this trend has been halted.' [See A. Giddens, *Where Now for New Labour?* (Cambridge: Polity Press 2002) p.72]. Ian Castles, former Australian Statistician, claims that 'most studies suggest that the past 25 years have seen a reversal in the trend towards widening global inequalities which had been proceeding for two centuries' [letter to *The Economist*, 26 May 2001]. See also P. Omerod, 'Inequality: the long view', *Prospect* August/September (2002); and R. Wright, 'Global happiness' *Prospect*, December (2002).

[15] In addition to the studies referenced elsewhere I draw on: G. Firebaugh, 'Empirics of world income inequality', *American Journal of Sociology*, (1999) 104; C. Jones, 'On the evolution of world income distribution' *Journal of Economic Perspectives*, (1997) 11; L. Pritchett, 'Divergence: big time', *Journal of Economic Perspectives*, (1997) 11; D. Quah, 'Empirics for growth and distribution: stratification, polarization, and convergence clubs' *Journal of Economic Growth*, (1997) 2; UN Development Program, *Human Development Report 1999*; R. Kanbur, 'Conceptual challenges in poverty and inequality: one development economist's perspective', WP2002-09, Dept. of Applied Economics, Cornell University, April (2002); R. Korzeniewicz and T. Moran, 'World-Economic Trends in the

Distribution of Income, 1965–1992' *American Journal of Sociology*, 102, 4, (1997) 1000–1039; R. Korzeniewicz and T. Moran, 'Measuring World Income Inequalities', *American Journal of Sociology*, 106, 1, (2000) 209–14.

[16] *Globalization and Development*, ECLA, April (2002) p.85. The dispersion of per capita GDP/PPP is measured as the average logarithmic deviation, the dispersion of growth rates as the standard deviation.

[17] The Penn World Tables provide purchasing power parity and national income accounts converted to international prices for 168 countries for some or all of the years 1950–2000. They are prepared by the Center for International Comparisons at the University of Pennsylvania.

[18] See S. Reddy and T. Pogge, 'How not to count the poor' available at www.social analysis.com (2002).

[19] See J. Kynge, 'Pyramid of power behind numbers game', *Financial Times*, 27 February (2002) drawing on work of Thomas Rawski. As another example from Rawski's analysis, Chinese government figures show total real GDP growth of 25 per cent between 1997 and 2000, whereas energy consumption figures show a drop of 13 per cent. (Some of the fall may be due to replacement of inefficient coal-fired furnaces.) Another source of major inaccuracy in the output and growth figures is that local bureaucracy remains strong enough to base promotion decisions on local increases in agricultural and factory production, providing incentives to falsify. See further A. Waldron, 'China's disguised failure: statistics can no longer hide the need for Beijing to instigate painful structural reforms', Personal View, *Financial Times*, 4 July (2002).

[20] World Bank sources who request anonymity.

[21] P. Babu and P. Khanna, 'Environmental Evaluation of Economic Growth: An Agenda for Change', *Yojana* (1997) pp. 13–18; K. Hommann and C. Brandon, 'The cost of inaction: valuing the economy-wide cost of environmental degradation in India', presented at the *Modelling Global Sustainability Conference*, United Nations University, Tokyo (1995).

[22] Evidence for rising inequality in India over the past two decades is set out in R. Jha, 'Reducing poverty and inequality in India: has liberalization helped?' *World Institute for Development Economics Research—Paper 204* (2000). Deaton agrees that inequality in India has been increasing 'in recent years', and that consumption by the poor did not rise as fast as average consumption.

[23] See S. Dowrick and M. Akmal, 'Explaining contradictory trends in global income inequality: a tale of two biases', Faculty of Economics and Commerce, Australia National University, 29 March (2001). Available on http://ecocomm.anu.edu.au/economics/staff/dowrick/dowrick.html. They find that world inequality increased between 1980 and 1993 using Gini, Theil, coefficient of variation, and the variance of log income.

[24] B. Milanovic, 'True world income distribution, 1988 and 1993: first calculations based on household surveys alone' *Economic Journal*, 112 (476), January (2002) 51–92. Milanovic is currently working on 1998 data.

[25] See P. Krugman, 'For richer' *New York Times*, 20 October (2002).

[26] More doubts are cast on the falling inequality hypothesis by trends in industrial pay inequality within countries. Pay inequality within countries was stable or declining from

the early 1960s to 1982, and then sharply increased from 1982 to the present. 1982 marks a dramatic turning point towards greater inequality in industrial pay worldwide. See the work of James Galbraith and collaborators in the University of Texas Inequality Project, available at http://utip.gov.utexas.edu.

CHAPTER 16

globalization: economic stagnation and divergence

alan freeman

Conventional economic wisdom holds that globalization was an economic success, and that its main problems arise from political opposition. It would be closer to the mark to say that globalization was a political triumph but an economic catastrophe.

The years 1980–2000 were the closest to a world free market that the 20th century saw, under a single world economic policy, which has regulated world trade—above all trade in capital—with few dissenters and even fewer exceptions. Critics of this policy are widely mythologized as idealistic, utopian, and standing in the way of progress. A closer examination suggests the critics were perhaps more realistic than the policy-makers.

stagnation and divergence: shaping a new political geography

In 1988, the GDP of the world in dollars was $4839. In 2002, it was $4748. These figures, like all others in this article, were extracted from GDP data published by the IMF in its *World Economic Outlook* database, with data before 1992 on the countries in transition from the Groningen Growth and Development Centre, and population data from the US Bureau of the Census. These rates are in constant 1995 dollars at current (period average) market exchange rates. They thus measure the income of the world in terms of its power to purchase global products—specifically those of the United States—unlike published figures, which are generally expressed in terms such as Purchasing Power Parity (PPP) dollars, which reflect purchasing power in local markets. This measure provides a great deal more insight into the underlying processes, which led both to the Iraq war, and to the increasingly protectionist rhetoric and practice of the advanced powers.

The absolute growth rate of the world economy has been falling systematically. Table 16.1 summarizes the outcome.

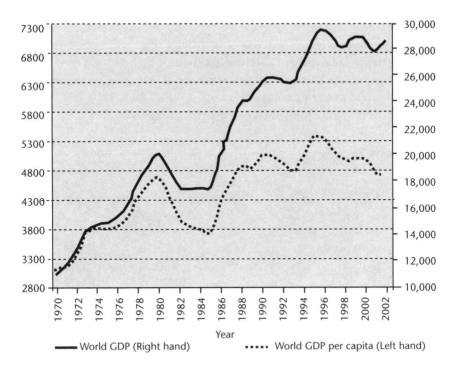

Figure 16.1 World GDP and GDP per capita in constant 1995 dollars, converted from national currencies at current exchange rates.

Source: World Economic Outlook April 2003 database, University of Groningen Growth Project

Table 16.1 Growth rate of world GDP and GDP per capita in constant 1995 dollars converted from national currencies at current exchange rates

	World GDP	World GDP per capita
1970–80	5.51%	3.76%
1980–90	2.27%	0.69%
1990–00	1.09%	−0.19%

Source: World Economic Outlook April 2003 database, University of Groningen Growth Project

But in parallel with this, the world is diverging as Figure 16.2 shows. From 1984 the industrialized and 'other advanced' countries pulled away from the rest of the world. In the 1990s, GDP per capita in the countries in transition fell between 50 per cent and 75 per cent depending on the measure adopted, catapulting them into the ranks of the developing countries. In a further development, during the 1990s the Major Industrial Countries (the G7) pulled away from the other advanced economies, comprising basically the South-East Asian Newly-Industrialized Countries (NICs).

As Figure 16.2 shows, this differential growth did not speed up the growth of the advanced countries relative to the rest of the world. It slowed down the growth of the rest of the world, relative to the advanced countries.

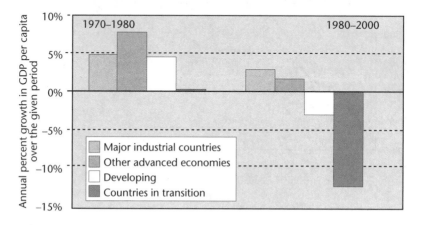

Figure 16.2 Stagnation plus divergence

Source: World Economic Outlook April 2003 database, University of Groningen Growth Project

absolute impoverishment

In terms of world political geography, this has decisive consequences and marks a sharp change compared with the 'Golden Age' of the late 1940s, 1950s, early 1960s, and even the 1970s. In periods when world output as a whole was rising, the continued relative divergence of rich from poor countries did not produce mass impoverishment on the scale now being witnessed. Divergence appeared largely as 'differential rates of growth' and thus, in some sense, the great majority of the world was becoming better off. Divergence combined with stagnation has a completely opposite effect. The countries at the bottom of the pile suffer the combined effect of getting poorer relative to the average, at the same time that the average is declining. Absolute impoverishment is back.

Thus in 1980, 118 million people lived in nine countries where GDP per capita declined absolutely over the previous decade. In 1998, there were 60 such countries with a combined population of 1.3 billion. Impoverishment on such a scale is politically unsustainable and it is the basic driver behind the collapse of the world bloc, which drove through the financial policies of the 1980s.

the measure of growth

These judgements depend on the measure adopted. World GDP, measured in dollars, rises and falls with exchange rates. Does the dollar, as a unit of measurement, not merely report its fortunes on the foreign exchange markets, rather than offering a real indicator of growth?

Measures such as PPP dollars, in which the world financial institutions report world output, are adjusted to reflect the local cost of living. Since costs are generally lower in poorer countries, these provide higher estimates of the income of poor people. The problem is that in order to grow and prosper, a country requires not cheap local produce but access to technologically advanced products and services, and their use and production are concentrated in the rich countries. By assessing output in real dollars, we obtain a more accurate measure of the true cost of development, namely the cost of obtaining advanced country products. It should not be forgotten, moreover, that securing access to world products was one of the main arguments advanced to persuade the political elites of the poor countries to open their doors to world markets.

The very fact that exchange rate GDP is diverging from PPP GDP signifies that something new is going on. 30 years ago, world output was rising unambiguously. Now it is not. Anyone wishing to argue that world output is still rising, can support this view only if output is measured in one particular way.

It is hard to sustain the argument that real-dollar GDP understates long-term growth, or that the fall in output reported above is a consequence of foreign exchange effects alone. It is true that, when the dollar appreciates against other currencies, the output of other countries measured in dollars will *ceteris paribus* fall. But over the whole of the period in which world output has fallen, the dollar has not appreciated against any major currency by more than 18 per cent—little more than 1 per cent per year—and it has by no means appreciated against all leading currencies. If, for example, growth is measured in yen, the result is an even more decisive decline in world GDP, as Table 16.2 demonstrates.

To say the least, if IMF and World Bank reports were drawn up in yen, there would be some explaining to do.

No matter how rosy the picture displayed in a succession of World Bank reports in terms of PPP dollars, there has been no suggestion that countries

Table 16.2 Annual growth of world GDP per capita in yen

	World GDP	World GDP per capita
1970–80	47.11%	44.60%
1980–90	31.54%	29.34%
1990–00	–6.45	–7.63

Source: World Economic Outlook April 2003 database, University of Groningen Growth Project

might settle their debts in PPP dollars—a step that would reduce debt payments for many Third World countries by 75 per cent and more. If PPP dollars really do measure wealth, why not use them as means of payment or at least settlement?

PPPs compare living standards in national economies independent of currency variations. They are fictitious exchange rates that take account of local national costs. Where these are low, the PPP exchange rate is higher than the actual market rate. Thus, the GDP of India measured in 1996 PPPs was $1783 billion but only $441.7 billion in real dollars. This is because, in India, a dollar buys four times as much as in the United States.

a genocidal decline in purchasing power

This offers a key insight into the increasingly strident and open argument between world development agencies, such as UNCTAD, and the international financial institutions. UNCTAD shares an analytical consensus to measure output in PPPs, which stretches across world institutions and many NGOs. The point is thus that, *even in PPPs,* a genocidal decline in purchasing power of the poorest third of the world's population is incontrovertible. The underlying trends are so stark that they impose themselves on any measure. In 2002, using PPPs, UNCTAD reported that, at the end of the 1960s, in the 39 Least-Developed Countries (LDCs) 211 million people were living on an income of less than $2 per day. By the end of the 1990s, there were 448 million, an increase of over 100 per cent.

This is the key to Table 21 from the UNCTAD report on LDC poverty, reproduced here as Table 16.3

It remains the case that even these measures obscure the underlying dynamics in output, which are probably a great deal worse. The principal cause of divergence between the two measures of world output, aside from the general tendency of PPPs to exaggerate poor country output, are the specific effects of China and India.

Table 16.3 Poverty trends in LDCs and other developing countries, 1965–1999
1985 PPP $2-a-day international poverty line

	1965–69	1975–79	1985–89	1995–99
Population living on less than $2-a-day (%)				
39 LDCs	80.8	82.1	81.9	80.7
Of which: African LDCs	82.0	83.7	87.0	87.5
Of which: Asian LDCs	78.8	79.6	73.4	68.2
22 other developing countries	82.8	76.5	61.6	35.3
Number of people living on less than $2-a-day (millions)				
39 LDCs	211.1	277.5	360.5	449.3
Of which: African LDCs	131.7	174.4	239.5	315.1
Of which: Asian LDCs	79.1	102.9	120.3	133.3
22 other developing countries	1,405.00	1,639.70	1,599.00	1,084.20
Total	1,615.80	1,917	1,958.80	1,532.60
Average daily consumption of those living below $2-a-day (1985 PPP $)				
39 LDCs	1.07	1.07	1.06	1.03
Of which: African LDCs	0.95	0.96	0.90	0.86
Of which: Asian LDCs	1.27	1.27	1.37	1.42
22 other developing countries	1.17	1.30	1.53	1.65

Source: UNCTAD, *The Least Developed Countries Report 2002,* (Geneva: UNCTAD, 2002)

china and india—exceptions to the globalization rule

These two enormous Asian countries are in a special relation to the world market by sheer virtue of their size and hence the extent of their internal market. Moreover, China is a very specific case, singled out precisely by the fact that, unlike the USSR, she did not follow IMF prescriptions, has not transformed herself into a model IMF economy, and has an entirely different ownership structure in which over two-thirds of her production remain outside the private market in capital. There is no room for doubt that China has undergone a prodigious and, in terms of world history, highly exceptional phase of growth. This can hardly, however, be attributed to globalization; the whole point is that the role of the Chinese state has indeed dominated over market and global processes. If, therefore, one wishes to assess the impact of the market and of global processes as such, exception should be made of China.

During the last two decades, the proportional contributions of China and India to world real GDP, according to the PPP measure, have more than doubled. They are now counted at four times the worth that their product fetches on the world market. Measured peak to peak, if GDP is presented including India and China, its growth rate shows no decline between 1979 and 1985 and falls by only 0.5 per cent from the 1979 to the 1996 peak. Without China and India, growth nearly halves over the latter period, from 5.3 per cent to 3.3 per cent.

This exception proves the rule. The global decline in world GDP is understated in PPPs only because of the specific situation of the two largest countries in the world. Therefore, it is the exception to globalization, *not* the impact of globalization that offsets its general impact on world poverty. In all those countries that do not enjoy the very particular advantages of China and India, the trend to poverty and differentiation is accelerated.

the globalization of divergence

Impoverishment is only one aspect of a more extended process of *differentiation*, which is not confined to the impoverishment of a relative 'minority' of the world's people in the LDCs. It is this differentiation, rendering the globalized world less and less homogenous, which is literally tearing apart the globalization bloc. Two developments accompanied the impoverishment of the Third World. One was the Asian crisis at the end of the millennium, which led to a significant deterioration in the condition of even that small group of developing countries such as the NICs that had been catching up with the advanced nations in the preceding 30 years. The other was the outbreak of increasingly hostile competition, even among the advanced countries, leading to significant deterioration in the Japanese and European economies, relative to the United States.

Between 1980 and 2000, the relationship between the advanced or advancing countries as a whole (comprising North America, the Eurozone, Japan, and the

Table 16.4 GDP per capita in constant 1995 dollars

	1982	2000
Rest of the World	1,457	1,116
Advanced or advancing countries	15,383	26,134

Source: UNCTAD, *The Least Developed Countries Report 2002,* (Geneva: UNCTAD, 2002)

advanced South-East Asian countries) and the rest of the world went through a qualitative evolution. GDP per capita of the rich nearly doubled; that of the rest of the world fell by around 30 per cent from its 1980 peak of $1683 to its 1999 trough of $1116.

It should further be noted that this divergence is less affected by currency fluctuations in that it would be the same whether measured in dollars, yen, pounds, or euros. Only if the output of each region is measured in a *different* unit, masking their differentiation, does the divergence appear to be reduced.

Differentiation has proceeded at every level of the world economy. Most significantly, *within* the advanced and advancing countries a wholly new development took place in the 1990s. The United States took the lead in growth, not by raising its own contribution to the growth of the world's wealth but by reducing everyone else's. US growth became, for the rest of the world, synonymous with its own stagnation.

Table 16.5 Growth rates in the advanced countries

	Growth 1980–90	Growth 1990–2000
South-East Asia	68.40%	19.50%
Eurozone	25.20%	–8.40%
North America	24.80%	21.20%

Source: World Economic Outlook April 2003 database, University of Groningen Growth Project

This type of world growth is the opposite of that which took place during the 'Golden Age'. Then, not only did the United States manifest qualitatively higher growth rates; it took the rest of the world with it. The United States was in surplus. It was the most productive country in the world and, at the same time, the most technologically advanced, the richest, the greatest capital exporter, and the military and financial guarantor of the rest of the advanced world. Its military and financial dominance were in balance with its productive dominance.

This situation has reversed. The last quarter of the century has been dominated by the relative decline of the United States and its inability to hegemonize the rest of the world by raising its productive capacity. Instead, the United States is ever more insistently driven to use its military and financial weight to offset its productive weakness, which is manifested most starkly in its in-eradicable trade deficit and also in the brutal fact that the world is being torn apart by the United States' fundamental economic incapacity to act as a catalyst for its greater prosperity.

rise of the finance sector

introduction

Part 04 examines how globalization has led to *the rise to dominance of the finance sector* of the global economy. Peter Warburton, a distinguished economist who once called himself a monetarist, examines the explosion in debt, globally, and highlights the inconsistency of central bank policies that ruthlessly suppressed the rate of inflation but failed to check the alarming growth of credit. Romilly Greenhill explains how banks create credit.

Michael Hudson explains (in an extract from his latest book) how the link was broken between the dollar and gold convertibility. Instead of gold, the US Treasury bill is now the global economy's key currency standard. He analyzes how this happened and its implications. Wynne Godley examines the exceptionally large and growing US balance-of-payments deficit, and concludes that the United States will not recover properly in the medium term, but rather enters a prolonged period of 'growth recession' with a high risk of financial implosion.

Dani Rodrick explores the misbehaviour of financial markets and Franklin Serrano demonstrates how dollarization has caused instability and ravaged Central and Latin America. David Boyle looks at a trend going in the opposite direction—the creation of local or barter currencies. Finally, Ann Pettifor reviews the structure of the 20th century international financial system and Jane D'Arista proposes a new international financial architecture for the 21st century.

debt and delusion

peter warburton

introduction

Over the past three or four years, the incidence of debt default and delinquency has escalated in the developed world. Corporate bond defaults (see Figure 17.1) have rocketed, both in number and size, as the telecommunications and energy sectors have plunged into loss. Personal and corporate bankruptcies are increasing across the developed world as hapless borrowers seek protection from their creditors. The so-called sub-prime mortgage sector in the United States is experiencing its worst-ever default rate and unpaid consumer credit debts are mounting in Europe as well as North America. European banks and insurance companies are nursing huge write-offs against their profits.

While banks price their loans to allow for a certain degree of non-payment, or delinquency, in a competitive environment it is difficult to resist the temptation to trim this margin in order to win business. In truth, the tolerance limits in the world financial system are very fine. Once annual default rates approach 1 per cent (of the value of the debt) across the whole lending

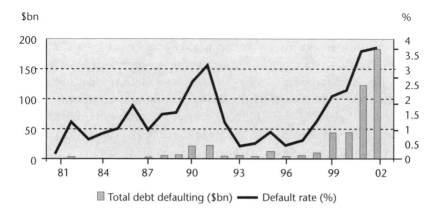

Figure 17.1 Characteristics of global bond defaults

Source: Standard & Poors, *Special Report on Ratings Performance in 2002*

spectrum, banks' profitability is called into question. If default rates reach 2 per cent, then the probability of a financial crisis rises appreciably. By my calculations, the first of these landmarks has already been reached.

There are many different kinds of debt in the world today. Debt is most simply defined as borrowed money, although debts can be settled in many other ways. Sometimes, interest is charged and sometimes not. Sometimes there is an appointed time for the debt to be repaid, sometimes not. Children borrow from their parents and, occasionally, parents borrow from their children. Work colleagues borrow from each other, as do friends and families. While these informal debts are important to society, they are impossible to measure. The debts I will describe are those that can be measured because they have the force of law behind them; that is to say, the creditor, who owns the debt, has a legal right to the payment of interest and the prompt repayment of the debt by the debtor, who owes the debt. There is one other important omission from the debts discussed here and that is governments' and companies' pension liabilities to individuals. Properly speaking, these are obligations or promises rather than debts.

the big picture

The best estimate of the total amount of legally enforceable debt in the world today is about $100 trillion ($100,000,000,000,000). About 90 per cent of this debt is owed by governments, companies, or individuals in one of the 25 richest countries. Most of this debt is also owned by entities in the same group of rich countries. The sum of all the debts of low- and middle-income countries accounts for approximately 10 per cent of the world debt total. Of this $10 trillion, about one-quarter is external debt and the remainder is internal. In other words, governments and commercial businesses in low- and middle-income countries owe about $2.5 trillion to foreign governments, banks, and businesses in other countries. All the debates about Third World debt are contained within this portion of the debt universe. Although it represents a small proportion of global debt, the burden of the debt is often extremely heavy in relation to the very low levels of income in the countries concerned, particularly in Angola, Congo, Nicaragua, Mauritania, and Sierra Leone.

You may already be asking: 'Why do people in rich nations owe so much to each other?' The answer is that the debts are contracts between different groups of people. A highly developed financial system offers the opportunity for individuals, small businesses, large firms and corporations, non-profit organizations, and governments to borrow money. At the same time, other people, companies, and governments will have surplus funds that they wish to lend or invest. Over time, the financial system has evolved smarter and smarter tricks to allow almost every potential borrower to have access to credit. Indeed, most individuals and companies in Western countries are active as borrowers and savers at the same time. For example, a householder may have a mortgage on her home and a savings plan, and a typical multinational company will have net borrowings in one currency and net deposits in another.

The facility to borrow can be a blessing or a curse. At one extreme, there is the loan that enables an act of investment from which there is a reasonable expectation of a continuing stream of income. Here, the loan represents capital that has been preserved by its careful use and, potentially, enhanced by the success of the enterprise. At the other extreme, there is a loan whose explicit purpose is to transform capital into consumption. Inefficient or corrupt capital markets deny adequate borrowing opportunities at affordable cost. Highly sophisticated, but yet distorted, capital markets make credit facilities too generally available and promote the wasteful or indulgent use of capital. This gives rise to a paradox—that poor countries often save proportionately more than rich ones.

who are the biggest borrowers?

As far as the developed world is concerned, corporations and financial institutions carry the largest debts. They have gross borrowings of around $45 trillion, composed of loans and bonds, followed by government borrowing ($23 trillion) and household borrowing ($22 trillion). As the largest nation by some distance, the United States accounts for some $12 trillion of corporate and financial debt and $10.5 trillion of government and agency debt, while US households have mortgages totalling $6 trillion within total liabilities of $8.5 trillion. Japan has the next largest accumulation of debts, with a total of $17 trillion, and the 12 countries of the Eurozone account for approximately $22 trillion.

Such vast numbers can be difficult to comprehend. The $90 trillion total, equivalent to more than three years' income for large developed nations, represents the sum of all domestic and international bank loans, monetary instruments, and bonds. There is an unavoidable element of double counting, as some types of debt security are simply bank loans that have been repackaged. However, the bank loans and the bonds still have independent lives, and each has a separate capacity to cause trouble for the universe of debt, more usually referred to as the credit system.

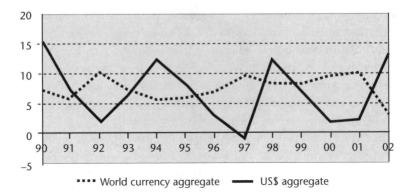

Figure 17.2 Annual growth of bank loan and private sector debt securities, percentage pa

Source: Author's calculations using data from IMF and BIS

Over the past ten years, the credit system in the developed world has been expanding much faster than its income and output. On average, nominal GDP in the OECD area has increased by less than 5 per cent per year since 1992, whereas growth in credit (see Figure 17.2) has averaged 8 per cent. In 2001, total credit growth, measured in world currency, reached 10 per cent and nominal incomes grew by less than 3 per cent. This means that the developed world economy has become progressively more highly geared. In theory, this process could continue for many years before the absolute limits are reached. But this assumes that the new debt is of the same high quality as the old debt. The concept of the quality of credit—reflecting the likelihood of the lender being repaid in full—is central to an understanding of the modern financial system.

how banks make money

romilly greenhill

A bank is not an institution that passes the savings of one individual to another; it is a shop that sells credit. But it is a very special shop: the product it is selling costs virtually nothing to produce and can be sold virtually without limit. When it mis-sells this product, it is not so much the shop-owners but the customers—and even the economy at large—that suffer.

Households and firms use the banking system primarily as a means to hold transactions balances to meet likely expenses in the course of day-to-day life. These balances are the main financial liability of the banking system. The crucial point to recognize is that the operational liability of a bank is not the same as this balance sheet liability. The operational liability of a bank is, instead, to be able to provide customers with cash when it is demanded and to meet its obligations to clear its liabilities to other banks, by a transfer of some of its deposits at the central bank ('bankers' deposits').

For a number of reasons, the quantity of 'reserves' (cash and bankers' deposits) required to meet this operational liability is small compared to the total liabilities on the balance sheet. Firstly, many transactions (usually the largest ones) are paid for without cash—through cheques, debit cards, and standing orders. These may give rise to clearings with other banks, but the net amount is small compared to the volume of transactions, and the money stays in the banking system. Secondly, the amount of cash an individual requires at a single point in time is low relative to the actual balance of the account (for example, the amount of cash held relative to a monthly salary). Thirdly, nearly all cash returns to the banking system very quickly (for example, once cash is spent in a shop, the shop will deposit it in a bank). Cash losses are usually small and quickly reversed.

Each of these reasons is underpinned by a broader 'confidence' that the public has in the banking system. The point in history when the public became confident that a deposit in the bank was as good as holding cash was pivotal for the ability of the banking system to create credit on a large scale.

Since the operational liability is a small fraction of total bank liabilities, banks need only keep a small reserve against the probability of a cash drain. Any new cash that comes into the banking system can give rise to a much larger credit expansion.

Banks' ability to create credit therefore derives from their reserves, the probability of cash losses, and the size of their total balance sheet—that is, they can either hold cash or other assets that earn a return. Overdrafts and other credits are assets to the banks. Suppose banks decide to expand their lending. When that credit is used (spent), the recipient will deposit the proceeds. Thus, for the banking system as a whole, credit creates deposits. But it may also cause the banks to be short of reserves, because for the system as a whole, bank liabilities have gone up.

Banks have developed a trade in reserves amongst themselves, but the role of the central bank in the context of credit creation operations is crucial here. In the United Kingdom, the Bank of England actively prints cash and supplies it to member banks in accordance with public demand.'[1] A central bank is hence engaged in the active creation of reserves. As a consequence, the banking system as a whole is not constrained by cash reserves but operates such that cash reserves are created to support lending. Banks create credit, and this action creates deposits. The central bank then supplies the necessary amount of cash to support this level of credit and deposit creation. They influence the banks by announcing the rate of interest at which they will provide this cash.

The question left unresolved is whether the quantity of credit generated in this way will be appropriate for economic activity more widely. It would be very easy for the banks to provide an excessive amount of credit in good times and tend to starve the economy of credit in bad times.

The apologists for the world's largest and longest credit boom would claim that the new credit was reaching frustrated, but creditworthy, households and companies. They would argue that commercial and savings banks had rationed credit according to their own whims in the past, and that deserving applicants had been turned away. However, the alternative interpretation is that, in a desire to build new loan books and to generate new business, the quality of the lending has been compromised. Access to affordable credit has become too easy and, in consequence, there has been a rise in the incidence of defaults and late payments.

do borrowers in rich countries always repay their debts?

In the mid- to late1990s, when the Asian financial crisis was raging, Russia had defaulted on its bonds, and Latin America was teetering on the brink, it seemed as though only low- and middle-income countries suffered from the blight of unpaid debts. When the Jubilee 2000 campaign was at its height, the rich countries opened their eyes—for a brief moment at least—to recognize the plight of highly indebted poor countries (HIPCs), and some valuable steps were taken to lighten these burdens.

However, over the past three or four years, debt default and delinquency have accelerated in the developed world.

Considering that the surge in corporate debt delinquency began when the developed world economy was still growing strongly, it is incorrect to blame the recent spate of corporate defaults and scandals on a downturn in the global economy. Nevertheless, a slowing economy is almost certain to aggravate credit quality problems for households, as unemployment rises, and for companies, as profitability suffers. While international organizations—like the IMF and OECD—are apt to take economic growth for granted when painting their scenarios, it is worth contemplating what will happen if the developed world slips into recession.

debt and delusion: the recent experience

Debt and Delusion, first published in 1999, warned about the dangerous expansion of debt in the world financial system and its likely consequences. It highlighted the inconsistency of central bank policies that suppressed the rate of inflation but failed to check the alarming growth of credit. Throughout the 1990s, central banks encouraged the development of a sophisticated infrastructure for financial markets without proper consideration of its implications for the overall stability of the system.

> *Despite the Basel Capital Accord of 1988 and its planned successor, central banks have effectively abdicated their role as guardians of the credit and financial system. They have retained a role as trouble-shooters and lifeboat providers, as shown in the rescue of Long Term Capital Management (LTCM) in 1998, but have lost the ability to influence the overall quality of private sector credit decisions. Their well-known commitment to preventing a financial collapse has had the perverse effect of emboldening risk-takers to take even larger risks. Enron is a case in point.*

In parallel to these developments, hedging and speculation in government bond markets and in their associated derivatives have contributed to large swings in the cost of risk capital. At times, the cost of corporate borrowing has been extraordinarily low, leading to excessive credit creation and poor investment decisions. The accumulation of excess capacity in the semi-conductor and fibre-optics industries, for example, was facilitated by an abundance of risk capital. Critically, the long-running inflation of the global stock market was a by-product of the global credit cycle. In 1999-2000, private sector financial asset prices exploded far beyond their sustainable values, creating the illusion of mass prosperity and inducing even more foolish borrowing based on the collateral of these temporary capital gains.

These arguments are sometimes countered with the view that those who lost heavily in technology and mobile phone investments were matched by others who sold out and realized their profits. While equity investments can be considered in this way, corporate bonds and venture capital cannot. At the time, the expenditures on additional, and now unneeded, economic capacity were expected to earn a return large enough to justify the original expenditure. When capacity is mothballed or destroyed prematurely, a large part of the original financial investment has been transformed into consumption. It is not available to be reinvested in another project or industry. When corporate bonds default, the typical recovery rate is only 20 to 30 per cent of the face value of the bond. The balance has been lost and must be written off on someone's balance sheet. When it is a bank that is forced to accept a loss, the bank's shareholders have lost some of their capital. They may well be called upon to subscribe to a new issue of shares in order to replenish the bank's capital resources.

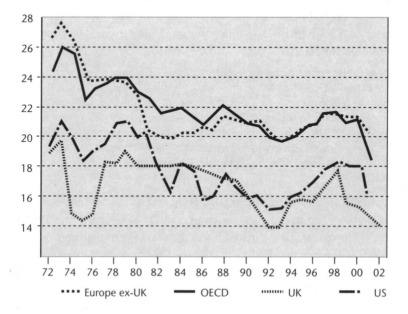

Figure 17.3 Gross national savings rate as a percentage of nominal GDP

Source: OECD Economic Outlook, volume 2002/2, no.72, December, Annex Table 25

An economy that suffers heavy financial losses in this way, as a result of the mis-allocation of capital, will discover that its scope to increase its productive capacity has diminished. Its national savings rate will have fallen, as it has done throughout the developed world since 2000 (see Figure 17.3). In order to rebuild the national savings rate, public or private consumption must be reduced for a temporary period. Otherwise, the decline in the savings ratio will render the economy incapable of replacing capital equipment and buildings when they wear out. The typical consequences of over-borrowing, capital wastage, and debt defaults are far-reaching and long lasting.

conclusions

Three years on from the peak of the global stock market, our debt perspectives are rather different. The house that debt built, with its innovative features and fancy derivatives, has fallen into disrepair and disrepute. There is a real danger that corporate and personal balance sheets have been damaged so badly as to cast the developed world, and thereby, most probably, the whole world, into a depression—a multi-year recession—where standard policy remedies are impotent.

The big mistake, in my view, was not the liberalization of the global economy, but the collective and personal enslavement to debt. An unwillingness to acknowledge the risks, as well as the rewards, of capital accumulation, has led to a highly distorted capital market and millions of deluded private investors. Through the late 1990s, the disciplining effects of losses and bankruptcies were suspended because of the ample opportunities for debt extension. The purging of bad debts from the credit system is a painful but essential phase in the development of the world's largest and richest nations. If nothing else, it should transform our attitudes to debt cancellation in the developing world.

further reading

Bank for International Settlements annual report available at www.bis.org/publ/arpdf/ar2002e.pdf.

Standard and Poor's website at www.standardandpoors.com.

Warburton, P. *Debt and Delusion* (London: Penguin Books, 1999).

World Bank *World Development Report 2003: Sustainable Development in a Dynamic World* available at http://econ.worldbank.org/wdr/wdr2003/.

references

[1] *Fact Sheet* on 'Bank Notes' from http://www.bankofengland.co.uk/banknotes/fact note.pdf.

CHAPTER 18

the dollar bill: who picks up the tab?[1]

michael hudson

By the early 1960s, it became clear that the United States was approaching the point at which its debts to foreign central banks would soon exceed the value of the Treasury's gold stock. This point was reached and passed in 1964, by which time the US payments deficit seemed to derive entirely from foreign military spending, mainly for the Vietnam War.

It would have required a change in national consciousness to reverse the military programs that had come to involve the United States in massive commitments abroad. The United States seemed to be succumbing to a European-style imperial syndrome, and was in danger of losing its dominant world position in much the way that Britain and other imperial powers had done, weighed down by the cost of maintaining its worldwide empire. And just as World Wars I and II had bankrupted Europe, so the Vietnam War threatened to bankrupt the United States.

If the United States had followed the creditor-oriented rules to which European governments had adhered after the two World Wars, it would have sacrificed its world position. Its gold would have flowed out and Americans would have been obliged to sell off their international investments to pay for military activities abroad. This was what the US officials had demanded of their allies in World Wars I and II, but the United States was unwilling to abide by such rules itself. Unlike earlier nations in a similar position, it continued to spend abroad, as well as at home, without regard for the balance-of-payments consequences. One result was a run on gold, whose attraction rose as America's military fortunes in Vietnam sagged. Foreign central banks, especially those of France and Germany, cashed in their surplus dollars for US gold reserves almost on a monthly basis.

Official reserves were sold to meet private demand and so hold down the price of gold. For a number of years, the United States had joined other governments to finance the London Gold Pool. But by March 1968, after a six-month run, America's gold stock fell to the $10 billion floor beyond which the

Treasury had let it be known that it would suspend further gold sales. The London Gold Pool was disbanded and informal agreement (diplomatic arm-twisting) was reached among the world's central banks to stop converting their dollar inflows into gold.

the creation of the dollar debt cycle

This broke the link between the dollar and the market price of gold. Two prices for gold emerged, a rising open-market price and the lower 'official' price of $35 an ounce at which the world's central banks continued to value their monetary reserves.

Three years later, in August 1971, President Nixon made the gold embargo official. The key-currency standard, based on the dollar's convertibility into gold, was dead. The US Treasury bill standard—that is, the dollar-debt standard based on dollar inconvertibility—was inaugurated. Instead of being able to use their dollars to buy American gold, foreign governments found themselves able to purchase only US Treasury obligations (and, to a much lesser extent, US corporate stocks and bonds).

As foreign central banks received dollars from their exporters and from commercial banks that preferred domestic currency, they had little choice but to lend these dollars to the US Government. Running a dollar surplus in their balance of payments became synonymous with lending this surplus to the US Treasury. The world's richest nation was enabled to borrow automatically from foreign central banks simply by running a payments deficit. The larger the US payments deficit grew, the more dollars ended up in foreign central banks, which then lent them to the US Government by investing them in Treasury obligations of varying degrees of liquidity and marketability.

The US federal budget moved deeper into deficit in response to the guns-and-butter economy, inflating a domestic spending stream that spilled over into spending on more imports and foreign investment and yet more foreign military spending to maintain the hegemonic system. But instead of US citizens and companies being taxed or US capital markets being obliged to finance the rising federal deficit, foreign economies were obliged to buy the new Treasury bonds being issued. America's Cold War spending thus became a tax on foreigners. It was their central banks who financed the costs of the war in South East Asia.

There was no real check to how far this circular flow could go. For understandable reasons, foreign central banks did not wish to go into the US stock market and buy Chrysler, Penn Central, or other corporate securities because this would have involved the kind of risk that central bankers are not supposed to take. Real estate was no more attractive. What central banks need are liquidity and security for their official reserves. This is why they had traditionally held gold as a means of settling their own deficits. To the extent that they began to accumulate surplus dollars, there was little alternative but to hold them in the form of US Treasury bills and notes without limit.

economic rules turned on their head

This shift from asset money (gold) to debt money (US Government bonds) inverted the traditional relationships between the balance of payments and domestic monetary adjustment. Thanks to the $50 billion cumulative US payments deficit between April 1968 and March 1973, foreign central banks found themselves obliged to buy all of the $50 billion increase in US federal debt during this period. In effect, the United States was financing its domestic budget deficit by running an international payments deficit. As the St. Louis Federal Reserve Bank described the situation, foreign central banks were obliged 'to acquire increasing amounts of dollars as they attempted to maintain relatively fixed parities in exchange rates'.[2] Failure to absorb these dollars would have led to the dollar's value to fall vis-à-vis foreign currencies, as the supply of dollars greatly exceeded the demand. A depreciating dollar would have provided US exporters with a competitive devaluation, and at the same time would have reduced the domestic currency value of foreign dollar holdings.

Foreign governments did not want to place their own exporters at a competitive disadvantage so they kept on buying dollars to support the exchange rate—and hence, the export prices—of Dollar Area economies. 'The greatly increased demand for short-term US Government securities by these foreign institutions resulted in lower market yields on these securities relative to other marketable securities than had previously been the case,' explained the St. Louis Federal Reserve Bank. 'This development occurred in spite of the large US Government deficits that prevailed in this period.' Thanks to the extraordinary demand by central banks for government dollar-debt instruments, yields on US Government bonds fell relative to those of corporate securities, which central banks did not buy.

This inverted the classical balance-of-payments adjustment mechanism, which for centuries had obliged nations to raise interest rates to attract foreign capital to finance their deficits. In America's case, it was the balance-of-payments deficit that supplied the 'foreign' capital, as foreign central banks recycled the dollar outflows—that is, their own dollar inflows—into Treasury securities. US interest rates fell precisely because of the balance-of-payments deficit, not in spite of it. The larger the balance-of-payments deficit, the more dollars foreign governments were obliged to invest in US Treasury securities, financing simultaneously the balance-of-payments deficit and the domestic federal budget deficit.

rest of the world finances america's boom

The stock and bond markets boomed as American banks and other investors moved out of government bonds into higher-yielding corporate bonds and mortgage loans, leaving the lower-yielding Treasury bonds for foreign governments to buy. US companies also began to buy up lucrative foreign businesses. The dollars they spent were turned over to foreign governments, which had little option but to reinvest them in US Treasury obligations at abnormally low interest rates. Foreign demand for these Treasury securities drove up their price, reducing their yields accordingly. This held down the US interest rates, spurring yet further capital outflows to Europe.

The US Government had little motivation to stop this dollar-debt spiral. It recognized that foreign central banks could hardly refuse to accept further dollars, lest the world monetary system break down. Not even Germany or the Allies had thought of making this threat in the 1920s or after World War II, and they were not prepared to do it in the 1960s and 1970s. It was generally felt that such a breakdown would hurt foreign countries more than the United States, thanks to the larger role played by foreign trade in their own economic life. US strategists recognized this, and insisted that US payments deficit was a foreign problem, not one for American citizens to worry about.

further reading

Hudson, M. *Super Imperialism: the origins and fundamentals of US world dominance* (London: Pluto Press, 2003)

references

[1] Extracted from Michael Hudson's book, *Super Imperialism*, published by Pluto Press http://www.plutobooks.com/.

[2] Federal Reserve Bank of St. Louis (1973) 'Interest Rates end Monetary Growth', *Review*, January. See also 'Will Capital Inflows Reduce Domestic Interest Rate Changes?' in *ibid*, July 1972.

the US economy: a changing strategic predicament[1]

wynne godley

introduction and summary

Right through the boom years prior to 2001, the US economy was facing a strategic predicament. The main engine of growth—credit-financed private expenditure—was unsustainable and it followed from this that the whole stance of fiscal policy would have to be radically changed if the New Economy was not to stagnate. The experience of the last two years has partially vindicated this view. The boom was indeed broken because, as predicted, private expenditure fell relative to income. And the potentially dire effects on the level of activity were mitigated by a transformation in the stance of fiscal policy, accompanied by a radical change in attitudes to budget deficits, which suddenly became respectable. The expansionary fiscal policy initiated by President Bush was reinforced by a further aggressive relaxation of monetary policy so that (real) short-term interest rates have fallen almost to zero, thereby giving the consumer boom a last gasp. Yet, with all this help, the recovery from the recession of 2001 has not been robust. Growth has generally been below that of productive potential and there is a widespread sense that all is not well.

This analysis argues that a new strategic predicament is on the horizon as a result of the exceptionally large and growing balance-of-payments deficit, to which the public discussion attaches very little importance. In testimony to Congress on the state of the economy on 11 February 2003,[2] Alan Greenspan, Chairman of the US Federal Reserve, made no reference whatever to the balance of payments. The models embodying the 'New Macroeconomics', which have suddenly become so influential,[3] do not even contain a foreign sector or any representation of stocks of foreign debt, which the United States is now rapidly accumulating. The Economic Report of the President[4] has a section on the balance of payments but considers that the deficit has no immediate policy implications, on the grounds that the cost of servicing the US net foreign liabilities is negligible.

The central argument of this essay can be simply stated. The primary balance of payments[5] in the fourth quarter of 2002 was equal to about 5 per cent of

GDP—easily a post-war record. If, as all official documents assume, the economy grows fast enough during the next six years to generate some reduction in unemployment, there is a presumption that the primary balance will deteriorate further, to at least 6.4 per cent. This would cause the US foreign debt to rise to nearly $8 trillion or 60 per cent of GDP. And if, as the ERP assumes, the stance of monetary policy reverts to neutral so that short-term interest rates rise to 4.3 per cent, the net flow of interest payments out of the country could well rise to $200-$300 billion a year, thereby raising the deficit in the overall balance of payments to about 8.5 per cent of GDP. As the private sector's financial deficit is likely to revert towards its usual state of surplus, it follows as a matter of accounting logic that the government would have to run a deficit at least as large as the balance-of-payments deficit—that is, the budget deficit would have to rise from some 3 per cent of GDP as now projected for 2003 to perhaps 9 to 10 per cent of GDP in 2007-2008. For a number of reasons this is not a credible scenario—if only because such a position would not itself be a stable one; the rate at which foreign debt would be accumulating would be such as to generate a further, accelerating, flow of interest payments out of the country, requiring even larger budget deficits in subsequent years.

The default conclusion is that the US economy will not recover properly in the medium term, but rather enter a prolonged period of 'growth recession'. The only lasting solution will be to get US exports to rise much faster than imports over a prolonged period. But how is this to be achieved? Whatever the politics of the matter, there was no *technical* obstacle to changing fiscal policy. But any policy to generate an adequate expansion of net export demand will likely encounter far more intractable obstacles.

more precisely

It is well known to students of the National Accounts that the surplus of private disposable income over expenditure is equal to the government balance (written as a deficit) plus the current balance of payments (written as a surplus).[6] While these balances are related to one another by a system of accounting identities each has, to some extent, a life of its own, which is reconciled with the other two via the aggregate income flow. The way the balances evolve provides a useful armature around which to organize a narrative account of economic developments, because any one of them is necessarily implied by the other two. Furthermore, the balances may give an early warning that unsustainable processes are taking place, for any high or rising balance implies a change in public, private, or foreign debts, which cannot grow without limit relative to income.

Figure 19.1 shows how the three financial balances have moved, relative to GDP, since 1960. Vertical lines mark the points at which the 1990s boom really started (at the beginning of 1992) and when it came to an end (in the third quarter of 2000).

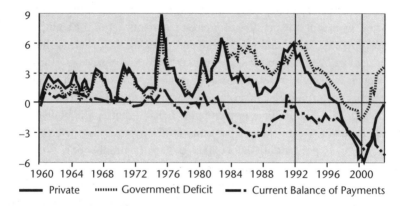

Figure 19.1 The three financial balances (percentages of GDP)

Source: The Levy Economics Institute

The figure shows how the configuration of balances during the 1990s was quite unlike anything that had happened before. It illustrates[7] how the boom took place despite strong contractionary forces from the government's fiscal stance and also from net export demand; and hence how the expansion of aggregate demand was driven by an unprecedented growth of private expenditure relative to income. By the end of the boom, private expenditure was far in excess of disposable income, an excess made possible by a huge accumulation of debt, both by the personal sector and by corporations. The turning point came in the second half of 2000, when (and because) private expenditure started to fall back relative to income. Deprived of what had been its motor during the previous eight years, the economy would have suffered a severe recession had the government not stepped in with a series of stimulatory fiscal packages. The private sector balance reverted towards its historical mean (a substantial surplus) but the pace at which this happened slowed down during 2002 because a reduction in interest rates, to levels not seen for 40 years, encouraged households to borrow huge sums of money and spend the proceeds. But disturbingly, the balance of payments continued its deterioration apace through 2001 and 2002, almost impervious to the brief recession and subsequent period of weak growth.

the new strategic problem

Figure 19.2 below does not contain a forecast. It shows what we believe to be the true implications of the growth path for the economy, which is mapped out in the Economic Report of the President and is designed to show what can't happen, rather than what will.

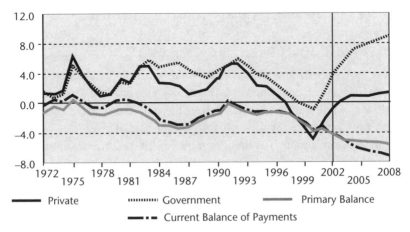

Figure 19.2 Financial balances, actual and projected

Source: The Levy Economics Institute

The assumptions underlying this chart are as follows. It is assumed, in line with the projections in the ERP, that the economy grows at an average rate of 3.3 per cent between now and 2008. This is the growth rate considered necessary to bring the unemployment rate down slightly from 5.7 to 5 per cent. With such a growth rate, we have taken the view that, provided there is no major devaluation of the dollar, the primary balance of payments will certainly not improve and will likely deteriorate, at least to some extent, over the next five or six years. We have aimed to be conservative in our assumptions. For example, the growth rate of 3.3 per cent is somewhat higher than that actually achieved during the past five years, which was 2.8 per cent, and the prospect for world growth outside the United States over the next six years seems, if anything, less favourable than during the past five. Japan is mired in a seemingly endless stagnation and Europe the victim of perverse rules governing fiscal policy; countries in the rest of the world, not merely Japan, but China, South East Asia, and Latin America all have an urgent need to expand their exports and many of them will be prepared to shade their prices in order

to raise their share of the large, open, and well organized market for manufactures in the United States.

To come down to it, we have assumed that the US primary deficit, having
risen by 3 percentage points (of GDP) during the last five years, will deteriorate
by a further 1.3 percentage points in the next five (notwithstanding the faster
growth rate). A small further decline thereafter takes it from 4.9 per cent at the
end of 2002 to 6 per cent at the end of 2007 and 6.4 per cent at the end of 2008.
Obviously the deterioration could be much greater than this.

the private sector

Figure 19.1 showed how the financial balance of the private sector moved,
during the boom, from its historically normal range of about 3 to 4 per cent of
GDP, to a wholly unprecedented minus 5.5 per cent of GDP in the third
quarter of 2000. Since then there has been a substantial reversion towards the
historical norm, although in the fourth quarter of 2002 it was still minus 1.1
per cent, implying that private expenditure at that point was still higher than
private income. We start with a general presumption that, looking to the
medium term, the private balance will continue to recover and eventually move
back into surplus. It helps to separate out the corporate and personal sectors.

The corporate sector has normally been in deficit, with outflows exceeding
income (gross of capital consumption) and therefore has normally been
dependent for funds on external borrowing. By this criterion, there has been
nothing unusual about the corporate experience during the whole period since
1992. Corporations increased their deficit by a large but not extraordinary
amount during the boom and reduced it (again by a large but not abnormal

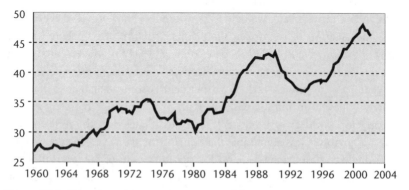

Figure 19.3 Corporate debt as a percentage of GDP

Source: The Levy Economics Institute

amount) in the subsequent slowdown. Nevertheless, corporate debt *levels* relative to GDP rose to record highs, as shown in Figure 19.3. This was at least partly because the corporate sector was borrowing to buy back equity; corporations taken as a whole have been net purchasers of equity presumably with the aim of maintaining share prices and financing stock options.

It was the behaviour of the personal sector, which has been truly exceptional. Figure 19.4 shows how, during the boom, the personal sector's financial balance[8] became negative to an unusual extent; and how, since the slow recovery in the economy began, the sector has remained in heavy deficit. Spending in recent quarters was below normal (relative to income) by an amount roughly equal to 5 per cent of GDP. Figure 19.4 also shows that personal expenditure has been financed throughout the last ten years by a rise in the flow of net lending, which continued right up to the third quarter of last year.

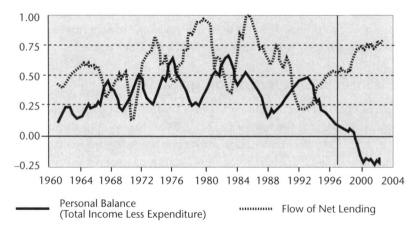

▬▬▬ Personal Balance (Total Income Less Expenditure)	┉┉┉┉ Flow of Net Lending

Figure 19.4 Personal financial balance and net lending (percentages of GDP)

Source: The Levy Economics Institute

The Fed has just published a comforting assessment of the present financial position of households,[9] which emphasizes that, with interest rates so low, the burden of debt service is generally quite tolerable. We have no quarrel with the Fed's assessment of the present position, but personal expenditure cannot be financed forever by a growing flow of net lending—that is by a continuing rise *in the rise* in debt. The drastic fall in interest rates and the extreme ease with which equity in houses can now be 'cashed out', has given a new lease of life to personal expenditure. But a rise of net lending cannot, by its very nature, be an abiding motor for growth of the economy; it can continue for a long time, but it cannot continue forever. Equity can be cashed out only for so long as it exists; the process is a once-and-for-all affair. At some stage, perhaps when interest rates increase, the growth of debt will slow down so that it rises no faster than income; and as that happens, the flow of net *lending* must fall from 10 per cent of disposable income at the last reading to perhaps 4 or 5 per cent, bringing a substantial check to the growth of personal expenditure relative to income and a corresponding reversion of the personal sector's financial balance towards its historical norm.

In making the projection of the balances shown in Figure 19.2, it has been assumed that, over the next few years, any return by the corporate sector to deficit will be more than offset by a significant recovery in the personal sector balance. Taking the private sector as a whole, we have assumed that the financial balance becomes slightly positive, rising to about 1 per cent of GDP between now and 2008, still far below its long-term average.

Is it conceivable (one must ask oneself) that the private sector will provide the motor for expansion by plunging deeply once again into deficit? This seems improbable if only because of the unusually high level of debt that has already been incurred both by corporations and by the personal sector.

an unprecedented drag on growth

There is no escape from the conclusion that, if the primary balance of payments reaches 6.5 per cent of GDP in 2008, if the overall balance reaches 8.5 per cent, and if the private deficit moves into moderate surplus, the general government deficit[10] must, by accounting identity, reach between 9 and 10 per cent of GDP—a story of twin deficits with a vengeance. Deficits in the balance of payments are usually feared because they have to be financed by external borrowing, which may not be forthcoming on acceptable terms, and because foreign debts have to be serviced. The argument put forward here is an entirely different one—that the developing balance-of-payments deficit is going to act as formidable drag on demand. The present haemorrhage from aggregate demand, at 5 per cent of GDP, is already far in excess of anything that has ever been experienced before (in modern times) though this is still being masked by the highly unusual private deficit, which is likely to go further into reverse. The rise in the government's deficit is no more than is needed to offset these negative forces.

growth recession and financial implosion?

Surely the government deficit cannot be allowed to reach 9 per cent of GDP with the corollary that government debt would increase by some 30 per cent of GDP compared with current levels? Surely insuperable obstacles would be encountered long before that point? Such a position would be highly unstable,[11] with foreign debt so high and rising so rapidly, that the economy could be kept going in later years only by ever larger injections from the public sector.

So what gives? In my view, the most likely outcome is simply that the US economy will not recover properly[12] but rather will enter a long, depressing era of 'growth recession' with increasing unemployment and the ever-present risk—with corporate and personal debt so high—of financial implosion.

The one antidote to this predicament is that exports provide the motor for sustained growth in the future; US exports must rise faster than imports by very large amounts and for a long period of time. The most congenial way to achieve this is for the rest of the world somehow to expand rapidly and spontaneously. Yet this, given present attitudes and institutions, is a hollow suggestion; it would be madness for the United States to base its economic strategy on the assumption that it will be hauled out of stagnation by others. Not merely is the rest of the world itself locked into stagnation; it is looking to the US economy to be the world's growth motor.

The classic remedy for chronic external balance is, of course, devaluation. It is not inconceivable that devaluation of the dollar will come to the rescue, but there is no obvious policy gesture that the US authorities can now take, with real short-term interest rates close to zero, which will bring this about on the huge scale necessary—even if this is what they wanted to do. Although the dollar has notoriously been weak against the euro in recent months, the more relevant 'broad' index of the dollar's value[13] has hardly fallen since the beginning of 2002. It seems that surplus countries (for example, Japan and China) are accumulating mountainous reserves, which they have been using to prevent any natural rebalancing process from taking place. It is unclear what, if any, limits there are to this process. And it is doubtful whether a fall in the dollar, however large, could in practise generate the required (enormous) rise in net exports given that the market is so stagnant.

The use by the United States of non-selective tariffs, conditionally under Article 12 of the WTO, should be mentioned. It is possible to imagine circumstances under which recourse to protective tariffs might be the only way in which the US strategic problem can be solved.

conclusion

This essay has identified a major strategic predicament for the US economy.[14] The most likely consequence of the massive and growing leak out of the circular flow of income will be, given present national and international policies, that there will be no proper recovery from the recent recession; and that this stagnation will eventually have grave consequences for the rest of the world, which has come to look to the United States to give it momentum. A number of solutions have been outlined, but none of them can be relied on and some of them carry serious disadvantages. At some stage, it will have to be recognized that a new world solution must be found.

further reading

Further papers by Professor Godley can be seen at http://www.levy.org/ and at www.cerf.cam.ac.uk.

references

[1] This essay is a shortened version of an essay by the same title published by the Levy Economics Institute, New York, USA, in February 2003. It is available on www.levy.org/does/stratan/stratped.html.

[2] Federal Reserve Board's semiannual monetary policy report to the Congress Before the Committee on Banking, Housing, and Urban Affairs, US Senate.

[3] See, for instance, B.S Bernanke and M. Gertler, 'Monetary policy and asset price volatility' in *New Challenges for Monetary Policy*, proceedings of the symposium sponsored by the Federal Reserve Bank of Kansas City, Jackson Hole, Wyoming (1999) p. 77–128.

[4] Council of Economic Advisers, *Economic Report of the President*, (Washington DC: USGPO, 2003) Chapter 1, (2003) p. 59–62.

[5] The primary balance of payments is defined as the overall balance less net payments abroad of interest, dividends and profits. It is equal to the balance of trade in goods and services plus net unilateral transfers.

[6] To spell it out, $Y = PX + G + X—IM$ where Y is GNP, G is government expenditure, X is exports including net income from abroad and IM is imports. Deducting taxes and government transfers, T, from both sides and rearranging we have the relevant identity $Y—T—PX = [G—T] + [X—IM]$.

[7] It illustrates but obviously does not prove any of these things; the diagram cannot distinguish between the effect of the budget on the economy and the effect of the economy on the budget—and so on. But a careful analysis of the causal factors at work confirms that the propositions which follow are correct.

[8] This differs from the conventional concept of personal saving in that income is defined gross of capital consumption and expenditure includes capital expenditure. If the personal sector's financial balance is negative, this necessarily implies that there is a net acquisition of debt or net realization (by the sector as a whole) of assets.

[9] Recent Changes in US Family Finances: Evidence from the 1998 and 2001 Survey of Consumer Finances.

[10] There are differences (definitions, timing and coverage) between the deficit of the general government which we are tracking here and that of the federal government, but these pale into insignificance given the huge figure we now tussle with.

[11] On the assumptions used, the situation is not formally unstable since real interest rates are below the growth rate. The foreign debt would eventually stabilize at about five times GDP and the balance-of-payments deficit at about 15 per cent—hardly an appetizing prospect.

[12] Assuming that geo-political developments do not give rise to military expenditure on a scale far larger than anything so far indicated.

[13] The Fed's broad trade weighted index, corrected for inflation.

[14] All the conclusions depend on the assumption that the official figures are broadly correct.

why financial markets misbehave

dani rodrik

Former US President Clinton's campaign manager, James Carville, famously quipped: 'I used to think if there was reincarnation, I wanted to come back as the President or the Pope or a .400 baseball hitter. But now I want to come back as the bond market. You can intimidate everyone.' What Carville had in mind, of course, was the constraint placed on economic policy by financial markets: the slightest departure from 'conservative' fiscal policies, and the markets apparently stood ready to heap punishment in the form of higher interest rates.

This may be something of a joke in the United States, but it is very serious business indeed in much of the developing world where financial markets have been freed up and the pursuit of 'market confidence' has become the *sine qua non* of public policy. Financial markets are quick to penalize any perceived mis-behaviour, whether current or in the future. During the summer and autumn of 2002, interest rates on Brazil's public debt climbed to punishing heights as left-wing presidential candidate Lula's fortunes in the polls rose. Investors were in effect telling the electorate: you have the vote, but we have the ability to crush the economy. Once elected, Lula was faced with a choice between exacerbating the financial crisis or outdoing the fiscal conservatism of his predecessor. He chose the latter.

the disproportionate power of the bond markets

It is easy to understand why government leaders act this way. Even small changes in market sentiment can result in large swings in interest rates, putting fiscal solvency in doubt. Consider an economy with a debt-to-GDP ratio of 60 per cent (roughly the level of Brazil's). At a reasonable real-interest rate of 5 per cent, the servicing cost of this debt is a non-negligible, but manageable, 3 per cent of GDP. When the real-interest rate rises to 20 per cent (as it did for a while in Brazil), the debt-servicing cost climbs to 12 per cent of GDP—an amount that is more than half of all tax revenues and vastly greater than public spending on health and education combined.

The cruel irony in this is that real-interest rates can be high for no other good reason than that they are expected to be high. There is always a level of interest rates at which debt service is too costly and hence default is likely. Expectations of default can be therefore purely self-fulfilling. This is the kind of logic that led John Maynard Keynes to despair about the functioning of financial markets and to the conclusion that the real economy cannot be safely entrusted to their whims and fancies. It is also the reason why the standard remedy of further fiscal tightening is so ineffective in these situations. In any democracy, a reduction in the budget of a couple of percentage points requires large amounts of political capital and difficult political manoeuvring. Yet movements in interest rates, which can be much larger, can, in no time, swamp the beneficial effects on debt sustainability. Furthermore, fiscal tightening has adverse effects on economic growth, threatening a downward spiral in economic activity as fiscal retrenchment chases after the ever-retreating goal of solvency.

financial liberalization backfires

It wasn't meant to be this way. The promise of financial liberalization was that it would lead to the mobilization of domestic savings, a more efficient allocation of investment funds, a flow of resources from rich to poor countries, and enhanced discipline on government behaviour. None of these expectations have materialized. Savings, investment, and productivity growth rates have all been lower in Latin America during the 1990s than in the days before free finance. Net private capital inflows (excluding foreign direct investment) have exhibited boom-and-bust cycles rather than a sustained upwards trajectory. As for market discipline, its quality has left much to be desired. During the boom phase of the cycle, access to international capital flows has facilitated rather than constrained spending binges. During the bust phase, the reversals in capital flows have been unnecessarily drastic and costly.

For countries that haven't yet unleashed the financial market genie out of the bottle, such as India and China, the implication is clear: Don't do it. Today's advanced countries have learned through painful experience that financial markets need to be reined in by high-quality regulatory institutions that moderate these markets' excesses. Poor countries are not yet there, and will not get there until they are significantly richer. Economic development requires finance, but not free finance. None of the success stories of the past 40 years—South Korea and Taiwan since the 1960s, or China since 1978—were based on financial liberalization early on.

how best to erect defences against the market

For countries that have already opened up their financial markets, the implications are less obvious and depend on circumstances. Countries that have low debt and are not already entangled in the financial confidence game have to institute precautionary regulations to guard against excessive inflows and debt cycles. But those that are not in this comfortable position (like so many in Latin America) must seriously consider the costs and benefits of stumbling along under the existing rules versus making a clean break. The latter would involve an extensive restructuring of public debt accompanied by capital controls and other regulatory measures to reduce financial integration.

The clean slate approach has many costs. It would be inherently messy, as it is very difficult to insulate the domestic financial system from the consequences of default on foreign liabilities. On the other hand, the net benefits of the 'business-as-usual' strategy are quite unclear as well. Under current rules of good behaviour, these countries are effectively precluded from taking on additional debt anyhow—removing the main benefit of financial integration even if one assumes that capital flows will revive soon. Many of them are engaged in highly costly self-insurance efforts, which would not be necessary if there were reduced financial openness. For example, a common strategy is to build up official foreign reserves as insurance against reversals in capital flows. However, this entails exchanging low-yielding US Treasury securities for high-cost debt—a boon for the US Treasury but a rotten deal for the home economy.

Debt restructuring is not a growth strategy; it is at best a mechanism for making room for such a strategy. Countries that articulate credible growth strategies are likely to find themselves the recipients of capital inflows even if they buck the trend of financial openness. Capital markets, unlike academics or policy advisors, do not mind eating their words as long as there is money to be made in doing so. When Malaysia imposed controls on capital outflows in late 1998, the country was written off by financial markets and the IMF. But when the Malaysian economy recovered swiftly, against market expectations, foreign investors were happy to flock back in. So the good news is that putting the real economy ahead of the financial sector may be good not just for the former, but for the latter as well.

further reading

Krugman, P. 'The Confidence Game' *The New Republic*, 5 October (1998).

Ocampo, J.A. *International Financial Reform: The Broad Agenda* (Santiago, Chile: ECLAC, 1999).

Rodrik. D. 'Governing the World Economy: Does One Architectural Style Fit All?' in S. Collins and R. Lawrence (eds) *Brookings Trade Forum: 1999* (Washington, DC: Brookings Institution, 2000).

CHAPTER 21

globalizing money: dollarization in latin america

franklin serrano

Dollarization means the use of the US dollar instead of the locally issued currency to perform some or all functions of money. A process of dollarization can be informal if people simply increasingly start using the dollar as money. Official dollarization, our concern here, occurs when the government of the country in question allows (or requires) by law that the public use the dollar instead of the local currency.

Official dollarization takes various forms. It can mean no more than the legal permission to make transactions and hold deposits denominated in dollars, co-existing with the local currency that still fulfils all of its traditional roles. It can mean that the government decides that it will only issue the local currency to the extent that it is backed with its dollar reserves and thus sets up what is known as a currency board system. Or it can mean that the dollar legally becomes the official currency used in the country, effectively replacing the domestic currency altogether.

Official dollarization has historically been uncommon in Latin America except for some small (*de jure or de facto*) colonies and protectorates. However, since the early 1990s, some independent countries have dollarized. For many decades, Panama, Puerto Rico, and the Virgin Islands have used the dollar as currency and Bermuda and the Cayman Islands have had dollar-based currency boards. From 1991 to early 2002, Argentina operated a dollar-based currency board. In 2000, Ecuador made the dollar its official currency, followed in 2001 by El Salvador. In that same year, Guatemala allowed the dollar to circulate in parallel with the local quetzal.

where are the benefits of dollarization?

The main (and arguably the only) benefit of dollarization is that it tends to bring low rates of inflation. Since, by definition, the dollarized country ceases to be able to devalue its exchange rate relative to the dollar, foreign competition prevents local producers from raising local prices in the sectors of the economy exposed to foreign trade (the tradable sector) much faster than they are increasing in the United States.

Most advocates of dollarization claim that it will bring many other benefits such as a decrease in the country's sovereign risk (the risk that a country will default on its external debt), elimination of balance-of-payments crises, budgetary discipline (since the government cannot print money to pay for its expenses), and, when coupled with a full opening of the financial sector to foreign capital, increased efficiency of the local banking system.[1]

In reality, dollarization for an independent country usually does not bring any of these extra benefits and entails very high costs in terms of low and unstable economic growth and a substantial weakening of the power of the state to manage the economy. Under dollarization, inflation tends to fall to very low levels but only with a considerable lag, especially due to increases in the prices of the sectors that are not easily subjected to foreign competition, including certain parts of agriculture and industry and most non-financial services and utilities. As a consequence, the costs of domestic products increase substantially relative to imports and exports lose competitiveness. This tends to bring about slow growth of exports and high growth of imports, increasing current account deficits that have to be financed through external debt.

Dollarization thus tends to worsen the balance-of-payments position of the country while at the same time removing the instruments that the government could use to mitigate it, as the dollarized country cannot change the exchange rate to improve the competitiveness of exports and discourage imports.

the loss of economic policy independence

Under dollarization, the local government suffers serious constraints on its ability to pursue stabilizing fiscal and monetary policies. Since the central bank cannot print dollars, it ceases to be able to play the role of 'lender of last resort' of the local banks when these face liquidity problems. This often leads to bank runs when depositors suspect the banks will not have enough dollars in their safes.

The government loses the ability to finance a budget deficit by issuing money (something that in a recession has no inflationary impact) and it also becomes much more difficult to finance fiscal deficits by borrowing. A government that prints its own money is an agent whose debt has zero internal default risk since it cannot possibly involuntarily run out of (its own) money. It is this special status that makes the central bank able to control the basic interest rate of the economy. Under dollarization, the government becomes a debtor that can go broke like any other and thus loses the ability to control the interest rate it pays on its internal debt.

Moreover, since the government in a dollarized country needs to borrow dollars even to pay domestic expenses, such as public sector salaries, help to troubled local banks, or the electricity bill of a school, government deficits tend to be increasingly financed by an increase in the public external debt.

These tendencies for the public and private external debt to rise sooner or later leads to an increase in sovereign risk and of the rate of interest the country has to pay on its external debt. The difficulties in servicing the external debt and paying for imports then tend to force the government to pursue contractionary credit and fiscal policies that slow growth and generate unemployment and that creates a vicious cycle. Fiscal problems are aggravated because slow growth or recession cuts tax revenues and often requires increased social spending. This leads the government to have to borrow more dollars, which worsens the situation and leads to a further dose of fiscal contraction. The bargaining position of both private and public sector workers is eroded, leading to nominal- (and real-) wage cuts and the only group that really benefits is the local financial sector.

argentina—proof imperfect

Over time these imbalances are unsustainable and, unless the country receives foreign exchange injections from multilateral organizations or the US government, the experiment with dollarization ends up provoking an internal and external financial crisis. This is precisely what happened in Argentina in early 2002 when the level of output fell 11 per cent and inflation shot up to 40.6 per cent per year.[2] Ecuador seems to be going along the same route. Inflation fell from 91 per cent in 2000 to 9.7 per cent in 2002 but, on the other hand, its current account surplus of $916 million in 2000 quickly turned to a deficit of $1703 million in 2002. Even in a country like Panama, dollarization has only worked with continuous support from outside: since 1973, Panama had no less than 17 IMF adjustment programmes.[3]

The folly of dollarization is that it tends to be adopted in countries that suffer from a chronic shortage of dollars due to weak structural competitiveness. All that dollarization does is to increase dramatically the local *demand* for dollars (since dollars are used for a large number of purposes besides the usual one of paying for the necessary imports), while doing nothing to increase the *supply* of dollars.

In recent Latin American experience, there have been two different motivations for dollarization. In the case of highly externally indebted economies such as Argentina and Ecuador, which have recently been through traumatic episodes of very high inflation, dollarization was seen as a solution to control inflation by any means.[4] Then, there are smaller Central American economies such as El Salvador and Guatemala that did not necessarily have a particular problem with inflation but which opted for dollarization because they were becoming increasingly integrated with the United States through trade, remittances from émigrés, and financial transactions. These are independent countries whose ruling elites seem to want to turn into some sort of protectorate of the United States in the context of fuller economic integration through the Free Trade Area of the Americas. In these cases, the loss of sovereignty and policy autonomy and the weakening of the State seem not just to be unwelcome by-products of a misguided policy but sadly the very purpose of the dollarization. For the same reason, because of NAFTA, more discussion in favour of the dollarization of Mexico is to be expected in the near future. The prospect for the region, if this policy spreads, is even more economic instability and hardship.

further reading

Calcagno, A. and S. Manuelito, 'Argentine convertibility: is it a relevant precedent for the dollarization process in Ecuador?' *Estudos Estadísticos y Prospectivos* (Chile: Economic Commission for Latin America, 2001).

Edwards, S. 'Dollarization and economic performance: an empirical investigation', *NBER Working Papers*, (Cambridge, Mass: National Bureau of Economic Research, 2001).

O'Connell, A. 'The recent crisis of the Argentine economy: some elements and backgrounds', presented at the *METU Conference*, Ankara, Turkey (2002).

Schuler, K. 'The basics of dollarization', *Joint Economic Committee Staff Report US, Congress* (2000).

references

[1] See K. Schuler 'The basics of dollarization' (2000) for these (and a few other) claims.

[2] For a thorough analysis of the Argentinean experience see A. O'Connell, 'The recent crisis of the Argentine economy: some elements and backgrounds' (2002).

[3] For a critical assessment of the case of Panama see S. Edwards, 'Dollarization and economic performance: an empirical investigation', *NBER Working Papers*, (2001).

[4] For a critical comparative analysis of the Argentinean and Ecuadorean cases see A. Calcagno & S. Manoelito, 'Argentine convertibility: is it a relevant precedent for the dollarization process in Ecuador?' *Estudos Estadisticos y Prospectiuos*, (2001).

localizing money: alternative currencies

david boyle

Singapore and Hong Kong, which are oddities today, have their own currencies and so they possess . . . built-in advantage. They have no need of tariffs or export subsidies. Their currencies serve those functions when needed, but only as long as needed. Detroit, on the other hand, has no such advantage. When its export work first began to decline it got no feedback, so Detroit merely declined, uncorrected. Jane Jacobs, *Cities and the Wealth of Nations*

Currencies are, among other things, measuring systems. We live in a world of big currencies that are designed to measure the value of companies, corporate or national risk, and occasionally the people who work there, with minute accuracy, from moment to moment. But they just don't measure these very well.

They are information systems that respond to the values that Wall Street and the City of London feel are important, but they don't measure—or circulate—nearly so well when it comes to people, places, or things that the global finance system doesn't have at the forefront of its mind. One of the tragedies of the modern world is that an increasing amount of its component parts—notably its people—do indeed fall into the category that escapes the attention span of finance. Euros, dollars, and pounds do not measure very well—and therefore protect the interests of—for example, manufacturing areas or poorer suburbs or economically outlying regions or subsistence farmers or agricultural commodities. As far as the big currencies are concerned, these are all infinite resources. The same goes for those aspects of modern economies that are known as social capital—the trust, know-how, and care embedded in neighbourhoods that make them work.

The result of this is that these vital people and places are forgotten economically. They are discounted, sidelined, and finally driven out. Big currencies are often massive engines of monoculture. They don't deal very well with diversity. Yet those marginalized places may have everything they need for success—people who want to work, people who need jobs done, raw materials that can be put to use—except the cash they need to bring them all together. The banks won't create it for them, and the investment money may prefer to shoot down the wires to the City or Wall Street to frolic among the hedge funds or dot.coms or whatever clever scheme is in vogue at the time.

One solution may be to find ways of introducing new kinds of currency that measure differently because they circulate locally, or just in the required sector. Creating one's own currency has a long and honourable tradition. It wasn't until the 12th or 13th century that kings tried to get control of all the money. Even after these times, tea and tobacco have been traditional currencies. Modern electronic barter currencies like trade dollars are now used by two out of three of the Fortune 500 companies—and for exactly the same reason. The big currencies do not value some of their assets: toothpaste in last year's colours, excess stock, 486 computers, airline seats or hotel rooms on specific dates that are coming up rather soon. They can't sell those for dollars, but they can for trade dollars.

If large corporations can do it, why should impoverished towns and communities wait helplessly around for governments to rescue them, when they know perfectly well they won't and when they may have all the necessities they need locally? They can issue their own money and start using their own assets more efficiently.

In fact, there are plenty of examples that prove this phenomenon is already beginning to emerge:

1. There are getting on for 1000 time banks or time dollar systems in the United Kingdom, United States, and Japan, which measure and reward people for their efforts in the local community using an electronic points system (www.timedollar.org).

2. The town of Ithaca in upstate New York prints its own money, accepted in a third of local businesses, which keeps money and spending power circulating locally. Nearly 100 other towns or regions in North America are following suit (www.ithacahours.org).

3. The latest loyalty card from Boots has space on it for more than 20 different loyalty currencies. Until recently, Northwest Airlines used to pay its entire worldwide PR account in frequent flyer points.

4. The Swiss parallel currency Wir now has an annual turnover equivalent to $12 billion, providing low-cost finance mainly in the restaurant and building trade.

5. There are at least 5000 LETS- and SEL-style local currencies providing mutual credit in local currencies all over the world, including the Global Barter Clubs in Argentina, which have more than one million members

and are struggling to survive because the demand on them for basic needs is so strong.

6. Many of the local government bodies of Argentina have launched printed notes and bonds to serve as currency but, unfortunately, many of them without the necessary backing to survive long-term.

7. In Rotterdam and Curitiba in Brazil, electronic credits are used to pay people for recycling, which they can spend on the buses, so imaginatively using spare capacity in public transport to clean up the city.

8. There are plans to launch a new currency for London based on the 'community way' model that has been successfully tested in Canada (www.openmoney.org).

Whether these new currencies should be local, regional, or sectoral, and whether they should be fiat currencies, mutual credit, or underpinned by the value of some local product, depends entirely on the local circumstances. But they do provide a potential way out of complete dependency on global currencies, and they can provide the basic liquidity any community requires to sustain life.

further reading

Boyle, D. *The Money Changers: currency reform from Aristotle to e-cash* (London: Earthscan, 2002).

Greco, T. *Money* (Vermont: Chelsea Green, 2002).

Lietaer, B. *The Future of Money* (London: Century, 2001).

financial architecture in the 20th century

ann pettifor

The virtue of the free flow of international capital is normally presented as a self-evident truth. In reality, this 'liberalization' effected under Margaret Thatcher and Ronald Reagan is only one of a series of resolutions of a complex and still unsolved debate over the structure of international finance.

At the turn of the 20th century, the *gold standard* was the self-evident truth of the day. Capital markets were dominant, and free to invest where they saw fit. To protect the value of financial assets invested in the 'emerging markets' of that time (countries like South Africa, India, Argentina, and Brazil) governments of these countries were obliged to maintain the value of their currencies relative to gold. In other words, the economy (in particular the currency and domestic interest rates) was oriented towards the interests of foreign creditors, via 'exchange rate stability'. Capital markets expected central banks to be independent of government, and so it was central bankers who maintained exchange rate stability via the all too familiar means of manipulating short-term interest rates. As a global system, the gold standard lasted about 30 years.

the breaking of the gold standard

However, the gold standard system buckled when war imposed extreme financial pressures on governments. In 1917, the British were forced to suspend their commitment to exchange sterling for gold. However, even before World War I drew to a close, committees of bankers and their allies from academia and the Civil Service were drawing up plans for an immediate return to gold, but this time important and informed voices were raised in protest. In Europe, the first was that of Reginald McKenna, the Liberal Chancellor of the Exchequer throughout the first coalition British Government from May 1915 to December 1916 and subsequently Chairman of Midland Bank. The second was economist John Maynard Keynes, already famous through his bitter opposition to the Treaty of Versailles in the *Economic Consequences of the Peace*. Both argued that developments in national banking systems meant that the gold standard was no longer relevant—Keynes called it a 'barbarous relic'. Both argued that central banks should instead 'manage' domestic exchange rates through buying and selling currency between a fixed and pre-announced range of exchange parities, rather than supporting a single fixed rate through interest rate manipulations. Such arrangements required controls over capital.

While the Chancellor of the Exchequer Winston Churchill gave sympathetic hearing to their views, the overwhelming force of the financial establishment's pressure for maintenance of the gold standard could not be resisted. On 20 March 1925, Churchill announced his intention to take sterling back onto gold. Four and a half years later, the Wall Street Crash marked the start of the Great Depression.

financial establishment versus the people

For everybody that lived through it, the Great Depression was irrefutable proof that the preferred policy and interests of the financial establishment were very much opposed to the interests of society at large. As the British Labour Party's 1944 policy document *Full Employment and Financial Policy* emphasizes: 'Blame for unemployment lies much more with finance than with industry. Mass unemployment is never the fault of the workers; often it is not the fault of the employers. All widespread trade depressions in modern times have financial causes, successive inflation and deflation, obstinate adherence to the gold standard, reckless speculation, and over-investment in particular industries.'

On 21 September 1931, Britain again suspended its membership. The following Sunday, Keynes wrote: 'There are few Englishmen who do not rejoice at the breaking of our golden fetters.' He was immediately co-opted into an advisory role to the Prime Minister, and shortly afterwards the new National Government took the advice Keynes and McKenna had been giving all along. The Budget of April 1932 announced the institution of the 'Exchange Equalization Account' to manage the sterling exchange. This arrangement included capital control, administered through approval of applications for foreign currency.

While the UK economy was gradually restored to life, on the international stage most other countries attempted to cling to gold whatever the cost in unemployment, committing deeds that Keynes later described as 'crucifying their countries in a struggle which is certain to prove futile'. However, on 20 April 1933, the newly elected Franklin Delano Roosevelt took the United States off gold. Keynes soon offered advice on the stabilization of dollar exchange policy, advice that Roosevelt accepted. At this point, the world was split between a 'gold block' and a 'managed block' led by the British Empire and the United States. The tensions reached their peak on 3 July 1933 at the World Economic Conference, called to bring order to international finance. Roosevelt firmly and famously rejected a proposal for the worldwide re-establishment of the gold standard, which he said, reflected the 'old fetishes of so-called international bankers'. The following day, Keynes responded in the *Daily Mail*, under the banner 'President Roosevelt is magnificently right'.

The final collapse of the gold block began on 26 September 1936, when the newly elected Leon Blum took France off gold. Non-gold countries all adopted exchange equalization type arrangements including capital control, and were brought close together through the US, British, and French Governments' 'Tripartite Agreement' to aid each other with the management of their exchanges. Over the next months, Switzerland, The Netherlands, Greece, Latvia, and Turkey extended the membership of the new system.

a proposed international clearing union

World War II interrupted the evolution of this architecture, but provided policy-makers with an opportunity to approach the global financial architecture problem as a whole. Nobody saw this more clearly than Roosevelt, who, in turn, encouraged Keynes to develop a 'free, fertile economic policy for the post-war world excluding nothing in advance'.[1] The result was his plan for an international 'Clearing Union', published as a British Government Command Paper on 7 April 1943.

But the world was not ready to go so far. The Bretton Woods Agreement was essentially a compromise policy between the British and the Americans. Nevertheless, while a compromise, the Bretton Woods agreement preserved the one feature that Keynes thought essential to prosperity: 'In my view the whole management of the domestic economy depends upon being free to have the appropriate rate of interest without reference to the rates prevailing elsewhere in the world. Capital control is a corollary to this.'

Bretton Woods was unable to tolerate the exchange rate pressures created as a consequence of the Vietnam War. With 'globalization', the capital controls Keynes saw as so essential to preserving monetary policy autonomy were abandoned. The cost to prosperity is evident in most of the developing world; it is now increasingly so in the developed world itself.

references

[1] D. Moggridge (ed), *The Collected Writings of John Maynard Keynes*, Volume XIII, (London: Macmillan Press Ltd, 1973) p.228.

financial architecture in the 21st century?

jane d'arista

As the crises that erupted in the mid-1990s spread from Mexico to Asia, to Russia, and back to Latin America, the need for a new 'international financial architecture' became a frequent subject for discussion among a wide spectrum of academics and policy-makers. However, most proposals that emerged offered changes in the current system but failed to question its underlying structure. None addressed the most basic component of any international system: how do the citizens of one country pay for the goods or financial assets they buy from another country? Are there rules that decide how these payments are made? If so, what are the rules and how do they work?

What might be reasonable objectives and institutional structures for an international monetary system in the 21st century? Which currency regime would be consistent with keeping international trade and investment open to all nations on equal terms? One objective that should be explored is the possibility of creating a system in which all currencies could be used in international as well as domestic transactions, regardless of the size of the economies in which they are issued. Equally important, the governing institutions in a new, more egalitarian system must be designed to give equal weight to both population and economic output in the decision-making process. And the international reserve asset itself must respond to the need for inclusiveness: its value must be based on a trade-weighted basket of currencies of all member countries.

dollar dominance in the post-war world

The international monetary systems in use over the past two centuries have been constructed out of the failures of the systems that preceded them. The agreement to make international payments in gold—the gold standard so widely accepted in the 19th century—was finally abandoned in the 1930s as depression, deflation, and looming hostilities forced countries to horde their limited supplies of gold. During the war that followed, the United States and the United Kingdom created a new system—the gold/dollar exchange standard—that gave the US dollar a central role in the post-World War II world. Under this new (Bretton Woods) agreement, all countries other than the United States were encouraged to hold dollars as reserves and use them in trade, while the United States was committed to exchange dollars for gold at a fixed rate of $35 an ounce.

The design of the Bretton Woods monetary agreement was appropriate for the hegemonic role the United States had to play in a war-ruined world. With 60 per cent of the world's output and most of its gold, only the United States could supply both the goods and the financial liquidity needed for reconstruction. Using the dollar as the primary international currency made it possible to revive trade among all nations and facilitated US efforts to rebuild other national economies by making grants of unprecedented size—2 per cent of its GDP annually for five years—under the Marshall Plan.

However, as the rapid recovery of Europe and Japan revived a more balanced distribution of economic strength, the dollar shortage of the 1950s turned into a dollar glut by the 1960s. Excess dollars held abroad were being cashed in for gold and US gold stocks were dwindling. In 1971, the United States unilaterally ended the Bretton Woods monetary agreement when President Richard Nixon 'closed' the gold window, declaring that the United States would no longer exchange dollars for gold.

This decision ushered in a new international monetary system—one in which international payments would be made by private banks in the national currencies of the so-called 'strong' currency industrial countries rather than exchanges of gold by central banks. Moreover, the value of the dollar—the currency used for most of these transactions—would no longer be fixed in relation to gold. Its value would 'float' in response to changes in the supply and demand for dollars.

Since 1973, the dollar has had its ups and downs: a substantial fall at the end of the 1970s, a big rise beginning in 1983, an engineered decline after 1985, and a period of steady strength from 1994 until 2002. By the 1990s, however, the dollar's dominant role in the global economy was unchallenged. Measures of that dominance included the rising amount of dollar debt owed both to foreign and domestic creditors by borrowers in countries other than the United States, the share of dollar assets in international reserve holdings, the amount of US currency held and exchanged outside the United States by residents of other countries, the impact of changes in US interest rates, and the value of the dollar on developments in other economies around the world.

dollar dependency and the pressure to export

The product of little thought or planning, the current international monetary system has had important consequences for the global economy. It has been the driving force behind the export-led growth paradigm that has elevated trade surpluses to priority status as an objective of economic policy in all countries except for the one that can always pay for imports and foreign investments in its own currency. Most countries cannot, not least because, until recently, all OPEC countries demanded that oil be paid for in dollars. Non-dollar countries must 'earn' the dollars they cannot issue in their own economies by exporting more than they import. Moreover, if they are emerging economies that need to attract investment from abroad to finance development, they must borrow in dollars or other strong currencies—not in the money issued and earned at home. But if they have borrowed in dollars, their need to export intensifies, as they must acquire dollars both to pay for imports and to service debt.

Using strong currencies channeled through private financial institutions to fund development has been a major cause of the financial crises that have plagued emerging economies and the global financial system since the 1980s. In many cases, the evidence already strongly suggests, the build-up in debt and the share of export earnings required to service it ultimately reverse the faster rates of growth that borrowing initially produced. Moreover, capital inflows can themselves cause one of the problems—exchange rate appreciation followed by a rising trade deficit—that induce foreign investors to flee. And when capital outflows occur, the falling exchange rate increases the value of debts denominated in strong currencies and reduces the value of all the real and financial assets denominated in the home currency.

To protect themselves against these recurring events, emerging economies have been urged to build up their stocks of foreign exchange reserves and they have done so. From 1990 through 2000, total foreign exchange reserves grew by 142 per cent and dollar reserves by 236 per cent. Most of the increase was in the reserves of emerging economies (up 268 per cent) and their share of the total rose from 39 to 60 per cent over the decade. But this constituted an immense and expanding transfer of wealth out of these economies, as they invested their foreign exchange earnings in United States' and other strong currency countries' financial assets.

Such a system appears to confer significant advantages on those countries that issue currencies used by others in international transactions. As other countries invest their international reserves in credit instruments (government securities, bank deposits, and so on) issued in strong currency countries, their investments augment domestic savings, increase the availability of credit, and allow residents of a reserve-currency country to spend more and save less. However, the steady stream of capital inflows into a country that issues a reserve currency can only continue if that country remains willing to run the trade deficits that allow other countries to earn its currency.

america sucks in global savings

Throughout the 1990s, the dollar's role as a reserve currency had the effect of transferring a substantial amount of global savings to the United States. By the end of 2001, dollar reserves held in the United States constituted a stock of loans to the Treasury and private borrowers equal to 10 per cent of US GDP. Moreover, gross liabilities to all foreigners ($9.2 trillion) had risen to 90 per cent of GDP and net liabilities ($2.3 trillion) to 23 per cent. But the red ink was rising on the other side of the US balance-of-payments ledger, with annual trade deficits approaching 5 per cent of GDP. Clearly, the US economy's ability to absorb such substantial shares of both the world's goods and savings undermined traditional mercantilist expectations. Not only had the primary reserve-currency country become the world's largest nominal debtor, it had become richer as a net importer than the major net exporting economies among its trading partners.

Now, however, growing US indebtedness has raised new concerns about the sustainability of its trade deficit and how a shift away from the dollar would affect the global economy. So far, the discussion has not led to calls for reform, partly because of a widespread assumption that, after a period of financial and economic turmoil, the euro will replace the dollar and a modified version of the current system will continue.

But Europe is unlikely to assume the US role of importer of last resort and, unless the primary reserve currency country (or area) is willing to run the trade deficits that provide the opportunity for other countries to earn its currency, a continuation of the international monetary system based on national currencies will not even achieve lift-off. Within the current decade, it will either be replaced by conscious planning or transformed by the effort to adapt to the ever-larger crises that will impact industrial as well as emerging economies.

keynes and his international clearing agency

One way to achieve a rational replacement for the current system is to revive John Maynard Keynes' international clearing agency (ICA) concept as a basic structure for a new global payments system. For example, an importer in country A would pay for machinery from country B by writing a cheque on his bank account in his own currency. The seller in country B would deposit the cheque in his bank and receive credit in his own currency at the current rate of exchange between the two currencies. This would be possible because of the existence of an international clearing process that would route the cheque from the commercial bank to the central bank in country B and from there to the international clearing agency.

At the end of the day, the ICA would net all cheques exchanged between the two countries and pay the difference by debiting or crediting their reserve accounts. Meanwhile, the individual cheques would be returned to the countries of origin and paid in a similar fashion. In this example, the central bank would debit the reserve account of the bank in country A on which the cheque was written and the bank would deduct that amount from the buyer's account.

The process is simple but it does imply certain rules. It would require that all commercial banks receiving foreign payments exchange them for domestic currency deposits with their central banks. The central banks, in turn, would be required to deposit all foreign payments with the ICA. The result would be that all international reserves would be held by the ICA and that the process of debiting and crediting payments against countries' reserve accounts would provide the means for determining changes in exchange rates. As in national systems where the level of required reserves is determined at weekly or bi-weekly intervals, such a structure would greatly reduce the exchange rate volatility that currently plagues the system.

building an egalitarian monetary system

But it could do even more. If, like national central banks, the ICA held the government securities of its member countries as backing for international reserves, it could create liquidity by buying a country's securities and adding to its reserve holdings. By creating a true lender of last resort to replace the current ad hoc facilities that depend on taxpayer donations, the ICA would be able to contain damaging crises and maintain the financial stability needed for balanced growth in the global economy.

Although the ICA is only one possible means to address the flaws in the current system, it incorporates the still-valid objectives of the Bretton Woods agreement for an open international trading system while reforming the institutional framework to promote more egalitarian participation by all countries in the global economy. I offer it in the hope of focusing attention on the need for reform as the world's economies continue to slide into slower growth.

further reading

Blecker, R. A. *Taming Global Finance: A Better Architecture for Growth and Equity.* (Washington, DC: Economic Policy Institute, 1999).

Dam, K. W. *The Rules of the Game: Reform and Evolution in the International Monetary System.* (Chicago: University of Chicago Press, 1982).

D'Arista, J. *Reforming the Privatized International Monetary and Financial Architecture.* (Philomont, VA: Financial Markets Center, 1999) available at www.fmcenter.org.

Eichengreen, B. *Toward a new International Financial Architecture.* (Washington, DC: Institute for International Economics, 1999).

Helleiner, E. *The Making of National Money: Territorial Currencies in Historical Perspectives* (Ithaca, NY: Cornell University Press, 2003).

PART 05

new era?

framework for economic justice and sustainability

ann pettifor and romilly greenhill

This, the first edition of *Real World Economic Outlook*, has focussed on asset prices, on consumer prices, on debts, on global markets, on fossil fuel addiction—in short on economic and environmental phenomena. We have noted that economic 'shocks'—poverty, environmental degradation, debt-deflation—will inevitably cause feelings of anger, frustration, and powerlessness in people, communities, and states. When investors watch helplessly as their expensive assets collapse in value, when the elderly are made vulnerable by pension poverty, when families are evicted from their homes because of spiralling debts, and when no democratic institution appears responsible—then extreme reactions will invariably take root. 'Politics hates a vacuum. If it isn't filled with hope, someone will fill it with fear.'[1] We are already witnessing this phenomenon in the rise of fascist or racist parties in Europe and in the surge of US nationalism, Islamic fundamentalism, and anti-Semitism.

As we go to press, personal and corporate bankruptcies are accelerating in Western economies. Debt-deflation is no longer a theoretical phenomenon, but a reality.

The implications of a debt-deflation crisis for global economic and political stability are frightening. Financial crises spread fear and irrational behaviour. Some governments will react defensively. Others will simply walk away, blaming terrorists or despots or the poor or SARS or AIDS. Given the global divisions precipitated by the pre-emptive invasion of Iraq, co-ordination and co-operation may be weak.

But governments need not throw up their hands impotently. They could choose to take action, as they did under the influence of Keynes in 1944, to stabilize the international economy. They could claw back their right to policy autonomy from the financial markets. They could strengthen and democratize international institutions. They could re-localize global markets. In short, they could bring forward another 'Great Transformation.'

What would such a transformation involve? We do not claim to have all the answers. This book is an *outlook*; it is not a manifesto or a blueprint for reform. We can provide only a set of *first principles*, which, if they find acceptance, could be adopted by those with resources and translated into effective policy.

the second 'great transformation'

A starting point for such a transformation will be to reverse the most pernicious elements of the 'globalization' experiment. This will mean:

- **Taming financial markets** through the re-introduction of capital controls; restraints in the growth of credit; the establishment of an International Clearing Agency; and a Tobin Tax;

- **'Upsizing' the state**, empowering governments to respond to democratic mandates.

- **'Downsizing' the single global market**, by introducing an international trading system based on the concept of 'appropriate scale'.

Moreover, as noted in Chapter 4, if we are to maintain our environmental life support system, we will need a new, just, and sustainable mechanism for allocating fuel emissions: contraction and convergence.

the taming of capital markets

The reforms since 1970 have liberated financial markets from social, political, and environmental constraints. As a result the world has been turned upside down. *Those in the finance sector that should act as servants to the global economy have, instead, become its masters.* The tail is now wagging the dog. The legacy of this transformation is financial crises, debt, and deflation. It is now time for the people, through their elected governments, to oversee, monitor, and restrain invisible and unaccountable financial markets.

Capital controls across borders must be reinstated, co-ordinated, and orchestrated through a multilateral body such as the IMF. Though this may sound unlikely to seasoned IMF-watchers, the control of capital movements remains a central mandate of the IMF.

articles of agreement, article 6

Section 3. *Controls of capital transfers*
Members may exercise such controls as are necessary to regulate international capital movements, but no member may exercise these controls in a manner which will restrict payments for current transactions or which will unduly delay transfers of funds in settlement of commitments, except as provided in Article VII, Section 3 (b) and in Article XIV, Section 2.

International opinion, including IMF staff, is swinging back in favour of capital controls, if only for developing countries.[2] *The Economist* asserted boldly in May 2003 that 'Nobody seriously proposes that the United States should introduce exchange controls.'[3] Once financial crisis strikes, it may not be so convinced.

At a domestic level, there is an urgent need to reinstate government control over the supply of credit. This does not imply 'monetarist' policies; nor does it mean that governments should ration credit, under a Soviet-style centrally planned system. Instead, there needs to be a 'transmission mechanism' whereby governments can increase or reduce the rate of credit growth according to the needs of their economies. *RWEO* contributor Jane D'Arista, of the Financial Markets Center,[4] has been developing one such proposal. She argues that the current system, whereby banks hold reserve assets against their liabilities, needs to be radically altered. Rather than reserve requirements applying only to banks—thus allowing all forms of other financial intermediary essentially to create credit at will—these reserve requirements should be made mandatory for all institutions. Moreover, the reserve requirements should be measured against total assets, not total liabilities. This would put governments in a much stronger position to maintain a restraining hand over the rate of credit creation.

We must now urgently revive Keynes' conception of an International Clearing Agency (ICA). As Ricardo Hausman has argued, central to such an Agency would be the right, currently enjoyed exclusively by the United States, for countries to repay foreign debts in their own currencies, or in a mixture of emerging market currencies.[5] In Chapter 24, D'Arista develops this proposal, proposing that reserve assets would be held centrally by the ICA and would constitute a mix of currencies, weighted by the volume of trade with each country. This means that the US dollar would no longer need to be used as the main reserve currency—a trend that has deeply iniquitous consequences, as so many of *RWEO* contributors point out. The ICA would also act as an international 'lender of last resort', and would serve to reduce the volume of speculative flows between countries.

Complementing such a framework would be a 'Tobin Tax'—a very small tax on currency transactions, which, in the words of its instigator James Tobin, would put 'sand in the wheels of international finance'.[6]

'upsizing' the state

Reversing the 'Great Transformation' means that states act to regain political autonomy by clawing back the power they gave away to unaccountable markets; regaining the ability to pursue democratic agendas and once more to control their currencies, their interest rates, and their external balances. Governments must be given the freedom to tax and spend and so meet demo-cratically determined priorities. Elected governments must be liberated to introduce environmental and social standards and regulations that promote social and economic justice and sustain the life support systems of the planet.

Governments will also have to take remedial action to boost pension provision, in order to protect millions of the elderly from suffering and hard-ship in old age. In order to renew and sustain investment in vital infrastructure, governments may have to re-nationalize privatized transport and other infrastructure. The options open to governments are varied. It is not for us to prescribe what they should do. We only insist that governments should be freed up to respond to the democratic mandates of their people.

dismantling the global market

The utopian project of a single global market needs to be dismantled. For the purposes of sustainability—economic and environmental—production, distribution, and consumption need to take place at the 'appropriate scale'. This could mean a move towards 'localization'—keeping production and consump-tion within an appropriate area, such as a country or sub-region; or it could mean promoting trade and investment within and between regions, in order to ensure fairer competition and reduce transport costs while maintaining some of the advantages of scale. While inevitably some goods and services will be traded internationally, the bulk of these could be traded locally and regionally.

How does a system of 'appropriate scale' differ from, and how is it superior to, the current 'globalized' system? First of all, it takes into account the environmental costs of trade. As we have noted in this volume, free trade is being given a free ride by the global environment. As far back as 1995, trade accounted for 20–25 per cent of all carbon emissions from energy use. By 2004, it is estimated that transport caused by international trade will have grown by 70 per cent. Such trends 'make a mockery of the reduction targets [for carbon emissions] set for industrialized countries'.[7]

A system of 'appropriate' scale would allow for a more managed system of global trade. The trading system would not be based on bullyboy power politics, but on the needs of particular regions and countries, particularly developing ones. Rather than being forced to liberalize their markets under the threat of WTO sanctions, undermining their ability to develop their own industries or even ensure the food security of their people, developing countries would be free to pursue the trade policies most appropriate to their climate, economy, and stage of development. Trade negotiations would take place more within regions, reducing the glaring inequalities in bargaining power that undermine the current system of global negotiations.

Some may fear that developing countries would lose out under such a system but they have not benefited much from the globalized market. Instead, they have been stripped of their ability to provide for their own people, and rewarded for this sacrifice by collapsing export prices and recurring financial crises. As Jayati Ghosh writes of South Asia in Chapter 8, 'The process of increased integration with the global economy was not associated with higher GDP growth or more productive employment generation, or improved performance in terms of poverty reduction.'

contraction and convergence

Reducing international trade through a more localized or regionalized approach would do much to help ensure environmental sustainability. But it would not go far enough. Moreover, it would not necessarily provide for a fair global allocation of carbon dioxide emissions. Instead, we need a system of 'contraction and convergence', as promoted by the London-based Global Commons Institute.[8] 'Contraction and convergence' would cap total emissions, progressively reduce them, and share entitlements to so that, in an agreed timeframe, they converge to being equal per person.

getting there: the united states as our leader?

Which country would lead such a transformation? Ironically, the world's largest economy is also the world's biggest sovereign debtor. Jubilee Research has elsewhere dubbed the United States as a HIPC, a 'Heavily Indebted Prosperous Country'.[9] Unlike the HIPCs of Africa, Asia, and Latin America, however, the United States is not forced to pay off its debts; to experience the necessary painful 'structural adjustments'; or to face the wrath of its creditors. Instead, the United States is free riding on the rest of the world, sucking in resources, and increasing economic, financial, political, and ecological instability.

However this cannot go on forever. Faced by a crashing dollar, huge external debts, likely financial collapse, deflation, and debt defaults, the US government will soon have to face the music. Like other world leaders, the administration will then have choices. It could continue its current role, trampling the globe and leaving a set of emaciated global institutions—the UN, the WTO, the World Health Organisation—in its wake. Or, it could look for constructive, co-operative international solutions.

Either way, the United States may well become the first rich country to embrace the 'first principles' we outline above. If confidence in the dollar continues to wane, then the haemorrhaging of capital flows out of the country might oblige the United States to implement capital controls. Whether this will be done unilaterally or through the IMF, imposing controls would provide *carte blanche* for other countries, both developed and developing, to follow suit.

Second, the United States may become the world's first 'localized' economy. Even now, as well being the world's richest country, it is also one of the least dependent on international trade, with exports accounting for only 10 per cent of GDP, compared to 28 per cent in the Eurozone.[10] In response to external crises, the United States may well batten down the hatches further, turning inwards and reducing its dependence on the global economy. As it well knows, the United States can produce almost everything it needs from within US borders, with the notable exception of oil—and even oil supplies look set to be guaranteed by a compliant, newly 'democratic' Iraqi regime.

The United States may actually prosper in such a situation. Of course, levels of consumption will fall, as US citizens no longer thrive on the fruits of other countries' cheap assets and finance. But once the dollar starts to lose its shine, and the United States is no longer able to borrow in order to wage wars and cut taxes, a 'localization' scenario may start to look more favourable than any other. Employment may even increase, as US manufacturing industry, decimated by international competition, is reconstructed.

In the long run, (and hopefully, before we are all dead) the rest of the world may also do well out of this situation. In the short run, countries will complain about the loss of their export markets, the collapse of their foreign currency reserves, and the drying up of new dollar loans. But they may come to welcome the opportunity of weaning their economies off unhealthy dependence on the US consumer, and start producing more for expanding regional and local markets. Existing trends towards political integration at the regional level will be accelerated, such as through the newly enlarged EU, or through initiatives such as NEPAD and ASEAN. And such regionalization would bring substantial benefits, economically, politically, and environmentally.

conclusions

Which way will the world go? Will we have constructive international co-operation, a shift towards localization, regionalization, and control over capital markets? Or will history have to repeat itself in the form of financial crises, terrorism, and world war? We do not know and, in all honesty, lack confidence in the common sense, honour, and vision of powerful economists or political leaders. But then

> . . . *small wonder that confidence languishes, for it thrives only on honesty, on honor on the sacredness of obligations, on faithful protection, on unselfish performance; without them it cannot live.* Franklin D. Roosevelt.[11]

The absence of these qualities means that we are pessimistic about how US and other world leaders will respond under duress.

What we do know, however is that the world faces a choice between financial disintegration, random terror, and war on the one hand, and financial, social, and political stability on the other. We call upon the world's leaders to wake up to the alarm bells being rung; to shed their attachment to a defunct economic ideology; and to apply social values more noble than mere monetary profit.

The economic alternatives are there and are eminently practicable. Indeed, these changes have been made before, and the results are widely acknowledged to have resulted in a prolonged period of peace, stability, and economic health.

What is needed now is political will. We hope that this edition of *Real World Economic Outlook* will help to build that political will.

references

[1] N. Klein, 'From Pots to Politics; Argentina was eager for change, yet is about to elect a discredited has-been as president' *Guardian* 12 May 2003.

[2] See, for example, the IMF report of March 2003 'Effects of Financial Globalization on Developing Countries: Some Empirical Evidence', co-authored by IMF Chief Economist Kenneth Rogoff.

[3] 'A survey of global finance' *The Economist*, 3 May 2003.

[4] www.fmcenter.org.

[5] B. Eichengreen and R. Hausmann, 'How to Eliminate Original Financial Sin' *Financial Times*, 22 November 2002.

[6] J. Tobin, 'A proposal for international monetary reform', *Eastern Economic Journal*, 4, 1972.

[7] A. Simms, R. Kumar, and N. Robins, 'Collision Course: Free trade's free ride on the global climate', (London: New Economics Foundation, 2000).

[8] For more information, visit the Global Commons Institute website at www.gci.org.uk.

[9] R. Greenhill and A. Pettifor, 'The US as a HIPC—Heavily Indebted Prosperous Country', (London: New Economics Foundation, 2002).

[10] World Bank, *World Development Indicators*, (Washington DC: World Bank, 2002).

[11] Taken from Franklin D. Roosevelt's inaugural speech.

glossary

ASEAN Association of South East Asian Nations.

Balance of payments The total of all international transactions undertaken by a country during a particular time period. It is equal to the current account plus the capital account. The balance of payments must always be equal to zero. If it is not, the country must either accumulate or run down its foreign currency reserves.

Balance of trade The value of a country's exports minus the value of its imports. It is a component part of the current account and hence the balance of payments.

Basel Capital Accord An international regime for regulating banks.

Brady Plan Named after US Treasury Secretary Nicholas F. Brady, this plan was designed to address the developing country debt crisis of the 1980s. However, the success of the plan was limited.

Bretton Woods Agreement An agreement between delegates from 45 nations reached at the UN Monetary and Financial Conference in 1944 in Bretton Woods, New Hampshire. The main elements of the agreement were the construction of capital controls, the return of policy autonomy to states, and the liberalization of trade. The Bretton Woods Institutions were also formed as part of the agreement.

BWIs Bretton Woods Institutions.

Bretton Woods Institutions The World Bank and the International Monetary Fund (IMF).

Bubble A rise in the price of an asset not based on the current or prospective income that the asset is expected to generate, but on the expectation that the price will continue to rise in the future. When those expectations cease, the bubble bursts and prices rapidly fall.

Bundesbank The central bank of the Federal Republic of Germany.

Capital account liberalization The removal of regulations over the free movement of capital across national borders.

Capital account The total inflow of capital into a country in any particular time period, minus the total outflow of capital. Such inflows and outflows can include foreign direct investment; portfolio flows; aid flows; repayments of the principal of loans; and other capital flows.

CDF Comprehensive Development Framework. A new World Bank approach to lending which is supposed to put the recipient country in the 'driving seat'.

CEE Central and Eastern European region.

Central bank The institution in a country (or a currency area such as the Eurozone) responsible for managing the supply of the country's money and the value of its currency on the foreign exchange market.

Clearing system An arrangement among financial institutions for carrying out transactions amongst them, including cancelling out offsetting credits and debits on the same account.

Constant dollars Dollars of constant purchasing power, that is, corrected for inflation. It is usually used to refer to dollars of a particular year. For example, figures for 1995 expressed in '1992 dollars' would mean that the figures had been adjusted for changes in the value of the dollar between 1992 and 1995.

Core rate of inflation The consumer price index without the influences of changes in the prices of food and energy, which can fluctuate widely from month to month.

Currency board system An exchange rate system whereby every unit of domestic currency in circulation is backed by a specified amount of foreign currency. For example, in Argentina, prior to the devaluation in 2001, every peso in circulation was backed by one US dollar. A currency board is in effect an extreme form of pegged exchange rate, operating in a similar way to the Gold Standard.

Current account deficit The balance of debits minus credits on the current account.

Current account The balance of trade (exports minus imports), plus the net flow of interest payments, profit remittances and workers remittances. The current account, together with the capital account, makes up the balance of payments.

Deflation Deflation is usually defined as a generalized fall in prices, the consequence of which is often a fall in wages. It is the converse of inflation, a rise in prices. In a deflationary environment, when prices are falling, the real value of debts will rise. In a context of high levels of debt, even mild deflation risks triggering a 'debt-deflationary' spiral when people are forced to reduce expenditure or sell off assets in order to pay off debts, thereby forcing prices down, and causing debt to rise even further in real terms.

DEFRA Department for Environment, Food, and Rural Affairs (UK).

Derivatives Financial instruments whose value is 'derived' from the price of some underlying asset (for example, an interest level or stock market index). They are designed to help companies 'hedge' (protect themselves against the risk of price changes) or as speculative investments from which great profits can be made. During the South Sea bubble such speculation was known as 'selling the bearskin, before the bear'.

Dollarization The adoption of the US dollar as the domestic currency by a country other than the United States.

EBRD The European Bank for Reconstruction and Development. An investment bank operating in 27 countries from Central Europe to Central Asia, owned by its shareholder member countries, the European Community, and the European Investment Bank.

ECB European Central Bank.

ECLAC Economic Commission for Latin America and the Caribbean.

Econometrics A sub-discipline of economics which involves the application of mathematical and statistical techniques to economic analysis.

EMU European Monetary Union.

ERM Exchange Rate Mechanism.

ERP Economic Report of the President.

European Commission Executive body of the European Union.

European Monetary Union An agreement to increase monetary co-operation reached between 12 countries in 1999 as a result of the Maastricht Treaty. EMU countries share the euro as a common currency.

European Union A group of countries in Europe that have agreed to pursue further integration politically and economically. For example, they already form a customs union and have harmonized many of their rules and regulations. At present, the EU has 15 member countries. However, as from 2004, the EU will be expanded to include 10 mainly Central and European countries.

EU European Union.

Eurostat Statistical office of the European Union.

Eurozone An area comprising of 12 European countries, also members of the EU that have adopted the common currency, the euro. All current EU member states apart from Denmark, Sweden, and the UK are within the Eurozone.

Exchange rate GDP GDP as measured in nominal exchange rates rather than purchasing power parity exchange rates.

Exchange rate mechanism A system of exchange rate co-ordination within the European Union which predated European and Monetary Union. Central banks within the EU intervened in foreign exchange markets to limit the fluctuations between the currencies to within a pre-defined range. The exchange rate mechanism was wrenched apart in 1992 when the exchange rate became de-linked from the real economy of a number of countries.

FDI Foreign Direct Investment. Investment made by an individual or company resident in one country in productive capacity in another country - for example, the purchase or construction of a factory or the purchase of a complete company.

Fed The Federal Reserve Bank of the United States, or US central bank.

Fiat money A money whose usefulness results from the government's order (fiat) that it must be accepted as a means of payment, rather than from its intrinsic value or the fact that it can be converted into gold or another currency.

Financial Architecture A catchphrase for the policies, programmes, and institutions required to manage international financial markets.

FOREX markets Foreign Exchange markets.

Formal sector The formal sector comprises the public sector plus that part of the private sector and civil society that is not defined as the informal sector. The informal sector comprises small firms and organizations that are not officially registered or monitored and may not, as a result, pay tax or meet other government regulations.

FTA Free Trade Area. A group of countries that allow free trade between themselves (that is trade without tariffs or non-tariff barriers) without necessarily adopting a common approach to trade with other countries.

FTAA Free Trade Area of the Americas. The free trade area being negotiated between most of the countries within the Western Hemisphere.

G7 The seven most powerful industrialized countries whose heads of state meet annually in summit meetings to discuss economic and political issues. Member countries are the United States, Canada, the United Kingdom, Japan, France, Germany, and Italy.

G8 The G7 plus Russia. Since 1998, the G7 have been accompanied by Russia in their summit meetings.

GCC Gulf Co-operation Council. An agreement reached in 1981 between six countries in the Persian Gulf region with the aim of co-ordinating and integrating economic policies. The six countries are Bahrain, Kuwait, Oman, Qatar, Saudi Arabia, and the United Arab Emirates.

GDP Gross Domestic Product. The value of all goods and services produced within a country in a particular year. Gross Domestic Product differs from Net Domestic Product in that it does not deduct the depreciation of capital produced in previous years.

GERA Programme The Gender and Economic Reforms in Africa programme. It is a pan-African research and advocacy programme established in 1996 by women from across Africa in order to influence economic policies and decision-making processes in Africa from a gender perspective.

Gini Index A measure of income inequality within a population, ranging from zero for complete equality, to one if one person has all the income. It is sometimes also known as the Gini Coefficient.

Gold Standard Market liberals in the 19th century promoted maximal opportunities for markets internationally, but needed to find a way in which people with different currencies could freely engage in transactions, while protecting the value of their assets. They devised three simple rules: each country would set the value of its currency in relation to a fixed amount of gold, and buy and sell it at that price. Second, each country would base its money supply on the quantity of gold it held in reserves. Third, residents would be given maximal freedom to engage in international transactions. When the price structure diverged from international levels, the only legitimate adjustment was by deflation, and contraction, until declining wages reduced consumption enough to restore balance. This implied declines in wages, farm income, increases in unemployment, and a sharp rise in business and bank failures. It was first adopted in the 1870s but came crashing down in World War I. It was re-instated post-war, and only abandoned at the height of the Great Depression in September 1931.

Golden Age The period between 1950 and 1973 during which the advanced economies, on the basis of Keynesian policies for capital controls, free trade, and governmental policy autonomy, recovered to pre-war levels, and then proceeded to rapidly expand at almost unprecedented levels.

Greenfield FDI Foreign Direct Investment that involves the construction of new firms or machinery rather than purchase of existing firms or machinery.

Gross Domestic Product See GDP.

HIPC Heavily Indebted Poor Country. These countries, of which there are 42, are deemed by the IMF and the World Bank to be eligible for debt relief under the HIPC initiative.

Hoover Vacuum cleaner.

Human Development Index Developed by the UN, this index ranks countries in terms of their 'human development', including indicators such as life expectancy, literacy and maternal mortality.

ICA International Clearing Agency (see 'clearing agency').

IFO International Financial Organization.

ILO International Labour Organization. The UN specialized agency that seeks the promotion of social justice and internationally recognized human and labour rights.

IMF International Monetary Fund. An international organization founded as part of the Bretton Woods Agreement in 1944. Although its mandate is to promote international monetary co-operation, exchange rate stability, economic growth, and to provide assistance to countries in times of financial crises, it is often accused of promoting policies which serve the interests of the G7 and their financial centres.

IPCC Intergovernmental Panel on Climate Change. The IPCC was established by the World Meteorological Organization (WMO) and the UN Environment Programme (UNEP) in 1988. The role of the IPCC is to assess the scientific, technical, and socio-economic information relevant for the understanding of the risk of human-induced climate change.

IRBD The International Bank for Reconstruction and Development. One of the component organizations of the World Bank.

Kyoto Accord An international treaty whereby countries agree to reduce the amount of greenhouse gases they emit if their neighbours do likewise.

LDC Least Developed Country. A country that appears on the list of the 49 least developed countries in the world according to the United Nations. Criteria for inclusion on the list include a low income, weak human assets, and a high level of economic vulnerability.

Lender of last resort An institution that makes loans when no other organization is prepared or able to do so. Domestically, this role is often played by the central bank. There is currently no real international lender of last resort.

Less Developed Country Developing country.

LETS Local Exchange Trading Scheme. Essentially a barter scheme, LET schemes allow people to swap skills within a local area without exchanging money. Scheme members are given points for certain tasks undertaken, such as gardening or childcare, which can then be exchanged for services which they need.

Levy Institute The Levy Economics Institute of Bard College, founded in 1986, is a non-profit, non-partisan, public policy research organization.

M&A Mergers and acquisitions.

Maastricht Treaty The 1991 treaty among members of the EU to work towards a monetary union, or common currency, on the basis of market liberalism. This ultimately resulted in adoption of the euro in 1999, but with a 'growth and stability' pact that limits the policy autonomy of European governments.

Marshall Plan A programme led by the United States following the Second World War to assist certain European countries in post-war recovery and in particular to ensure that countries did not become communist as a result of economic hardship. Between 1947 and 1952, the Marshall Plan dispersed over $12 billion.

MDGs Millennium Development Goals. A set of international poverty reduction targets agreed by world leaders at the UN's Millennium Summit in September 2000. The most widely cited goal is to halve the proportion of people living in extreme poverty by the year 2015.

Meltzer Commission Influential US Congressional commission chaired by Allan Meltzer, in 1998 to study the role and effectiveness of the International Monetary Fund and the World Bank.

MENA Middle East and North Africa.

Mexican Peso crisis The first of series of financial crises which have plagued so-called 'emerging market' economies since the mid-1990s.

MFA Multi-Fibre Arrangement. A trade agreement between developed country importers and certain developing country exporters of textiles and garments. It serves to restrict quantities of imports into developed countries, thus artificially raising prices. It also serves to restrict exports from non-member countries.

MNC Multi-National Corporation. A firm that operates in at least two countries.

Monterrey Consensus An agreement reached in Monterrey, Mexico, in March 2002 during the United Nations conference on Financing for Development. Amongst other things, the Monterrey Consensus includes a commitment by rich countries to provide more financing to developing countries to help them to meet the Millennium Development Goals.

NAFTA North American Free Trade Agreement. A free trade area consisting of the United States, Canada, and Mexico, which came into effect in January 1994.

National income National income is more or less equivalent to GDP, apart from some adjustments that do not usually enter theoretical models.

National Sample Survey Surveys run by the National Sample Survey Organization, Department of Statistics, Government of India, New Delhi.

Neoliberalism A political and economic philosophy which tends to elevate markets to a dominant role, and which prioritizes privatization, efficiency and economic growth over other aims including redistribution and social justice.

NEPAD New Partnership for Africa's Development. A strategy for development in Africa prepared by African Presidents in 2000, in particular those from Senegal, Algeria, Nigeria, and South Africa. It aims to provide for more co-operation between African countries, and also to promote better governance in the continent in exchange for more aid and better access by African exports to rich country markets.

Net equity investment Foreign direct investment plus net portfolio investment.

Net portfolio investment Purchase of shares by foreign investors. In contrast to foreign direct investment, portfolio investors generally purchase less than 50 per cent of the shares in a company and thus do not have a controlling stake.

NIC Newly industrialized country.

Nominal (wages, interest rates) The value of something in absolute terms, that is not taking account of inflation.

Nominal exchange rate The actual exchange rate at which currencies are bought and sold in the foreign exchange markets at any particular point in time. It contrasts with the real exchange rate, which takes into account different inflation rates in each country; and the purchasing power parity exchange rate, which takes account of varying cost levels in each country.

OECD Organization for Economic Cooperation and Development. An international organization comprising of 30 of the richest and most industrialized countries in the world.

OPEC Organization of Petroleum Exporting Countries. An international oil cartel, or group of countries which attempts to regulate the price of oil. As of July 2002, it had 11 member countries, including many, but not all, of the largest exporters of oil.

Plaza Accord An agreement reached in 1985 between the United States and its major trading partners to bring down the value of the dollar, which had appreciated substantially since 1980.

Ponzi Finance A way of financing named after Carlos Ponzi that involves paying for old liabilities with new liabilities (see Introduction).

PPP Purchasing power parity. A way of measuring exchange rates between countries which takes into account the differences in prices between the countries.

Price-to-earnings ratio The price of a stock, divided by its earnings per share - a common way to gauge the value of a company.

Primitive accumulation The forceful expropriation of resources and wealth, the separation of people from their means of production, consumption, and survival.

Purchasing power The amount of goods services that can be bought with a given quantity of currency.

Real (interest rates, wages, and so on) The term 'real' is used to refer to the value of something once inflation rates are taken into account. For example, if nominal interest rates are 5 per cent but inflation is at 3 per cent, then the real interest rate is 2 per cent. Similarly, if nominal wages are growing at 10 per cent but the rate of inflation is 5 per cent, then the real growth of wages is 5 per cent.

Real dollars The value in dollars after taking inflation into account. Real measures are only used to compare figures over time. Measuring economic variables over time in real dollars involves taking out the changes in value accounted for solely by inflation.

Real exchange rate The nominal exchange rate adjusted for different inflation rates between countries over time.

Savings Any income after all taxes have been paid that is not used by a household in the form of current expenditures.

Sovereign risk The risk that a government or a body guaranteed by the government will not make a payment on its debt.

Stability and Growth Pact A set of economic 'austerity' rules which strips European governments of powers to set interest rates, powers that rest with an independent central bank. Under the pact, countries have agreed to limit their government spending, and to endure sanctions, should they breach these limits. These rules apply regardless of whether a government needs to reflate the economy to avoid a recession and cut unemployment, and they therefore strip elected governments, like Germany, of policy autonomy during a recession.

Stagflation A term coined by economists in the 1970s to describe the previously unprecedented combination of slow economic growth and rising prices

Sub-prime Prime and sub-prime are terms used to describe the risk of lending to a particular individual. A person considered a prime loan candidate has few or no negative entries in her credit history. Therefore, the risk of him defaulting on a loan is low. A sub-prime loan candidate has some negative qualities to his credit history. The risk of defaulting on debt is therefore considered higher.

Treaty of Versailles The peace treaty negotiated to end World War I in January 1919, at the château of Versailles near Paris.

UN United Nations. An organization of countries established in 1945 with 51 members, expanded to 188 countries as of July 2000. Its purpose is 'to preserve peace through international cooperation and collective security'.

UNCTAD United Nations Conference on Trade and Development. A United Nations body formed in 1964 that specializes in trade and development issues. It has traditionally been an advocate for the interests of developing countries within the international arena.

UNEP United Nations Environment Programme.

UNFCCC United Nations Framework Convention on Climate Change. An international framework adopted in 1992 in an attempt to stabilize atmospheric concentrations of greenhouse gases at a level that would prevent human action from leading to 'dangerous interference' with the climate system. The UNFCCC entered into force on 21 March 1994, and now has 186 Parties.

Washington consensus A short-hand phrase to describe the set of neoliberal policy measures advocated by the Washington-based institutions, most notably the IMF and the World Bank, including tight fiscal and monetary policies, free trade and capital flows, deregulation and privatization.

Wealth effect Refers to the tendency of people to spend more if they have more assets. The idea is that when the value of equities or other assets rises, so does our wealth, thus we feel more comfortable about spending money.

WMO World Meteorological Organization. An international organization that coordinates global scientific activity to allow increasingly prompt and accurate weather information and other services for public use.

World Bank One of the Bretton Woods institutions, the World Bank was formed in 1944 in order to provide loans and other forms of development assistance to developing countries. The World Bank consists of five separate institutions: the International Bank for Reconstruction and Development (IBRD); the International Development Association (IDA); the International Financial Corporation (IFC); the Multilateral Investment Guarantee Agency (MIGA); and the International Center for the Settlement of Industrial Disputes (ICSID).

WTO World Trade Organization. An international organization formed in 1994 which aims to promote free trade between its member countries. It is increasingly acting to promote liberalization in other areas as well, including investment and services. As of April 2000, it had 136 member countries.

index